DATE DUE			
16 5 3 90			
MAR 3 0 1998			
DEC 0 8 2000			

SAUDI ARABIA IN THE OIL ERA:
REGIME AND ELITES; CONFLICT AND
COLLABORATION

SAUDI ARABIA

- –·– International boundary
- – – – Province boundary
- ■ National capital
- + Railway
- Road

There are no provincial capitals; administration is from Riyadh. Province boundaries are approximate.

Damascus
Haifa SYRIA
Tel Aviv
Amman
JORDAN
Al Qurayyat
Baghdad
IRAQ
Dezful
Esfahan
IRAN
Bandar-e Shahpur
Abadan
Al Basrah
Iraq–Saudi Arabia Neutral Zone
KUWAIT
Kuwait
Shiraz
Bushehr
Persian
Elat
Haql
Al Muqata'ah
Tabuk
Ash Shamaliyah
Al Jawf
Al Hudud Ash Shamāliyah
Ha'il
Ha'il
Ash Sharqiyah
Ad Dammam
Dhahran
BAHRAIN
Manama
Bandar 'Abbas
Al Madinah
Buraydah
Al Qasim
Riyadh
QATAR
Doha
Ash Sharqiah
Dubayy
OMAN
Gulf
Gulf of Oman
Yabu al Bahr
Medina
Afif
Al Khasirah
Ar Riyēd
Al Hufuf
Harad
Abu Dhabi
UNITED ARAB EMIRATES
Al Buraymi
Suhar
Muscat
Makkah
Jiddah
Mecca
Al Bahah
Ranyah
Bishah
As Sulayyil
Ash Sharqiyah
OMAN
Red
Sea
Port Sudan
Al Qunfudhah
Asīr
Abha
Najrān
SUDAN
Jizan
Jizan
Salalah
Asmera
Mits'iwa
Sana
Arabian Sea
Al Hudaydah
YEMEN (SANA)
Ta'izz
YEMEN (ADEN)
Sayhut
Al Mukalla
ETHIOPIA
Mocha
Aseb
Aden
Gulf of Aden
DJIBOUTI
Djibouti
Bender Cassim
SOMALIA

Socotra
YEMEN (ADEN)

0   200 km
0   200 miles

Names and boundary representation are not necessarily authoritative

SAUDI ARABIA IN THE OIL ERA

REGIME AND ELITES;
CONFLICT AND COLLABORATION

MORDECHAI ABIR

WESTVIEW PRESS
Boulder, Colorado

Contents

Tables

Abbreviations

ANLF	Arab National Liberation Front
CGC	Council for Gulf Cooperation
CSM	*Christian Science Monitor*
EIU	*Economic Intelligence Unit*
FBIS	Foreign Broadcasting Information Service
FT	*Financial Times*
IHT	*International Herald Tribune*
IJMES	*International Journal of Middle Eastern Studies*
IRO	Organisation of the Islamic Revolution for the Liberation of the Arabian Peninsula
JP	*Jerusalem Post*
JQ	*Jerusalem Quarterly*
KFU	King Faysal University
KSU	King Saud University
MEED	*Middle East Economic Digest*
MEJ	*Middle East Journal*
MES	*Middle Eastern Studies*
NLF	National Liberation Front
NRF	National Reform Front
NYT	*New York Times*
OPEC	Organisation of Petroleum Exporting Countries
PDF	Popular Democratic Front (Saudi)
PDFF	Popular Democratic Front for the Liberation of Palestine
PDP	Popular Democratic Party
PDRY	People's Democratic Republic of Yemen
PFLOAG	Popular Front for the Liberation of Oman and the Arabian Gulf
PFLP	Popular Front for the Liberation of Palestine
PLO	Palestine Liberation Organisation
SABIC	Saudi Basic Industries Corporation
SAMA	Saudi Arabian Monetary Agency
SR	Saudi riyal
UAE	United Arab Emirates
UAR	United Arab Republic
UK	United Kingdom
UPAP	Union of the Peoples of the Arabian Peninsula
UPM	University of Petroleum and Minerals

ABBREVIATIONS

US	United States
USA	United States of America
WP	*Washington Post*
WSJ	*Wall Street Journal*

In Memory of Anat,
the Victim of her Father's Academic Career

Preface and Acknowledgements

When I began a survey of source material for this book in the early 1980s, I was somewhat surprised by the paucity of sources relating to socio-political dynamics in modern Saudi Arabia both in European languages and Arabic. Thus, William Rugh's article 'Emergence of a New Middle Class in Saudi Arabia' (1973), for instance, remains a classic to this day. In the field of social anthropology I found only a handful of serious studies of the Saudi population produced by western and Arab scholars (Katakura, Lancaster, Cole, Shamekh, and Hamzah's outdated work). Other sources in Arabic largely dealt with the kingdom's geography and tribal division, past history to the twentieth century, the reign of Abd al-Aziz ibn Saud, and the rise of the Wahhabi movement and its impact on the Arabian Peninsula. The contribution of Saudi scholars of good standing to the subject was minimal, as the Saudi modern elites were beginning to emerge in the middle of the century and only lately have they begun to publish worthwhile scholarly studies of their society and government — studies inhibited, unfortunately, by the character of the regime and its strict censorship laws.

It was not only that Saudi Arabia was a sparsely populated desert periphery of the Arab world, but travelling in the kingdom until the 1960s or early 1970s was technically difficult and the authorities, as well as the xenophobic Wahhabi-Saudis, were suspicious of foreigners (Hijaz is the exception) travelling in their country or researching its population. Indeed, with very few exceptions, foreigners were not permitted to conduct fieldwork in the rural areas (Lancaster's and Cole's experience) and until the 1970s were not supposed even to travel in the kingdom other than between its main towns and in the Eastern Province, where Aramco began to operate on a large scale after World War II (and became a major source of information on Saudi Arabia as well as of oil). The provincial governors (amirs) are, *inter alia*, in charge of security in their respective areas and it is their duty to prevent unauthorised foreigners from entering them. Thus, Saudi Arabia remained until recently *terra incognita*.

Many books, articles and news items dealing with the Saudi kingdom were published in different languages after the 1973–74 oil crisis. In most cases they relate to the Saudi royal family and government, to power politics and defence, and to oil and the Organisation of Petroleum Exporting Countries (OPEC). Very few serious studies of the Saudi society and institutions and the revolutionary changes which they have undergone in the last twenty-five years, were published even in the 1970s, although their number has grown in recent years.

I myself faced the dilemma common to all Israeli social-historians dealing with Arab countries, that of being unable to conduct field-work in the countries which they research. The situation was exacerbated by lack of suitable published material and by limited opportunities to exchange ideas and opinions with Saudi counterparts.

Having exhausted all the available published sources I turned to press and radio monitoring collections. I also examined about 120 theses in the humanities and social sciences relating to Saudi Arabia, the majority of which were written by Saudis, and submitted to American, and in some cases to European, universities. A large number of the theses that I have read were of little relevance to me. The 35 or so theses which appear in my bibliography are not necessarily the best, but rather the ones I found of special interest or cited. A few were written by offspring of the Saudi oligarchy, some by students who became cabinet ministers, some by high-ranking officials. Nearly all, when it came to matters relating to the Saudi regime or the royal family, I found biased or, in many cases, relying heavily on foreign sources and previous PhDs (preferably ones written by ministers and senior technocrats), in order to avoid expressing an opinion and offending the rulers. Each thesis which I used, nevertheless, contributed to my understanding of different aspects of modern Saudi Arabia. Only a few of the theses represented, directly or indirectly, the point of view of the militant nationalist opposition to the regime which, it seems, is not uncommon among Saudi students in western universities. These few theses were essential for understanding the phenomenon of a miniscule militant opposition in the kingdom on the one hand and the rapidly growing new middle-class elites which serve the regime, yet do not participate in decision-making, on the other.

I take this opportunity to thank the many Saudis whose works I have used and who unbeknownst to them have helped me to understand better their country, society, educational system, government and politics and the changes that these underwent due to modernisation. I am also grateful to the Woodrow Wilson International Center for its fellowship (1982/83), which enabled me to lay the foundation for this book: to the Brookings Institution and Dr William Quandt for hosting me in the summer of 1983; to the US Library of

Congress for providing its facilities; to the Truman Institute for Peace of the Hebrew University of Jerusalem for providing me with research assistance and library facilities in the last two years, and to several friends and colleagues in the United States, Europe and Israel, who were willing to exchange ideas with me or comment on parts of my work. I would like to mention David Furman (in Washington, DC), Judith Rakhmani and Hana Jerozolimski (at the Hebrew University in Jerusalem) who, with others, patiently served, in different periods, as my research assistants.

Dr Edward Ingram of Simon Fraser University (British Columbia) helped with the editing of my chapter 'Modern Education and the Evolution of Saudi Arabia', in his book *National and International Politics in the Middle East* (London, 1986) and agreed to my using an updated and revised version of it in my book (Part I, Chapter 3). The same goes for Dr Sylvia Haim (Kedouri), who not only edited my article 'The Consolidation of the Ruling Class and the New Elites in Saudi Arabia' (*Middle Eastern Studies* (MES), Vol. 23, No. 2 (April 1987)), but served, among others, as my consultant for Arabic terms and transliteration. My thanks go to both her and Prof. Elie Kedouri, my friends, for permission to use the above-mentioned in a revised and updated form (Part I, Chapter 1) and to their daughter Helen Grubin for editing the English part of the book. Special thanks are due to my friends Dr Judith and Dr Jacques Roumani for very substantial editorial assistance, to Prof. David Ayalon (whose *mamluk* I remain) and Prof. Pesah Shina'r, my teachers, who supported me and also helped with Arabic terms. All the above are, of course, not responsible for my mistakes. Dr Jacob Goldberg of the Dayan Center of Tel-Aviv University and Mr Keith Kyle of the Royal Institute of International Affairs (Chatham House) helped with important press cuttings. To Dr Reinhard Schulze of Friedrich-Wilhelms-universität, Bonn for permission to quote his paper (draft, not for quotation) and for most illuminating remarks (in a letter to me) on the cultural-Wahhabi aspect of the Najdi–Hijazi cleavage.

Last, but not least, this book, like all my previous works, could not have been produced without the help and partnership of my wife Rutha, who in addition to her usual talents and patience has now also acquired the skill to operate the computer used to produce this book.

I have followed, whenever possible, the established system of transliteration of Arabic words and names. In the case of names and words which have become common in European languages, the common European transliteration has been used. Because of

technical difficulties, diacritical signs have been kept to a minimum
and simplified.

Mordechai Abir
Jerusalem

Introduction

Saudi Arabia has a territory of about 865,000 square miles and a citizen population of about five million.[1] With the exception of Asir in the south and a score of oases, the largest of which is Al-Hasa in the east, it is made up of a largely arid plateau of varied desert landscapes. Officially declared a united kingdom in 1932, Saudi Arabia consists of five major regions. The core of the kingdom is Najd, the Central Region, the historical seat of the Wahhabi movement (*muwahhidun*) and the House of Saud. Al-Hasa, renamed the Eastern Province (Al-Sharqiyya), the Hijaz or the Western Region (the most populated), Asir or the Southern Region (the second most populated), and the Northern Region (the periphery of the Syrian desert) were conquered between 1913 and 1934 by the founder of modern Saudi Arabia, King Abd al-Aziz Al Saud (better known as Ibn Saud).

Administratively, the kingdom's five regions are subdivided into fourteen major provinces — *imarates* (the number has varied over time). The governor of each province is an amir (plural *umara*) who is a prince of the royal house, or a member of one of the aristocratic families related to it. Until the development of the modern central government in the 1950s and 1960s, the amir ruled the province in the king's name and was the head of its administration. The traditional government hierarchy included the heads of local 'dynasties', notables (*a'yan*), and above all tribal leaders or shaykhs, also known as *umara*.

With minor exceptions all the kingdom's citizens are Muslim Arabs who speak a variety of similar Arabic dialects; most are of tribal origin and the Arab culture is common to all. Yet Saudi society cannot be considered fully homogeneous. Although about 90 per cent of the Saudis are Sunni Muslims, a large proportion of the population of Al-Hasa are Shi'ite Twelvers (*ithna'shariyya*).[2] Small communities of Twelvers and Isama'ilis (seventh imam) are to be found in Asir and the Hijaz and Zaydis (fifth iman) in Asir. Although most of the population of Hijaz and Asir are now Wahhabi and adhere to the Hanbali school of theology and religious jurisprudence (*madhab*; plural *madhahib*), followers of the Shafi'i, Hanafi and Maliki schools are still to be found in the above provinces as well as in Al-Hasa. Culturally, historically and climatically, agricultural Asir is an offshoot of Yemen. Al-Hasa, with its large Shi'ite community and mixed coastal population, is also very different and more oriented to the population of the Gulf principalities and Iran. Historically, the Hijazi townspeople, considered by Najdis to be of mixed blood (an outcome of the settlement of non-Arab pilgrims and merchants and concubinage), are proud of their unique heritage having given Islam to the world and being continuously the guardians of Islam's holy cities. They are closely connected with the Muslim world through the Hajj and trade; they are more sophisticated, cosmopolitan and religiously moderate than other Saudis, the Najdis in particular.

Cultural variations exist between the nomads (*badu*) and the settled (*hadr*) but more so between the 'aristocratic', conservative and religiously puritan Najdis who consider themselves 'racially pure', and the population of the other regions. At mid-twentieth century, more than half the population of Saudi Arabia were still nomads, and perhaps 35 per cent settled and semi-settled. Barely 10 per cent lived in the major towns. The tribe and clan were still the most important socio-political substructures in Arabia. The tribal *umara* were considered *primus inter pares*; their position and the extent of their authority depended on their individual merit and leadership capability. The number of Bedouin had begun to decline in the first half of the century, a process sharply accelerated after the 1950s by massive urbanisation sparked by increasing oil wealth and modernisation. By the mid-1980s just about 5 per cent of the population was considered nomadic, while about 25 per cent settled or semi-settled cultivators. The major urban centres grew dramatically and claimed over 50 per cent of the total population, though towns of under 100,000 people had declined from 14 per cent of the total to 12 per cent.[3] As one observer put it in the 1980s:

> There are few poor Saudi left except for a dwindling minority of bedouins, who, resisting the lure of government largesse in return for sedentarization, live a life of voluntary semi-poverty for the sake of their social and spatial freedom.[4]

With urbanisation, traditional institutions began to decline, as oil wealth and modernisation increasingly bridged the differences between the population of the kingdom's provinces. Notwithstanding these processes, national integration and the stability of the regime in Saudi Arabia are largely the result of the kingdom's oil revenues and the delicate balance of power within the House of Saud, between the rulers and the religious leaders, the ulama (singular *'alim*), and between traditional elites and the expanding new middle class, led by the intelligentsia.

NOTES

1. *Area Handbook Series: Saudi Arabia A Country Study* (Washington, DC, 1982), pp. 45, 63; R. Knauerhase, *The Saudi Arabian Economy* (New York, 1975), p. 13. Saudi statistics are notoriously inaccurate.

2. Shi'ite mainstream followers of twelfth *imam*. Zaydis, nearest to Sunnis.

3. G.A. Lipsky, *Saudi Arabia: Its People, Its Society, Its Culture* (New Haven, 1959), p. 24; A.H. Said, 'Saudi Arabia: The Transition from a Tribal Society to a Nation', unpublished PhD thesis (Missouri, 1979), pp. 115, 137, 156–7. On urban population: Kingdom of Saudi Arabia, Ministry of Planning, *Third Development Plan 1400–1405 A.H. — 1980–1985 A.D.*, p. 56. Jedda and Riyadh each have a population of over one million. Mecca is the third largest town. Dammam, Al-Khobar, Dhahran and Hufuf in Al-Hasa follow it: T.H.T. Al-Hamad, 'Political Order in Changing Societies, Saudi Arabia: Modernization in a Traditional Context', unpublished PhD thesis (University of Southern California, 1985), p. 229; A.A. Al-Ibrahim, 'Regional and Urban Development in Saudi Arabia', unpublished PhD thesis (University of Colorado at Boulder, 1982), p. 299 (note 127).

4. E.B. Gallagher, 'Medical Education in Saudi Arabia: A sociological perspective on modernization and language', *Journal of Asian and African Studies*, Vol. XX, Nos. 1–2 (1985), p. 11.

Part One

Ruling Class and Elites in Saudi Arabia

1

The Consolidation of the Ruling Class in Saudi Arabia*

The Saudi population at the beginning of the twentieth century could be considered, with some exceptions, a classless society: there was no upper class to speak of in Arabia at the time. Only a small proportion of the merchants and the ulama in the towns of Hijaz and Najd could be described as 'middle class'. The great majority of the Arabians — townspeople as well as the rural nomads and agriculturalists — lived at or near subsistence level. The unification of the Saudi kingdom by Abd al-Aziz ibn Saud in the first decades of the century consolidated the power and authority of a new Saudi ruling class — the aristocracy. The development of the kingdom's oil industry since 1938 and the modernisation of Saudi Arabia after World War II, produced, moreover — in addition to existing regional and other differences — new classes and a relatively rigid social structure. The latter depends not so much on power, wealth and education as on affiliation to the ruling family and on regional (Najd), tribal (noble) and urban or rural origin and citizenship. This chapter will examine the evolution and composition of the Saudi aristocracy and whether it has changed in recent decades, under the impact of rapid modernisation and the rise of new elites.

THE EMERGENCE OF THE SAUDI RULING CLASS

The reconquest of Riyadh in January 1902 is considered in Saudi annals as the beginning of the modern Saudi kingdom. The small army of Abd al-Aziz ibn Saud was composed at the time of a few score brothers, uncles, cousins, other relatives and in-laws and some Bedouin followers. During this crucial stage, Abdallah ibn Jiluwi was said to have twice saved the life of his 'cousin' Abd al-

3

Aziz (henceforth also Ibn Saud). Subsequently, the Jiluwi family, a cadet branch of Al Saud,[1] gained a key position in the kingdom's ruling class. Such a development is typical of considerations which influenced the formation of that class in Saudi Arabia. Indeed, all of Ibn Saud's partners in the conquest of Riyadh, as well as members of his and other important families who helped him in the consolidation of his kingdom in the first decades of the century, were incorporated into the Saudi aristocracy[2]. At their side, the ulama led by Al al-Shaykh (the descendants of Muhammad b. Abd al-Wahhab, the founder of the Wahhabiyya), and important tribal and regional umara (singular 'amir) who joined Ibn Saud's camp at this stage also won a preferential status and can be considered part of the Saudi ruling class.

Ibn Saud continued to expand his powerbase by numerous matrimonial alliances with traditional regional rulers and important tribal shaykhs (umara)[3]. As a Muslim, he was limited to four wives but, acording to custom, he could frequently divorce them and marry others whose offspring were regarded as part of the royal family. Thus he incorporated into his regime an important element of the regional and tribal umara. Most significant, however, was his affiliation with the powerful Sudayris of northern Arabia, who had intermarried with the Sauds in the past.

Contrary to the Wahhabi-Saudi 'holy war' (or jihad) of previous centuries, Ibn Saud's military campaigns were not aimed at spreading the Wahhabiyya in the conquered areas but rather at re-establishing the authority of the House of Saud. The historical alliance between the Najdi ulama, at the head of which were Al al-Shaykh and the House of Saud, led by Ibn Saud, had not been automatically reinstated this time. The Najdi ulama viewed Ibn Saud's government with reservation, if not with suspicion. Some, who lived under the protection of other Wahhabi rulers even supported his enemies. Eventually, however, most of the Najdi ulama agreed to recognise the authority of the young ruler, only on condition that, at least temporarily, his father, Abd al-Rahman, would carry the title of imam.

Relations between Ibn Saud and the Wahhabi ulama were also somewhat soured by the fact that, in this period, they did not regard Ibn Saud as sufficiently pious. He toyed with technological innovations which they considered heretical innovation (a bid'a). He did not conduct jihads against the polytheists (mushrikun) in the region, and he was known to associate with the British infidel authorities in the Persian Gulf.[4]

4

The cementing of the relationship between Al Saud and Al al-Shaykh through matrimonial arrangements, and the preferential treatment accorded to the religious hierarchy, undoubtedly contributed to the improvement of relations between the king and the majority of the urban Najdi ulama. Moreover, in order to establish a loyal military force to carry out his plans and overcome the natural opposition of Bedouin tribes to law and order, about 1912 Ibn Saud revived, or took under his patronage, the Ikhwan movement. Ulama volunteers (*muttawwa'in*[5]), some of tribal origin, were sent to teach the Bedouin the principles of the Wahhabiyya, and land and funds were apportioned for their settlement. By 1930 this movement had led to the settlement of approximately 150,000 Bedouin in over 200 military-agricultural villages (*hujar*).[6]

After 1913 as the Ikhwan armies were principally responsible for Ibn Saud's conquests including Jabal Shammar, the Hijaz and Asir, they became the mainstay of his regime. As a result the importance of the tribal *umara* and the *muttawwa'in* who settled in the *hujar*, and the Najdi ulama in general, rapidly increased.

Thereafter Ibn Saud appeared to follow the Wahhabi code of behaviour more strictly, and frequently consulted the ulama and the Ikhwan leaders on different issues. But, as he became more dependent on them, the leading tribal *umara*, some of whom had been Ibn Saud's bitter enemies in the first decade of the century, and the more fanatic ulama, exploited their new leverage to coerce their *imam* to accept their extreme interpretation of the Wahhabiyya and their right to intervene in the running of the kingdom. Although the attitude of the Ikhwan leaders increasingly infuriated Ibn Saud's lieutenants, the Saudi ruler chose to overlook the Ikhwan's excesses in order to avoid an open breach with them.

After World War I, Ibn Saud accelerated his efforts to establish a united centralised kingdom in the Arabian Peninsula. For this purpose he planned to introduce aspects of modern administration and western technology which he considered essential for effective government and not contradictory to the principles of Islam.[7] Moreover, aware of the political realities in the region, he coordinated his activities as much as possible, with the British government and its local representatives.

Abd al-Aziz's policies were anathema to the Ikhwan and to most of the Najdi ulama. Their traditional xenophobia had been whipped up by British activities in the region and they also regarded Ibn Saud's internal policies as a betrayal of Wahhabi doctrine. The fact that the ruler had also begun to consolidate his dynastic rule and had taken to himself, instead of the traditional title of the Amir of Najd, the title of 'Sultan of Najd and its Dependencies' (1921) and later (1926) 'King of the Hijaz' only added fuel to the fire.[8] Indeed, both tribal shaykhs and the ulama, especially those connected to the Ikhwan, were convinced that time was working against them and if they were not to stop Ibn Saud, or at least limit his authority, they would be incapable of doing so in the future.

The Ikhwan rebellion (1927–30)[9] was thus not only a challenge to Ibn Saud's policy but also a desperate attempt on the part of the leading Ikhwan amirs and some fanatic ulama allied with them to preserve their power and the traditional socio-political frameworks from which they derived it. Ibn Saud's final victory over the Ikhwan in 1929–30, and the consolidation of the power of the Saudi state thereafter by establishing a national army and a centralised administration, deprived the tribal shaykhs and the ulama of the power to intervene, on their own initiative, in the conduct of state affairs.

CENTRALISATION AND THE DECLINE OF NON-ROYAL TRADITIONAL ELITES

There are about 50 senior tribal amirs and a few hundred shaykhs (*umara*) of secondary tribes and sub-tribes in Saudi Arabia.[10] The power and authority of these amirs has been gradually declining since 1930 as the power and authority of the Saudi kingdom and its government were consolidated and its administration expanded. The foundations for the Bedouin 'White Army' (later the National Guard) were laid by 1930, and the armed forces were established in the early 1940s. Most important, Ibn Saud's revenues increased from about £100,000 sterling annually to about £4–5,000,000 sterling after the conquest of the Hijaz and they spiralled to tens and soon to hundreds of million of pounds, following the commercial exploitation of oil in Saudi Arabia.[11]

The relatively substantial funds at his disposal enabled Ibn Saud to purchase armaments and transport, and to 'buy' the loyalty of the tribesmen. Thereafter the amirs' potential to resist the concentration of power in the hands of Al Saud was literally nullified. Subsequently, when faced with the choice of either integrating into the Saudi provincial administration and enjoying royal patronage, or resisting Ibn Saud and losing whatever authority was left to them, even the remnants of the Ikhwan leadership opted for the former course.[12] Henceforth, the tribal amirs became part of the power-base of the Saudi regime and have a vested interest in its continuity. Together with the royal house and the ulama they are considered to be a component of the ruling class. Their position within this class, however, is inferior to that of the ulama and depends as much on the relative importance of each amir in the Saudi tribal structure.

Notwithstanding his victory over the Ikhwan and the consolidation of his power after 1930, Ibn Saud continued to pamper the ulama, and especially the Al-Shaykhs. Their support was still essential for the legitimisation of his regime and its policy. It was also crucial for the process of national integration through religion (Wahhabiyya), law (*Shari'a*) and traditional education. Yet, consultations with the ulama rank and file during the king's daily council (*majlis;* plural *majalis*)[13] with them and with the senior ulama in a far more important weekly *majlis*, could no longer be viewed as a recognition of their supreme authority and their right to participate in the decision-making process. Indeed, in matters which he thought of secondary importance, Abd al-Aziz was still ready to accept the ulama's opinions, even when they were opposed to his own. But on more important problems, although he consulted them when he saw fit, he made his final decision according to what he considered right and, whenever necessary, in contradiction to the ulama's opinion.[14]

The ulama, who were coerced into accepting the new status quo realised that in the new phase of their alliance with the House of Saud, Wahhabi hegemony and their special position in the kingdom were still guaranteed, but their actual power and influence were to be dependent on the ruler's goodwill. However, even as junior partners of the Sauds, the ulama, led by Al al-Shaykh, enjoyed high prestige, privileges and substantial influence, and were consulted regularly by Ibn Saud. As the kingdom's government and administration developed they were given key positions in it, in addition to control of the religious establishment, including justice and the educational system.

Paradoxically, the role and authority of the ulama further declined after the rise of King Faysal whom they helped bring to the throne in 1964. Related through his mother to Al al-Shaykh, and known for his piety, Faysal, who promoted the pan-Islamic movement in his struggle against pan-Arabism, nevertheless deliberately eroded the ulama's power and independence. In addition to his modernisation programme, he left vacant and practically abolished the key positions of judicial power held by the ulama, such as the

7

Grand Mufti and Chief Qadi, held by Muhammad ibn Ibrahim Al al-Shaykh who died in 1969. Moreover, Faysal entrusted his newly established Ministry of Justice in 1970 to an *'alim* of Hijazi origin (usually more moderate than the Najdi ones) and gradually established secular administrative (non-*Shari'a*) tribunals of different kinds. Frequently he ignored the ulama's opposition to aspects of his accelerated modernisation, sometimes even in matters that they considered to be major issues.[15] Last but not least, he curbed the authority and activities of the Committees for Encouraging Virtue and Preventing Vice (*Hay'at al-Amr bi'l-Ma'ruf wa'l-Nahy 'an al-Munkar*) (henceforth the Morality Committees and the Morality Police).

The ulama, nevertheless, remain a component of the Saudi ruling class, although a junior one, and the Sauds' loyal partners; both the Sauds and the ulama, each for their own reasons, have a vested interest in the preservation of their historical alliance. On the one hand, it contributes to the regime's legitimisation, to stability and to national integration. On the other hand, it helps preserve the Wahhabi character of, and the role of the ulama in, the kingdom.

The rise to power of King Khalid and Crown Prince Fahd in 1975 signalled a reversal of Faysal's policy. Senior ulama, largely Al-Shaykhs, filled the positions previously left vacant at the head of the judicial and educational systems. Hijazi ulama were no longer preferred to the more strict Najdi ones (as was the case in other fields). The activities of the Morality Committees and the Morality Police were also somewhat stepped up, although their authority was still limited.[16]

The revival of Wahhabi fundamentalism (neo-Ikhwan) in the 1970s and the Mecca incident (1979), if anything, only brought the ulama and the Sauds closer together. The ulama, notwithstanding some extremist *'alims* who sympathised with neo-Ikhwan teachings,[17] considered the rise of fundamentalism not only a threat to the Wahhabi-Saudi kingdom but also a challenge to themselves as part of the Saudi establishment. They did sanction, therefore, the storming of the Holy Mosque and denounced the rebels for their action and their preachings. For their part, the Saudi rulers, intimidated by the neo-Ikhwan phenomenon and the impact of the rise of Iranian Shi'ite fundamentalism, reinforced somewhat the ulama's control of daily life in Saudi Arabia and tried to appear more devout and pious. Yet in matters of policy and substance, especially with regard to the kingdom's government, development or foreign policy, the ulama, as in the past, are rarely consulted. Important members of the Al al-Shaykh considered part of the Saudi *ahl al-ḥal wa'l-'aqd* (lit. those who loosen and bind),[18] but not necessarily *'alims*, however, often participate in the meetings of the informal royal *majlis al-shura* (Consultative Council).

Regardless of the decline in their power and influence, the ulama thus remain an important component of the Saudi ruling class. In the scale of importance of the traditional elites they come immediately after the royal house and its collateral and associated families, but above the *umara*. Indeed in contrast to the *umara* they are organised, have a hierarchy, leadership, state-supported institutions and common interests which bind them as a cohesive group.[19] The activities of the Al-Shaykhs, moreover, are no longer limited to the religious establishment and they are now to be found in key positions in the administration, educational system, security services, the armed forces as well as in the private sector of the Saudi economy. In fact, it appears that in the 1980s, only a small proportion of the numerous Al-Shaykhs are *'alims* and only a handful are among the senior Saudi ulama.[20]

THE SAUDI OLIGARCHY AND DECISION-MAKING

It was generally accepted that until the 1970s the House of Saud, the ulama and the *umara* — the most important components of the regime's powerbase — were in fact the Saudi ruling class. The size of this class is difficult to determine. Al Abd al-Rahman and the other 'recognised' branches of Al Saud, not to mention their associated important families, are generally estimated to be about 5000 strong. The ulama, their associates and all the members of the religious hierarchy in Saudi Arabia probably number in the tens of thousands. Indeed, Al al-Shaykh is intermarried with all the other branches of the ruling class, by itself believed to consist of 7000 to 10,000 people. As for the *umara* and their extended families, their number is probably equal to that of the religious establishment. Thus, in King Faysal's time, the traditional Saudi ruling class, in the wider sense, was quite substantial.

Some scholars classify the Saudi kingdom as an autocracy. Others call it a 'desert democracy'.[21] The more appropriate description of the Saudi regime after the death of Ibn Saud is probably an oligarchy whose pillars are the Saudi royal house, the ulama and the *umara*. The conduct of its government follows, especially since the last years of King Abd al-Aziz, the golden rule of consultation (*shura*) and consensus (*ijma'*), within the ruling class.

The monarch has a power of veto over all the decisions of the executive system (government and administration) which developed rapidly, and gained power after Faysal became Prime Minister in 1958. Indeed, notwithstanding the principles of *shura* and *ijma'*, the King can also veto, at least in theory, decisions of his informal Consultative Council (*majlis al-shura*),[22] the representative organ of the Saudi oligarchy. Yet in certain circumstances, the Saudi oligarchy, through its unofficial leadership (*ahl al-ḥal wa'l-'aqd*) may overrule the King, limit his authority, and in extreme cases even depose him. Such prerogatives, however, were exercised only in relation to King Saud (r. 1953–64) whose policies undermined the kingdom's economic structure, its stability and the hegemony of the House of Saud. Saud's incompetent governance unified most of the ruling class, led by Faysal's manipulations, against him. Thus in exceptional circumstances, if the policies of the King or a financial crisis caused by him were to threaten the stability of the kingdom and the power of the ruling class, a similar coalition to that which deposed Saud in 1962–64 could again emerge.[23]

Information concerning *ahl al-ḥal wa'l-'aqd* in Saudi Arabia is scarce. Most sources agree that membership in this authoritative and powerful body is informal and limited to about 100 members of Al Abd al-Rahman Al Saud and its cadet branches. Fifty additional members of this body are said to belong to the aristocratic families associated with the Sauds — Jiluwi, Sudayri, Thunayan, Al-Shaykh — and some outstanding ulama not related to the latter, and a handful of extremely important *umara*.[24] The criteria of membership in *ahl al-ḥal wa'l-'aqd*, it seems, are origin, seniority, prestige and leadership qualities (and in addition Islamic scholarship and piety for the ulama), according to Bedouin tradition.

Leading ulama have usually participated with the other components of *ahl al-ḥal wa'l-'aqd* in consultations which preceded dramatic developments in Saudi history: on Ibn Saud's succession in 1953, the appointment of Faysal as Prime Minister in 1958 and as Prime Minister with full decision-making powers in 1962, the forced abdication of Saud in Faysal's favour in 1964, the succession of Faysal by Khalid in 1975, and of Khalid by Fahd in 1982, and the crushing of the Mecca rebellion in 1979. In several such instances *fatwas* (religious-legal opinions) were also issued by the leaders of the ulama. Yet, the ulama's participation in the informal royal Consultative Council, the kingdom's decision- and policy-making organ, is *ad hoc* and conditional, it seems, on the need for religious sanction for specific decisions.[25]

The tribal shaykhs and the members of regional dynasties (*umara*) provide the third leg of the tripod of the Saudi dynasty's traditional powerbase. Yet, just a handful of the most important *umara* are considered *ahl al-ḥal wa'l-'aqd*. Indeed, since Abd al-Aziz's death, only a few exceptionally important amirs have been invited — largely in times of crisis or in relation to major policy debates — to consultations of the informal royal *majlis al-shura*.[26]

Despite the subsidies they received from Ibn Saud and their role in the provincial government, the importance of the *umara*, as mentioned above, has declined steadily since 1930 with the exception of a short period under King Saud. This process was accelerated with Faysal's rise to power and the reorganisation and strengthening of the central government. That, and the introduction of five-year development plans in 1970, continuously strengthened the new Saudi elites and the central government. Simultaneously, the strengthening of central government and the extension of its administration and welfare services to the provinces eroded the authority of the provincial governors (*umara al-manatiq*), the royal authority's sole representatives in the provinces and districts between 1930 and the early 1960s and, even more so, that of the tribal shaykhs (*umara*) and the regional and urban notables (*a'yan*).[27]

Moreover, the decline of the *umara's* authority gathered momentum after the 1960s also as a result of Faysal's policies and the rapid urbanisation of the Bedouins and agricultural population. Indeed, the average Saudi found himself increasingly turning to the central government's representatives for services and help rather than to his amir or headman.[28] However, the *umara*, still the link between the rural population and the Sauds, regained some of their lost influence when Fahd (then Crown Prince) began to strengthen the authority of the provincial government and court the tribal amirs after 1980.[29]

Obviously, the most important component of the Saudi ruling class and of *ahl al-ḥal wa'l-'aqd* is the royal family. It dominates the kingdom's decision-making apparatus through the King, his informal royal Consultative Council and *ahl al-ḥal wa'l-'aqd*. It is essential, therefore, to determine who can rightly be included in the term 'Saudi royal house'.

After its meteoric rise to power in the first half of the eighteenth and the beginning of the nineteenth centuries, the Al Saud had split into different branches who often fought each other for power. Such wars of succession led to the decline of the power of the Sauds and the flight to Kuwait in the last decades of the nineteenth century of Al Abd al-Rahman and other branches of the family.

The term 'royal house' in modern Saudi Arabia is exclusively used to describe the descendants of Abd al-Rahman ibn Faysal ibn Turki Al Saud, foremost among them the offspring of his son Abd al-Aziz, as well as a few cadet branches of the family. This definition received legal sanction in 1932 when only the descendants of Abd al-Aziz, his brothers and the branches of the Sauds allied to them by common history and marriage were to be considered royalty and to receive a stipend.

Abd al-Aziz and Faysal publicly denounced the use of royal titles and protocol which contradicted Wahhabi puritanism. In an emotional speech shortly after he came to power in 1964, Faysal said: 'I beg of you brothers to look upon me as both brother and servant. "Majesty" is reserved to God alone and "the throne" is the throne of the Heavens and Earth.'[30] Yet it was Abd al-Aziz who took to himself and to his family royal titles and his son Faysal enhanced them. Indeed, regulations instituted by the Saudi civil service during Faysal's reign demand that all the direct descendants of King Abd al-Aziz should be referred to as 'His Royal Highness'. Those of his brothers and some of his uncles should be referred to as 'His Highness', and members of other recognised branches of the Sauds as 'His Excellency', a title they share with cabinet ministers, non-royal district amirs and other senior officials.[31] All in all, it is estimated that between 4000 and 7000 members of Al Saud are considered today part of the royal family, and of those about 700 are direct descendants of Ibn Saud.[32] This substantial group is unquestionably the most important component of the Saudi ruling class. When Crown Prince Faysal reorganised the kingdom's financial and administrative systems in 1958 he also substantially reduced the stipends allocated to members of the royal family and removed from the list members of remote branches of the family. That, *inter alia*, caused a large part of the aristocracy including, ironically, the young Liberal Princes, to support his dismissal by King Saud at the end of 1960.

By late 1962 Saudi Arabia again faced another major political and financial crisis as a result of the revolution in Yemen (September 1962); Faysal was requested to resume the premiership with full powers. Among other things, Faysal instructed in 1963 his uncle and Finance Minister, Musa'id ibn Abd al-Rahman, to re-examine the royal list and to determine who among the Sauds would henceforth be considered 'royal family' and receive a stipend. Subsequently, Prince Musa'id limited the recognised membership of the royal family to the offspring of Abd al-Aziz and his brothers and Saud al-Kabir, Abd Al-Rahman's nephew, the Jiluwis, and the less important Thunayans, Abd al-Aziz's kinsmen and companions since the beginning of his career and also related to him through marriage.

The royal family (as defined above), the Sudayris[33] (the powerful Bedouin dynasty from northern Najd intermarried with all the branches of the Sauds) and the Al-Shaykhs, thus compose of the upper echelon of the kingdom's ruling class. This group is estimated at over 20,000 people. Together with their other non-royal partners in the kingdom's traditional elites (ulama, *umara*), they probably number nearly 100,000 (a very different situation from Iran, where the Shah could depend only on his immediate family).

Some scholars are of the opinion that until the rise of Faysal the non-royal traditional elites also included important merchant families and urban notables.[34] Yet, even if such a claim is valid, these groups are not part of the ruling class. Such differentiation is especially significant for our definition of 'ruling class' in view of the dramatic rise of the importance of the new elites in Saudi Arabia since the 1960s.

The crucial criterion for membership in the ruling class, we believe, should be the ability to participate in policy formulation and decision-making. In short, to be represented in ahl al-ḥal wa'l-'aqd. Wealth, education and key positions in the administration, military or the economy, proposed as additional yardsticks for inclusion in the Saudi ruling class, prove incorrect when examined against the criterion set out above and the history of the modern Saudi kingdom since its establishment in 1932.

Wealthy merchants, entrepreneurs or even tribal shaykhs very rarely participated during the reign of Ibn Saud in royal consultations in which important policy decisions were adopted. Indeed, merchants, tribal shaykhs, notables and ulama were present (and still are) in the daily and weekly *majalis* of Ibn Saud, his heirs and those of senior princes. They attended regional gatherings convened by the ruler to adopt formally decisions proposed by him.[35] Occasionally, individuals were requested to help in various matters and were later handsomely rewarded. Moreover, until the 1940s important merchants were frequently requested, if not obliged, to lend money to Ibn Saud. Their reward was the prestige which they gained and other advantages which enabled them, in many cases, to amass their present immense fortunes. But they were never considered *ahl al-ḥal wa'l-'aqd* nor members of the King's informal *majlis al-shura*. Not only was their influence on decision- and policy-making limited, but their success was, and still is, dependent on the rulers' goodwill.

Following in the footsteps of their father the great Abd al-Aziz, the Saudi monarchs carefully adhere to the golden principle of *shura* and *ijma'*. Until today, however, they apply this principle exclusively to the royal family and its traditional partners in the ruling class. Yet, the monarch's 'absolutism' is tempered by the fact that he consults with the informal *majlis al-shura* representing *ahl al-ḥal wa'l-'aqd* on every important issue and whenever policy decisions are required. In the case of a major crisis, moreover, a larger forum of *ahl al-ḥal wa'l-'aqd* is convened. The centralisation of the government, the expansion of the administration and the rapid modernisation of the kingdom, nevertheless, eroded the power of the non-royal traditional elites (tribal *umara* and ulama), and, to a lesser degree, that of the important families, such as the Jiluwis, Al al-Shaykh and the Thunayans. Thus the recognised main branches of the royal family dominate the ruling class and its informal consultative bodies.

NOTES

* This chapter is a revised and updated version of my article 'The Consolidation of the Ruling Class and the New Elites in Saudi Arabia'. *Middle Eastern Studies*, Vol. 23, No. 2 (April 1987).

1. Al, equivalent to *Ahl*, meaning family, clan or tribe. Until recently the Jiluwis governed the kingdom's oil-rich Eastern Province.

2. The leading families associated with Al Saud are: Jiluwi, Sudayri, Thunayan and Al al-Shaykh.

3. For example, the mother of Crown Prince Abdallah came from the defeated house of Rashid of Jabal Shammar. Amir could denote in Saudi Arabia: prince, provincial or district governor, tribal shaykh or village headman.

4. On Ibn Saud and the ulama following the reconquest of Najd, see B.O. Kashmeeri, 'Ibn Saud: The Arabian Nation Builder', unpublished PhD thesis (Howard University, 1973), p. 168; J. Goldberg, 'Abd al-Aziz ibn Saud and the Wahhabi doctrine: Thoughts about a paradox' (Hebrew), *Hamizrah Hakhadash*, Vol. 30 (1981), pp. 107–12. On Abd al-Rahman's imamship, see H. St John Philby, *Sa'udi Arabia* (Beirut, 1968), p. 240; G. De Gaury, *Faisal King of Saudi Arabia* (New York, 1966), p. 18. Ibn Saud destroying his beloved wind-up gramophone: R. Lacey, *The Kingdom* (London, 1981), p. 144.

5. The majority novice ulama, some of tribal origin. This archaic form (*muttawwa'in*) is common to this day in Saudi Arabia.

6. J.S. Habib, *Ibn Sa'ud's Warriors of Islam* (Leiden, 1978), p. 222; C. Moss Helms, *The Cohesion of Saudi Arabia* (London, 1981), pp. 137–8; also Philby, *Sa'udi Arabia*, p. 265.

7. The modernisation which Ibn Saud planned was in the fields of administration, communications and military technology.

8. On tension between Ibn Saud and the ulama and the reaction to the titles mentioned above: Al-Rihani's evidence (1922) in Lacey, *The Kingdom*, p. 178. Also H. Wahba, *Arabian Days* (London, 1964), pp. 127, 129, 131–6; G. Rentz, 'The Saudi Monarchy', in W.A. Beling (ed.), *King Faisal and the Modernisation of Saudi Arabia* (London, 1980), pp. 27–8; F. Hamza, *Al-bilad al-'Arabiyya al-Sa'udiyya* (Mecca, 1335 A.H., 1937 A.D.), pp. 90–1; A. Bligh, 'The Saudi religious elite (ulama) as participant in the political system of the kingdom', *International Journal of Middle Eastern Studies* (IJMES), Vol. 17, No. 1 (February 1985), p. 38.

9. On the Ikhwan rebellion, see Habib, *Ibn Sa'ud*: Moss Helms, *Saudi Arabia*; Philby, *Sa'udi Arabia*.

10. O.Y. Al-Rawaf, 'The Concept of the Five Crises in Political Development: Relevance to the Kingdom of Saudi Arabia', unpublished PhD thesis (Duke University, 1981), p. 329.

11. M. Abir, 'Saudi security and military endeavor'. *The Jerusalem Quarterly* (JQ), No. 33 (Fall 1984), p. 81. Ibn Saud already had the beginning of an air force in 1927: *Handbook* (1984), p. 290. On revenue: Philby, *Sa'udi Arabia*, p. 333; Ibn Saud's revenues in 1922 amounted to 780,000 dollars: M.E. Faheem, 'Higher Education and Nation Building. A Case Study of King Abdul Aziz University', unpublished PhD thesis (University of Illinois at Urbana-Champaign, 1982), p. 98.

12. Said, 'Saudi Arabia', pp. 126, 138; Wahba, *Arabian Days*, p. 299. On Bedouin settlement after 1930: 'Abd al-Amir al-Rikabi, 'Al-dawla wa'l-da'wa fi'l-'Arabiyya al-Sa'udiyya al-iftiraq shart al-tahaquq', *Qaḍaya 'Arabiyya* (June 1980), p. 73.

13. *Majlis*, lit. council or audience (reception room) — a forum for discussion and for petitions, held by every Saudi of consequence. Royal *majalis*, theoretically open to every Saudi; in practice, are limited by the size of the room, and admittance frequently depends on the rank of the person or his patron.

14. Wahba, *Arabian Days*, pp. 50–2, 170–1; T. Niblock, 'Social Structure and the Development of the Saudi Arabian Political System', in T. Niblock (ed.), *State, Society and Economy in Saudi Arabia* (London, 1982), p. 95; F.A. Shaker, 'Modernization of the Developing Nations. The Case of Saudi Arabia', unpublished PhD thesis (Purdue University, 1972), p. 138.

15. To placate the ulama, but also to continue the process of drawing them into the establishment, Faysal founded in 1970 and 1971, respectively, the Administration of Scientific Study, (religious) Legal Opinions, Islamic Propagation and Guidance (*Idarat al-Buḥuth al-'Ilmiyya wa'l-Ifta' wa'l-Da'wa wa'l-Irshad*) and The Council of the Assembly of Senior Ulama (*Majlis Hay'at Kibar al-'Ulama*) (see below Chapter 2, pp. 22–3). The monarch entrusted the Ministry of Pilgrimage and Awqaf, moreover, to a Hijazi

belonging to a merchant family: W Rugh, 'Emergence of a new middle class in Saudi Arabia', *The Middle East Journal* (MEJ, 1973), pp. 14–15. On non-*Shari'a* judicial tribunals: F.A.S. Al-Farsy, *Saudi Arabia: A Case Study in Development* (London, 1982), p. 68; also S.A. Solaim, 'Saudi Arabia's judicial system', MEJ, Vol. 25, No. 3 (Summer 1971). See above p. 7.

16. On the reversal of Faysal's policy by Khalid-Fahd after 1975: W. Ochsenwald, 'Saudi Arabia and the Islamic revival', IJMES, Vol. 13 (1981), p. 278; M. Field, *Financial Times* (FT, London), 24 April 1984, supplement; J. Buchan, 'Secular and Religious Opposition in Saudi Arabia', in Niblock, *Saudi Arabia*, p. 108. Also below.

17. Abd al-Aziz al-Baz, one of the leading Saudi ulama, a Najdi and an arch-reactionary, was known to harbour such sympathies before 1979. The Islamic universities in Al-Madina and Riyadh were, and possibly still are, centres for neo-Ikhwan activities. D. Holden and R. Johns, *The House of Saud* (London, 1982), p. 517; Buchan, 'Religious Opposition', pp. 122–3; M. Field, FT, 28 September 1982; Al-Rawaf, 'Five Crises'. pp. 359, 527; *Al-Mawqif al-Arabi* (pro-Libyan, Beirut), 20 April 1981.

18. The principle of representation, according to the *Shari'a* can only be selective: only the elite can represent the people in Islam. Muslim interpreters refer to such an elite as *ahl al-ḥal wa'l-'aqd*. Ibn Taymiyya, a forerunner of Wahhabism, limits membership in this body to amirs and the ulama. Other eminent interpreters of Wahhabism include in it also the notables (*wujuh al-nas*). The oath of allegiance (*baya'*) of *ahl al-ḥal wa'l-'aqd* confers legitimacy upon the ruler on condition that he consults them since they are supposed to speak for the people: G. Assaf, 'A constitution for Saudi arabia', *Plus* (Paris, 1985), No. 1, p. 40; also Prince Fahd to *Al-Hawadith* (Beirut), 7 September 1973.

19. The most distinguished ulama, in addition to the top judiciary and religious education systems are represented in the Council of Senior Ulama, the Administration of Scientific Study, (religious) Legal Opinions, Islamic Propagation and Guidance and the (Central) Committee for Encouraging Virtue and Preventing Vice. See Al-Rawaf, 'Five Crises', pp. 323, 326; A. Layish 'Ulamā' and Politics in Saudi Arabia', in M. Heper and R. Israeli (eds), *Islam and Politics in the Modern Middle East* (New York, 1984), p. 30.

20. Three Al-Shaykhs are cabinet ministers (1986). The Director of the General Security Services is General Abdallah ibn Abd al-Rahman al-Shaykh. The army's commander-in-chief in 1982 was General Muhammad al-Shaykh: T.R. McHale, 'The Saudi Arabian political system — its origins, evolution and current status', *Vierteljahresberichte*, No. 89 (September 1982), p. 203; Bligh, 'Religious elite', p. 39; S.S. Huyette, *Political Adaptation in Sa'udi Arabia* (Boulder, 1985), p. 98. On Al-Shaykhs in society: L. Blandford, *Oil Sheikhs* (London, 1976), p. 79. On Al-Shaykhs in the economy: Al-Rawaf, 'Five Crises', pp. 331–2.

21. Shaker ('Modernization', p. 169) and Van der Meulen (D. van Der Meulen, *The Wells of Ibn Sa'ud* (London, 1957), p. 255): 'desert democracy'. Wenner (M. Wenner, 'Saudi Arabia: Survival of Traditional Elites', in F. Tachau (ed.), *Political Elites and Political Development in the Middle East* (New York, 1975), p. 180): 'modernizing autocracy', Alyami

(A.H. Alyami, 'The Impact of Modernization on the Stability of the Saudi Monarchy', unpublished PhD thesis (Claremont Graduate School, 1977), p. 175): 'almost absolute autocracy'.

22. Called also *Al-Lajnah al-'Ulyah* — The Supreme Committee.

23. See Chapter 8 below on attempts to discredit King Fahd due to his foreign policy and the decline of oil prices, allegedly caused by his strategy.

24. Of the hundred Sauds considered *ahl al-ḥal wa'l-'aqd*, 50 are said to be descendants of Abd al-Aziz. The document sanctioning the deposition of King Saud and Faysal's enthronement (1964) was signed by 68 princes, of whom 38 were Ibn Saud's sons and twelve distinguished ulama of whom four were Al-Shaykhs: Al-Rawaf, 'Five Crises', pp. 320, 326; Ochsenwald, 'Islamic revival', p. 274. According to Dawisha (A.I. Dawisha, 'Internal values and external threats', *Orbis* (Spring 1979), p. 130) the above body is composed of 100 princes and more than 60 leading ulama (?!). Also D.E. Long, 'Inside the royal family', *The Wilson Quarterly* (Winter 1979), pp. 66–7.

25. Dawisha, 'External threats', pp. 129–30; Ochsenwald, 'Islamic revival', pp. 274, 277; Holden and Johns, *House of Saud*, pp. 173, 517–18, 522; Long, 'Royal family', pp. 66–7; Al-Rawaf, 'Five Crises', p. 320; Mashaal Abdullah Turki Al Saud, 'Permanence and Change: An Analysis of the Islamic Political Culture of Saudi Arabia with a Special Reference to the Royal Family', unpublished PhD thesis (Claremont Graduate School, 1982), pp. 161–2. This source is of special interest because the author is affiliated to a cadet (unprivileged) branch of Al Saud and thus had access to members of the ruling class.

26. Leading tribal amirs participated in the *majlis al-shura* before Ibn Saud's death. They were courted and consulted by Saud. They were consulted in the 1979 crisis and they are again courted by King Fahd: J. Kraft, 'Letter from Saudi Arabia', *The New Yorker*, 4 July 1983, p. 51; Chung In Moon, 'Korean contractors in Saudi Arabia: Their rise and fall'. MEJ, Vol. 40, No. 4 (Autumn 1986), p. 628. See also below.

27. On provincial and district *umara* (1930 to the 1950s and 1960s), urbanisation, rise of central government and decline of tribal shaykhs and *a'yan*: Said, 'Saudi Arabia', pp. 107–8; A.N. Abussuud, 'Administrative Development in Saudi Arabia: The Process of Differentiation and Specialization', unpublished PhD thesis (University of Maryland, 1979), pp. 45, 104–5, 126; also T.R. McHale, 'A prospect of Saudi Arabia', *International Affairs* (Autumn 1981), p. 640; Al-Rawaf, 'Five Crises'. pp. 428–9, 483, 503.

28. Said, 'Saudi Arabia', pp. 164–5, 132, 175–8; M.M. Deij, 'Saudi Arabia's Foreign Policy 1953–1975', unpublished PhD thesis (University of Idaho, 1979), p. 26; A.M. Al-Selfan, 'The Essence of Tribal Leaders' Participation, Responsibilities, and Decisions in Some Local Government Activities in Saudi Arabia: A Case Study of the Ghamid and Zahran Tribes', unpublished PhD thesis (Claremont Graduate School, 1981), pp. 151, 192.

29. J. Shaw and D.E. Long, *The Washington Papers*: *Saudi Arabian Modernization: The Impact of Change on Stability*, No. 89 (1982, pp. 64–5; J. Buchan, FT, 5 May 1981, supplement, p. V; M. Collins 'Riyadh: The Saud balance', *The Washington Quarterly* (Winter 1981), pp. 202–3; N.H. Hisham, 'Saudi Arabia and the Role of the Imarates in Regional Development',

unpublished PhD thesis (Claremont Graduate School, 1982), pp. 537, 543.

30. Al Saud, 'Permanence', p. 129; Kingdom of Saudi Arabia, Ministry of Information, *Faisal Speaks* (Jeddah, 1965), p. 17; J. Craig (UK Ambassador to Saudi Arabia until 1984), confidential report no. 5184 to the Secretary of State for Foreign and Commonwealth Affairs, *Glasgow Herald*, 9 October 1986.

31. On titles of royalty: Hisham, 'Imarates', p. 9. Instead of *imam* and amir Ibn Saud took in 1921 the title 'Sultan of Najd and its Dependencies'. In 1926 the title 'King of Hijaz' and in 1927 'King of Hijaz and Najd and its Dependencies'.

32. R. Braibanti and F.A.S. Al-Farsy, 'Saudi Arabia: A development perspective', *The Journal of South Asian and Middle Eastern Studies*, No. 1 (Fall 1977), p. 27: 2000 to 7000; Al-Rawaf, 'Five Crises', p. 319: 3500 to 5000 with Al Abd al-Aziz alone accounting for 700; Al Saud, 'Permanence'. p. 131: 4000 to 5000; *Sunday Times* (London), 2 December 1984: no fewer than 5000.

33. Al Saud, 'Permanence'. pp. 136, 146 (note 26); Al Rawaf, 'Five Crises', pp. 318-19; Dawisha, 'External threats'. p. 131; Holden and Johns, *House of Saud*, p. 461; Lacey, *The Kingdom*, p. 432. Muhammad Saud al-Kabir, the son of Saud, Abd al-Rahman's elder brother at first challenged Ibn Saud's leadership yet was married to his sister. Ibn Saud's mother was a Sudayri. Of his two Sudayri wives, Hassa bint Ahmad al-Sudayri was the mother of King Fahd and his six brothers.

34. Niblock, 'Political System', pp. 94-5 (1926-47); Buchan, 'Religious Opposition', pp. 108-9; Gh. Salameh, 'Political power and the Saudi state', *Merip Reports*, No. 91 (October 1980), pp. 16, 18; Lacey, *The Kingdom*, p. 443.

35. For example, the gathering at the oasis of Murat in 1944 before Ibn Saud met with President Roosevelt: Van Der Meulen, *Ibn Sa'ud*, p. 158.

2

'The Book and the Sword' — the Ulama and the Sauds

The term ulama is used in this book in its wider sense to include all recognised religious scholars: the judges (*gadis*) of the different ranks, religious lawyers and all the other *'alims* engaged in the judicial system; the various ranks of religious teachers (*mudarris*); *imams* and the other office-holders of consequence in the mosques. According to one source the Saudi ulama number in the mid-1980s 'at least 10,000', but it could well be that their number is far larger, now that the three religious universities[1] graduate several thousand students annually. Yet not all the above are recognised 'ulama', nor are they of equal importance.

At the head of the religious pyramid is the Council of the Assembly of Senior Ulama (*Majlis Hay'at Kibar al-'Ulama*), said to be composed of twenty-five members. Leading members of several other institutions are either included in the above or are equally, or almost as, important. Such institutions are: the Higher Council of Qadis (*Al-Majlis al-A'la li'l-Qada*); the Administration of Scientific Study (religious) Legal Opinions Islamic Propagation and Guidance (*Idarat al-Buhuth al-'Ilmiyya wa'l-Ifta' wa'l Da'wa wa'l Irshad'*, popularly *Dar al-Ifta' wa'l Ishraf 'ala'l-Shu'un al-Diniyya*) and the Committees for Encouraging Virtue and Preventing Vice (*Hay'at al-Amr bi'l-Ma'ruf wa'l-Nahy 'an al-Munkar*), whose Morality Police serve as the executive arm of the ulama.[2] The Najdi ulama are overwhelmingly dominant in all the above institutions.

Saudi Arabia's society is often described as a theocracy; its puritanical Islamic laws and regulations are maintained, it seems, more strictly than ever since the 1950s. This, however, does not reflect the power of the ulama and their influence, as this chapter tries to show. Moreover, one must make a distinction between the ulama in general, who although numerous and organised, exercise little power, particularly in politics and policy-making, and the handful of senior ulama who constitute the apex of the religious establishment and control the kingdom's religious institutions.

The latter, appointed by the ruler and numbering probably about 30 or 40 'alims,[3] have direct access to the King and all the senior princes. They are greatly respected, seem to be powerful, and are consulted on matters of importance, at least those that have a bearing on religious affairs. Thus, under certain circumstances, they may influence the decisions of the rulers. In general, however, they exercise only marginal influence, and other than the relatively unbinding consultations, their major role is to legitimise an act or a decision previously reached at by the senior princes of the informal royal *majlis al-shura* or *ahl al-ḥal wa'l-'aqd* and thus provide the required consensus (*ijma'*).

As referred to earlier, this relationship between the religious hierarchy and the royal house, and the general decline of the ulama's influence in modern Saudi Arabia are an outcome of a process which began in the days of King Abd al-Aziz ibn Saud and culminated with the suppression of the Ikhwan rebellion in 1930. Thereafter, particularly after the rise to power of King Faysal, the regime progressively decentralised the ulama's power concentrated at the time in the person of the Grand Mufti, Shaykh Muhammad ibn Ibrahim Al al-Shaykh. Until his death in 1969, the latter was recognised as the head of the ulama and second only to the King in power and influence, and he discharged the roles that were traditionally within the domain of the Saudi ulama. Although Faysal placed the old and new religious institutions which he created, as well as the Ministries of Justice and Education under the control of distinguished 'alims, such ulama were accountable to him and became *de facto* part of the establishment. Indeed, the most important fields of ulama activity — justice, education and Hajj — became formal ministries whose heads are members of the cabinet chaired by the King.

THE ULAMA AND SAUDI ARABIA'S MODERNISATION, 1930–70: AN OVERVIEW

The Ikhwan rebellion (1927–30), which gravely threatened the government of Abd al-Aziz ibn Saud, was the last serious bid of the tribal society to challenge Al Saud's centralist regime and re-establish the former's traditional independence and way of life. The rebellion was especially dangerous because its leaders, supported by a few prominent ulama[4] and many *muttawwa'in*, took on the mantle of defenders of puritanical Wahhabism. They also underscored the inherent right of the community to replace a leader who betrayed their principles or who was incapable of carrying out his duties.

The total defeat of the Ikhwan led to a sharp decline in the power of the Bedouin amirs. The tribal forces, including the remnants of the Ikhwan, were, after 1930, integrated into the 'White Army'[5] and became loyal supporters of the regime and an important component of the Sauds' powerbase. Simultaneously, the collapse of the Ikhwan movement deprived the ulama of their military leverage and eroded their political power. Before the Ikhwan rebellion, when Abd al-Aziz faced strong tribal opposition, he was practically obliged to consult the ulama on important policy decisions and his efforts to modernise the Saudi-Wahhabi state were often vetoed. After 1930, although he still consulted them on major issues (mainly on internal matters), Ibn Saud was able to disregard their vehement objections to his limited modernising measures, essential for the consolidation and development of his kingdom.

The ulama did not easily accept the decline of their power and bitterly fought the monarch's 'innovations' such as the motor car, telephone, telegraph and radio, adopted after the conquest of the Hijaz (1924–25). As late as the 1930s, they openly disapproved of the religious conduct of the ruler and his sons. In 1939, when the King attempted to establish a modern Saudi army, they opposed European-style uniforms, martial music and some of the weapons of the new army.[6]

Although he finally overruled their objections, Ibn Saud, nevertheless, always showed respect for and pampered the ulama in order to enhance the legitimacy of his regime. The more fanatic Najdi *'alims* who vehemently opposed the King's policies had to retire to their home towns or villages.[7] Others, though clashing verbally with Ibn Saud, accepted his ruling at the end. Otherwise Abd al-Aziz devoutly espoused Wahhabi principles, his kingdom's *raison d'être*, and confined the process of modernisation to the most essential. He also upheld whenever possible the golden rule of *shura* (consultation) and *ijma'* (consensus) concerning most non-political major decisions.

Modern education was slowly introduced by King Abd al-Aziz in Saudi Arabia from the 1920s onwards, despite the ulama's bitter opposition (Chapter 3). Until the 1950s the pace of educational reforms was restricted and hesitant and the country's modernisation effort depended heavily (and still does) on foreigners, mostly of Arab origin. However, after World War II the ulama gradually adapted to changing conditions, especially with regard to matters of organisation and technology. They not only 'modernised' the religious educational system up to university level, but also, during Faysal's reign (1964–75), extended their control over the modern system as well.

Several scholars have recently attempted to analyse the ulama's involvement in the Saudi political process after Ibn Saud's death (1953).[8] Evidently the conservatives, who at first largely rallied behind the 'reactionary' King Saud (r. 1953–64) rather than support the 'modernist' Crown Prince Faysal, played only a peripheral role in the dramatic developments in Saudi Arabia in the 1950s and early 1960s. However, in addition to the power struggle among Ibn Saud's sons, this period saw the rise of Arab nationalism and of new Saudi elites. Most writers agree that the ulama's involvement in various crises was necessitated by the regime's need to legitimise succession (1953, 1964, 1975, 1982), and/or other extraordinary political actions that required the issuing of a *fatwa* by the senior ulama. Such was the case when Faysal was appointed Prime Minister in 1958 and 1962, when the twelve leading ulama signed a *fatwa* which forced Saud to abdicate in Faysal's favour (after the *ahl al-ḥal wa'l-'aqd* agreed on this matter) in October 1964,[9] and when circumstances demanded the storming of the Ka'ba in 1979.

Most ulama have become realistic since the 1950s. They tend to accept, to some degree, the limited modernisation efforts and their subordinate position in the Saud–ulama traditional alliance, since they nevertheless do enjoy a relatively high status and exercise a degree of control over everyday life in Saudi Arabia. This somewhat revised form of alliance between the Wahhabi ulama and the Sauds was finalised by Faysal when he was Prime Minister (1958–60 and 1962–64) and clinched during his monarchy (1964–75).

Although he noticeably accelerated modernisation, Faysal, who believed in evolutionary rather than revolutionary changes, followed his father's golden rule of consultation and consensus and whenever possible attempted to gain the ulama's consent, if not support, for his reforms. Endeavouring to modernise and decentralise the religious hierarchy and to incorporate it in the Saudi establishment, Faysal created several very important religious institutions some of which replaced the broad authority of the Grand Mufti who died in 1969. The most important were: The Council of the Assembly of

Senior Ulama (*Majlis Hay'at Kibar al-'Ulama*), the Higher Council of the Qadis (*Al-Majlis al-A'la li'l-Qada*) and the Administration of Scientific Study, (religious) Legal Opinions, Islamic Propagation and Guidance (*Idarat al-Buḥuth al-'Ilmiya wa'l-Ifta' wa'l-Da'wa wa'l-Irshad*, traditionally *Dar al-Ifta' wa'l Ishraf 'ala'l-Shu'un al-Diniyya*).[10] Those institutions are today the centres of the ulama's authority in the kingdom and enjoy substantial prestige and influence.

Whenever the Wahhabi conservatives opposed his evolutionary reforms, Faysal did not hesitate to confront them. For instance, when he pioneered girls' education in Saudi Arabia in 1960 during his tenure as Prime Minister under his brother Saud (1953–64), Faysal encountered the fierce opposition from the ulama. This major innovation sparked off riots incited by the ulama in different parts of the kingdom which Faysal suppressed with an iron hand. In 1965, the King's nephew, Khalid ibn Musa'id ibn Abd al-Aziz, was killed by the police following a violent demonstration by fundamentalists against the opening of a television station in Riyadh.[11]

As long as he was able to achieve his essential objectives, Faysal compromised with the ulama. Once television was introduced, for example, Faysal agreed that its broadcasts would be restricted largely to religious programmes and news, and that it would be monitored by the ulama.[12] After establishing The Female Education Authority and expanding the kingdom's higher education, the monarch entrusted their development and supervision to senior ulama. Students not only study many religiously-orientated courses but are constantly reminded of the organic relationship within the kingdom between the Wahhabi movement and the regime, and that the rulers are the protectors of the Islamic state. This process of indoctrination was accelerated and the 'Islamisation' of modern education was expanded after the 1979 Mecca rebellion. Not surprisingly, the ulama-controlled religious education produces, with very few exceptions, conformist graduates and not militant fundamentalists.[13]

Notwithstanding all the above, and despite his acquired reputation as a devout ruler and *'alim*, his pan-Islamic policy (to counter President Nasser's pan-Arabism) and support of foreign fundamentalists, Faysal was bent on eroding, directly and indirectly, the ulama's position within the Saudi power equation. This was partly the outcome of their political weakness and in part of Faysal's modernisation policy. Important factors in this process were the reorganisation and expansion of authority of the central government after 1962, and the increasing number of western-trained technocrats and graduates of 'secular' Saudi universities who control most of the new ministries and government services, with the exception of the religious-oriented ones. Most important, however, was the launching of the regime's first three multi-billion dollar five-year development plans (1970–85) which dramatically transformed Saudi Arabia's backward economy and society into a modernising 'nation-state'.

THE 'INSTITUTIONALISATION' OF THE ULAMA AND FAYSAL'S ISLAMIC ALLIANCE (1958–70)

Having become more 'pragmatic' in the 1960s the ulama, rather than attempting to fight Faysal's accelerated modernisation, tried to limit the impact of westernisation on the special character and culture of the Saudi-Wahhabi kingdom. As time passed, the lower and middle ranks of the religious hierarchy, who enjoyed prestige and affluence, were gradually being filled with 'alims who had grown up in the new era and were, with some exceptions, willing to tolerate, if not support, the regime's policy as long as it did not undermine the kingdom's basic character.[14] It could be said that by the 1970s most of the ulama (in the wider sense) had progressively been co-opted into the system. Even if a disgruntled extremist minority expressed its views in the religious universities, institutions and publications, the main critics of modernisation were secure, relatively affluent, old school fundamentalists. While lashing out at the westernisation of Saudi Arabia and the erosion of the 'Saudi way of life' by foreigners and western-trained technocrats, and censuring other Muslim rulers for corrupting Islam, they absolved the Saud's regime of such guilt.[15] Such an ambivalence, typical of the Wahhabi ulama, was totally rejected by the new militant fundamentalists (neo-Ikhwan) which, as in other parts of the Muslim world, began to emerge in the 1970s in Saudi Arabia.

The development of secular nationalism and pan-Arabism in the Arab world brought to Saudi Arabia, between the 1940s and 1960s, Muslim Brothers (mainly Egyptian) and other salafi (neo-fundamentalists, largely militant movements) refugees, who were persecuted by their governments, or unwilling to accept official ideologies and reforms. All were given sanctuary and generous stipends by the Saudi authorities, on the understanding that they would refrain from criticising their hosts. Faysal, who was fighting Nasser's pan-Arabism, needed their support, moreover, for his pan-

Islamic policies. Faysal claimed that pan-Arabism was opposed to the idea of Islamic solidarity encompassing hundreds of millions of Muslims of which the Arabs were a small, though important, component. Subsequently, with the help of the foreign fundamentalists, he established in 1962 The World Islamic League (*Rabitat al-'Alam al-Islami*). The secretariat of this organisation and many of its institutions, funded by the Saudis, are located in Mecca and Jedda and have become an important tool of Saudi foreign policy which also promoted later the Islamic Conference Organisation. Moreover, in 1961 foreign fundamentalists in cooperation with the leading Wahhabi ulama were permitted to establish the Al-Madina University, meant to replace Al-Azhar in Cairo as an international centre of Islamic scholarship. Other expatriate *salafis* were also employed by the Riyadh and Mecca Islamic universities dominated by Wahhabi *'alims*.[16]

By the 1970s the Muslim world had experienced an upsurge of Islamic fundamentalism, which contributed to the growth of neo-*salafi* (jihad — ultra-militant) organisations which held socio-political ideologies, and set out to fight the 'unbelievers ruling the Islamic countries'. Some of these were the *Al-'yyat al-Islah* (Kuwait), *Jami'yyat al-Tabligh* (India-Pakistan) and similar organisations which adopted terrorist tactics and flourished in Egypt, Syria, Kuwait and the Indian sub-continent. Thus, 'the nuclei of isolationist organizations propagating the jihad against apostates and apostate regimes emerged', a movement that was bound to affect Saudi society.[17]

Following the far-reaching changes which the Saudi kingdom and society underwent in the 1960s and early 1970s, those centres of foreign *salafis* and students began to attract Saudi supporters. Aware that their society was rapidly disintegrating under the impact of urbanisation, students of tribal origin and some of their urban brethren and foreign colleagues, disillusioned with their extremist ulama teachers, began to develop their own brand of militant neo-fundamentalism, strongly critical of the westernisation of Saudi Arabia, the 'moral corruption' of its ruling class and the hypocritical Wahhabi ulama.[18]

MODERNISATION, THE MECCA UPRISING (1979) AND ITS RAMIFICATIONS

King Khalid (r. 1975–82) succeeded Faysal in 1975. Yet Crown

Prince Fahd, because of the monarch's poor health and in line with pre-agreed succession arrangements, practically ruled Saudi Arabia in the ensuing years with the ulama's blessing. Fahd, the leading modernist in Faysal's camp, had been restrained by Faysal's determination to preserve a fine balance between modernists and conservatives. After his accession to power and given the kingdom's increasing oil revenues, Fahd launched vast development projects necessitating the substantial expansion of the foreign workforce, thus disregarding the ulama's apprehensions concerning the rapid changes that the kingdom was undergoing. By the late 1970s the foreign workforce in Saudi Arabia numbered nearly three million, of which about 100,000 were westerners.[19] This phenomenon — especially the presence in the Wahhabi kingdom of the large western community with its abhorred lifestyle — was anathema to the conservative population. The ulama in particular feared that, together with western technology, western cultural influences would subvert the Wahhabi-Saudi 'way of life'. Hence, some Najdi *alims* even began openly to criticise the Saudi ruling class for betraying the principles of (Wahhabi) Islam.

In 1977, as Khalid's health declined, the struggle for succession surfaced again. Criticism of the regime's uncontrolled modernisation and pro-western policy increased among both traditional and new elites.[20] The Crown Prince, also aware of the rise of militant fundamentalism in the Muslim world, now strove to improve his relations with the ulama, curbing the more flagrant aspects of westernisation. Wahhabi laws and a puritanical code of behaviour were more strictly enforced by the Morality Police, now endowed with additional authority. The slow process of women's emancipation in Saudi Arabia was practically halted, and westerners, even Aramco employees, who violated the kingdom's religious prohibitions were now dealt with more harshly. Nevertheless, Fahd refused to slow down the kingdom's modernisation programmes and, unlike Faysal, he rarely consulted the ulama even on internal problems, unless they were directly related to religion.

While militant, socially-oriented, fundamentalist ideologies were by the 1970s spreading rapidly and, to some extent, replacing pan-Arabism in the Arab world, this was far less the case in Saudi Arabia (the Shi'ites of the Eastern Province excepted). Here, on the one hand, the standard of living of the largely unsophisticated, conservative population was rapidly rising; on the other hand, the cooperation between the Sauds and the establishment ulama, including the tame ultra-conservatives, produced a 'pragmatic fundamentalism' which accepted modern technology and state organisation, closed its eyes to other aspects of modernisation, yet openly rejected western culture, its material values, consumerism and permissiveness. It also provided a legitimate outlet for Wahhabi xenophobia and the anti-western sentiments of many Saudis.[21] Moreover, by the late 1970s the regime had succeeded in its efforts to solve most of the problems which were causing hardship to the newly urbanised population. Thus the spontaneous mass uprising of enraged puritans, which Juhayman bin Muhammad al-'Utaybi hoped to spark off when he and his followers occupied the Mecca *haram* in 1979, did not materialise.

The Mecca rebellion of 1979, rather than exposing the regime's vulnerability, underlined its strength and the dependence of the establishment Wahhabi ulama on their traditional alliance with the Sauds. The rebels may have enjoyed the sympathy of some extreme Najdi *'alims* and of unimportant elements among the conservative urban lower middle class and some Bedouin. Yet the fact remains that the Mecca uprising remained an isolated incident and the rebels did not win any overt support.[22]

The critical attitude of the Ikhwan toward the establishment, which neo-*salafi jihad* groups in the Muslim world propagated, is nevertheless consistent with the Wahhabi world-view. It has been hinted that some frustrated senior Najdi ulama sympathised with, and may have even encouraged, neo-Ikhwan groups and their criticism of the regime.[23] However, after the initial shock and within a few days of deliberations, thirty senior ulama, headed by Shaykh Abdallah ibn Humayd and including several arch-conservatives such as Abd al-Aziz ibn Baz and Shaykh Salim ibn Muhammad b. Lahidan, produced a *fatwa* on 24 November 1979 permitting the storming of the Ka'ba and condemning the rebels who had violated the sanctity of the *haram*. They also condemned the claims of the Ikhwan as 'sedition, insurrection, atheism, and a perversion of the ideas of Islam'. The Saudi regime, they concluded, 'had done nothing to warrant the rebellion'.[24]

Interestingly enough, of about thirty signatories of the *fatwa*, only three were Al-Shaykhs, indicating the change in the social composition of the Saudi ulama by the late 1970s and the decline of this family in the ranks of the senior ulama. None the less, Al-Shaykhs were still to be found among the heads of the religious hierarchy and three held ministerial positions (although only two were *'alims*). Following the suppression of the rebellion, General Al-Awfi, the Director of Public Security, was replaced by General Abd al-Rahman al-Shaykh — a sign, as one observer saw it,[25] of the rising power of the Al-Shaykhs ironically at the time that the influence of the ulama as a whole was declining.

The historic alliance between 'church and state' in Saudi Arabia and the regime's golden rule of consultation and consensus in its relations with the ulama thus clearly guaranteed the latter's legitimisation of the Sauds. Despite the continuous erosion of the ulama's influence in the kingdom's power equation, their role was still indispensable despite criticism of the Saud's policy and behaviour by fundamentalist circles. Moreover, the relatively prosperous settled and nomadic population of Bedouin origin were not attracted by the neo-Ikhwan ideologies and stood firmly by the Sauds.

REGIME AND ULAMA IN AN ERA OF SOCIAL CHANGE AND GROWING MUSLIM EXTREMISM

The success of the Islamic revolution in Iran and the Mecca affair (at a time when American credibility in the region was sharply declining) had put the Saudi regime, and especially Crown Prince Fahd, on the defensive. Saudi 'institutionalised puritanism' was now facing the challenge of the new militant fundamentalism. The Saud rulers, therefore, decided to strengthen their cooperation with the religious establishment. In practice, this meant that the rulers would enforce more strictly the Wahhabi code of behaviour on citizens and foreign residents alike. They also expanded, once again, the authority of the ulama-controlled Committee for Encouraging Virtue and Preventing Vice, and its Morality Police.[26] Through this measure Crown Prince Fahd hoped to ensure the continued support of the ulama to his regime as well as to his watered-down modernisation programme.

The alliance between the regime and the ulama has been even more carefully cultivated in recent years because of Teheran's revolutionary anti-Saudi propaganda and the Iran–Iraq War. In line with his predecessors, King Fahd, who succeeded Khalid to the throne in 1982, meets with the senior ulama every week and with lesser *'alims* during his regular *majalis*.[27] The monarch consults senior ulama on a variety of internal matters and tries to win their consent, whenever possible, regarding reforms and other matters that may relate to religion. Since his accession to the throne, moreover, King Fahd had reversed the hesitant liberalisation of the early 1970s concerning the status of women and further increased the Morality Police's control over the behaviour of the foreign community. Education has become more 'Islamic' and the ulama's control of it has increased. Separation of the sexes in the universities is now absolute, as it is in all public places in the kingdom. But although he bows to their wishes on matters connected with religious and moral conduct and the curtailment of 'westernisation', which he considers of secondary importance, Fahd does not permit the ulama to interfere in the running of the kingdom, its development or its foreign policy.

Despite the increased respect which the ulama enjoy and the fact that King Fahd frequently underscores his devotion to Wahhabi principles through the media, it seems that the ulama's influence and power under Fahd is continuing to decline, supporting the conclusion that

It is noticeable that the activities of the ulama are socially and not politically orientated. The ulama have exercised very little or no influence over major policies concerning foreign affairs, internal security, economic development, oil production and pricing, wealth distribution and regional allocation, or political participation.[28]

The Wahhabi movement emerged in the periphery of the Arab world where it was adopted by an impoverished and backward society, largely tribal or of tribal origin. Once Ibn Saud had unified his kingdom it became increasingly evident that it was impossible to govern a twentieth-century political body according to the principles of an extremist, unsophisticated, fundamentalist religious movement. Ibn Saud attempted, therefore, to win the ulama's consent to the introduction of essential elements of modernisation, especially in the field of technology and government. Even after the Ikhwan rebellion, however, the ulama strongly resisted any attempt at modernisation. Yet the King, in matters which he considered of special importance to Saudi Arabia, did not hesitate to overrule them. Nevertheless, by adhering to the principles of consultation and consensus in their relations with the ulama, Ibn Saud and his heirs won the continued legitimisation of their regime and, somewhat unwillingly, of the socio-economic revolution which they instituted.

The pace of modernisation initiated by Faysal from the late 1960s onwards, sustained by increasing oil wealth, led to important changes in Saudi society and, to a lesser extent, in its cultural values.

The monarch's devoutness, combined with coercion, 'bribery' and manipulation, enabled Faysal to win the acquiescence of the ulama for his evolutionary reforms. Faysal used the Wahhabi ulama and the foreign *salafis*, moreover, to launch moderate pan-Islamic policy which, *inter alia*, helped consolidate the Saudi state by countering Nasser's pan-Arabism. As long as Faysal and his successors carefully maintained the 'Wahhabi character' of their kingdom, the ulama increasingly adapted to the new situation and became integrated into the Saudi establishment. Paradoxically, while individual *'alims* became cabinet ministers and their traditional institutions were modernised and granted expanded responsibilities, the group's real power, if not status, declined.

All social changes run against elements which cannot, or will not, adapt. That partly explains the 1979 'neo-Ikhwan' reaction, which protested the corruption of the fundamentalist *jihad*ist Wahhabi state by modernisation and gradual westernisation. But in the age of jet airplanes, sophisticated weaponry and a complex security apparatus, such elements cannot hope to overthrow a regime, unless they enjoy widespread support. By the late 1970s, the Saudis were no longer an impoverished people ready to embrace extremist puritan ideologies, but rather a society composed largely of an affluent urban middle class. Indeed, Saudia's educational system continues to produce annually school graduates by the hundreds of thousands. Coupled with modernisation and rapid urbanisation, these changes have made militant Wahhabi fundamentalism (neo-Ikhwan) unattractive to the Saudi masses (obviously the new elites included), although being essentially conservative they continue to support the existing diluted version of Wahhabism.

The Wahhabiyya was always an antithesis of sophisticated religious philosophy. **What is now left of its original fundamentalist-*jihad*ist message, besides old-fashioned unitarianism, is largely its traditional puritan moral code of public behaviour, feigned asceticism and xenophobia, merged with tribal customs and heritage, popularly referred to the as 'Saudi way of life', it was sanctified by the Sauds and the ulama and transformed into a national ethos.** This unique combination, coupled with oil wealth, provides the regime with a working formula for countering militant fundamentalism on the one hand and radical nationalism on the other. As long as the Sauds continue to nourish the above ethos and respect the special position of the ulama in the Saudi-Wahhabi kingdom, they are assured of the continuity of their historic alliance with the ulama, notwithstanding the continuous erosion in the latter's influence. That, and economic prosperity (if renewed), ensures the Sauds of the support of most of their subjects and particularly the less sophisticated ones.

NOTES

1. D. Ottaway, *Washington Post* (WP), 27 November 1984. On Islamic universities, see Chapter 3 below.

2. A. Bligh, 'The Saudi Religious Elite (ulama) as Participant in the Political System of the Kingdom', *International Journal of Middle East Studies*, Vol. 17, No. 1 (1985), p. 42; Layish, 'Ulama and Politics in Saudi Arabia', in M. Heper and R. Israeli (eds), *Islam and Politics in the modern Middle East* (New York, 1984), pp. 35–6; M. Field, FT, 24 April 1984, supplement, p. XII; Ottaway, WP, 27 November 1984.

3. O.Y. Al-Rawaf, 'The concept of the Five Crises in Political Development', PhD thesis (Duke University, 1981), pp. 326–7; Bligh, 'Religious elite', pp. 10–15.

4. For instance Abdallah b. Blayhid (the *Qadi* of Mecca after the Hijaz's conquest) and Abdallah b. Hassan Al al-Shaykh (*khatib* of the Grand Mosque of Mecca, who became *Qadi* of Mecca after Blayhid resigned and returned to Najd in 1927): A. Bligh, *From Prince to King. Royal Succession in the House of Saud in the Twentieth Century* (New York, 1984), p. 34; also Bligh, 'Religious elite', p. 38. On Ikhwan: Chapter 1 above, p. 15. Najdi ulama were, and still are, known for their extremism.

5. Later the National Guard: M. Abir, 'Saudi security and military endeavour', *The Jerusalem Quarterly*, No. 33 (Fall 1984), pp. 91–3.

6. Bligh, 'Religious elite', p. 40; also M. Abir, 'Modernisation, reaction and Muhammad Ali's "empire"', MES, Vol. 13, No. 3 (October 1977), p. 298: on similar criticism by the ulama of Muhammad Ali's European style army in the 1830s.

7. The case of Abdallah b. Blayhid: Bligh, 'Religious elite', p. 38.

8. Ibid.; Layish, 'Ulama'; Ochsenwald, 'Saudi Arabia and the Islamic revival', *International Journal of Middle East Studies*, Vol. 13 (1981).

9. The ulama leadership (principally Al al-Shaykh), participated in the final deliberations leading to Saud's dethronement. Saud's removal from office — an extreme step — was in line with tribal custom and Muslim concepts: — S.S. Huyette, *Political Adaptation in Sa'udi Arabia* (Boulder, 1985), p. 82. Faysal wished, nevertheless, to legalise the procedure by a *fatwa*: F.M. Zedan, 'Political Development of the Kingdom of Saudi Arabia 1932–1975', unpublished PhD thesis (Claremont Graduate School, 1981), p. 24; T.R. McHale, 'The Saudi Arabian political system', *Vierteljahresberichte*, No. 89 (September 1982), p. 201; A. Assah, *Miracle of the Desert Kingdom* (London, 1969), p. 123. Layish ('Ulama', p. 49) identifies the signatories of the *fatwa* as the crust of the Saudi religious hierarchy. See also A. Lateef, 'King Faisal: From obscurity to international status', *Pakistan Horizon*, Vol. 28, No. 4 (1975), p. 120; G. De Gaury, *Faisal King of Saudi Arabia*, (New York, 1966), pp. 130–5. For text of the *fatwa*, see

W. Khalidi and Y. Ibish, *Arab Political Documents* (Beirut, 1964), p. 441.

10. Founded in 1953, the Institute for the Issue of (religious) Legal Opinions and the Supervision of Religious Affairs (*Dar al-Ifta' wa'l-Ishraf 'ala'l-Shu'un al-Diniyya*), was expanded and institutionalised by Faysal in 1970 after the death of the Grand Mufti. In 1962 Faysal helped in establishing a council of 22 senior ulama, which served as the foundation for the 1971 body of Senior Ulama, to help adapt the *Shari'a* to present-day requirements: Layish, 'Ulama', pp. 30, 34–5; R. Schulze, 'The Saudi Arabian 'ulama and their Reaction to Muslim Fundamentalism', a paper prepared for a Colloquium on Religious Radicalism and Politics in the Middle East, The Hebrew University (Jerusalem, May 1985), pp. 1, 22 (cited with the author's permission).

11. Especially in Najd: A.H. Said, 'Saudi Arabia: The Transition From a Tribal Society to a Nation', PhD thesis (University of Missouri, 1979), p. 105; M.A.T. Al Saud, 'Permanence and Change', PhD thesis (Claremont Graduate School, 1982), p. 140. Ten years later King Faysal was assassinated by Khalid's brother, Faysal. A different version of the above incident: Huyette, *Adaptation*, p. 74.

12. The conservatives claimed that TV has become a channel for western influence. A. Tash, 'A Profile of Professional Journalists Working in Saudi Arabian Daily Press', unpublished PhD thesis (Southern Illinois University at Carbondale, 1983), pp. 51–3; Al-Rawaf, 'Five Crises', pp. 358–60; Lacey, *The Kingdom* (London, 1981), p. 512.

13. Said, 'Saudi Arabia', p. 111; Al-Rawaf, 'Five Crises', pp. 187–8; Huyette, *Adaptation*, p. 117.

14. Bligh's (Bligh, *Succession*, p. 100) claim of a growing rift between the senior and younger radical *'alims*, need substantiation. The few extremist *'alims* who publicly challenged the authorities were quietly deprived of a public platform by the establishment: M. Field, 'Why the Saudi royal family is more stable than the Shah', *Euromoney* (October 1981); FT, 21 April 1986, supplement, p. VIII.

15. R. Schulze, 'The Saudi Arabian ulama and their Reaction to Muslim Fundamentalism', paper prepared for a Colloquium on Religious Radicalism and Politics in the Middle East, The Hebrew University (May 1985), pp. 9–10, 20, 23; Al-Rawaf, 'Five Crises', pp. 359–60; Ochsenwald, 'Islamic revival', pp. 277, 283; Layish, 'Ulama', pp. 46–7; F.A. Shaker, 'Modernization of the Developing Nations: The case of Saudi Arabia', PhD thesis (Purdue University 1972), p. 138.

16. Schulze, 'Ulama', pp. 11–12, 18.

17. Ibid., pp. 22–3; also D. Holden and R. Johns, *The House of Saud* (London, 1982), pp. 516–17; Layish, 'Ulama', p. 50.

18. The tribes of the above participated in the Ikhwan rebellion: Holden and Johns, *House of Saud*, p. 517; *Al-Mawqif al-Arabi*, 20 April 1981. See also below, Chapter 6, pp. 148–52.

19. On foreign workforce: M. Abir, 'The Manpower Problem in Saudi Arabian Economic and Security Policy', Colloquium Paper, Woodrow Wilson International Center for Scholars (Washington, DC, April 1983).

20. See below Chapter 6, pp. 137–8, 140.

21. J. Shaw and D.E. Long, *Saudi Arabian Modernization (The Washington Papers*, No. 89, 1982), p. 44; Holden and Johns, *House of*

Saud, pp. 402, 519; T. Sisley, *The Times* (London), 22 May 1980; FT, 24 April 1984, supplement, p. II. Ironically, Saudi society became one of the world's largest *per capita* importer of consumer goods.

22. Al-Rawaf, 'Five Crises', pp. 356, 359; *New York Times* (NYT), 25 February 1980; *Al-Mawqif al-Arabi*, 20 April 1981; also Huyette, *Adaptation*, p. 37. See below Chapter 6, pp. 151–2, 159.

23. Schulze, 'Ulama', pp. 22–3; J.A. Kechichian, 'The role of the ulama in the politics of an Islamic state: The case of Saudi Arabia', IJMES, Vol. 12, No. 1 (February 1986), pp. 59–60.

24. Ochsenwald, 'Islamic revival', p. 277.

25. J.A. Kechichian, The role of the 'ulama', *International Journal of Middle East Studies*, Vol. 12, No. 1 (February 1986), p. 62.

26. The status of Saudi women also suffered a reverse. Huyette *Adaptation*, p. 35; NYT, 24 March 1980; Sisley, *The Times*, 22 May 1980; *International Herald Tribune* (IHT), 22 November 1983, 22 August 1984; *The Times*, 4 January 1985; FT, 22 July 1980, 5 May 1981, 23 May 1984, 22 April 1985, 21 April 1986; *Wall Street Journal* (WSJ), 19 July 1985; Collins, 'Riyadh: the Saudi balance', *The Washington Quarterly* (Winter 1981), p. 202; *Al-Madina* (Saudi Arabia), 30 November 1983, 29 July 1984. On Morality Police: Layish, 'Ulama', p. 35–6.

27. P. Mansfield, FT, 21 April 1986; Huyette, *Adaptation*, p. 93.

28. Al-Rawaf, 'Five Crises', p. 527; also Field, FT, 21 April 1986, supplement, p. VIII; Huyette, *Adaptation*, p. 117; Layish, 'Ulama', pp. 54–7.

3

Modern Education and the Rise of New Elites in Saudi Arabia*

MODERN EDUCATION AND THE ULAMA — THE INITIAL PHASE

The implantation of modern education in the Saudi-Wahhabi state

Traditionally the ulama, in addition to their religious and judicial duties, were the teachers of the devout, and of the sons of the ruling elites. The puritanical Wahhabi ulama, however, limited themselves to the study of the *Shari'a* and its recognised interpretations and totally ignored all other subjects. On the other hand, the Hijaz, the most populated province with its holy cities was of old a centre of Islamic scholarship in the broader sense, and in the first quarter of the twentieth century it benefited from the development of 'modern' education in the Ottoman Empire. Yet, except for Arabic and geography, the curriculum of its handful of 'modern' schools remained almost exclusively based on the study of the Koran and related subjects.[1]

In 1926, Ibn Saud created in the kingdom of the Hijaz (conquered in 1924) a directorate of education (*Mudiriyyat al-Ma'rif*) under his Egyptian adviser, Hafiz Wahba, who opened the first secondary school, reformed the public schools, and introduced modern subjects into the curriculum. For this purpose Wahba hired teachers from Egypt, and between 1926 and 1931 sent some young Hijazis to study there. His activities naturally aroused substantial opposition among the Wahhabi ulama, whose leaders strongly protested against his policy. But the King supported Wahba's programme which he considered essential for national integration and his kingdom's development.

34

Ibn Saud, however, prudently tried to avoid a confrontation with the ulama, and sought a compromise whenever they protested at his innovations. As his meagre revenues suffered in the 1930s from the world economic recession and its aftermath, the development of modern education in Saudi Arabia was slowed and largely confined to the Hijaz, leaving the ulama with a *de facto* monopoly on education. Thus, illiteracy in Saudi Arabia was said to have remained as late as the middle of the twentieth century as high as 95 per cent.[2]

Political-economic dynamics and the growth of modern education, 1946–58

As Ibn Saud increasingly recruited Arabs from outside the kingdom to help with the running of his modernising government, he realised that ultimately he needed the support of educated Saudis who would eventually replace the traditional administrators and foreign experts. Accordingly, despite the financial difficulties of the early 1940s, Ibn Saud, in an effort to advance Saudi education, hired many more Egyptian and other Arabic-speaking teachers, and sent more Saudis to study in Egypt. Commercial exploitation of oil in Saudi Arabia after 1946 speeded up these efforts and eventually caused the progressive Egyptianisation of Saudi education.

In 1949 Aramco launched a five-year plan for the development of the skills of its employees, and by 1952, 8000 company workers had benefited from this training. Selected Saudi employees were sent to the American University in Beirut (AUB) and later to the United States. Aramco also provided modern education for their children and for other children in the Eastern Province.[3] Of course, Aramco was not motivated exclusively by philanthropy: its investment in education was necessitated by its operations and the need to Saudi-ise its workforce. Yet its contribution to the development of modern Saudi education, especially in the Eastern Province, should not be underestimated.

In 1949 and 1952 respectively, an Islamic College and a teachers' training college were founded by the Directorate of Education in Mecca to offer subjects including Arabic language, history and civilisation, although the curriculum of schools and colleges continued to be dominated by religious and Arabic studies.

The ulama, led by the kingdom's Grand Mufti, resenting state invasion of their domain, countered the administration's move by 'modernising' and reorganising their own traditional system of education. Thus, the Grand Mufti founded in Riyadh a college of Islamic jurisprudence (1953) and one for the Arabic language (1954) which also offered courses in Arab history and civilisation. This pattern of adding related subjects to religious studies and adopting a modern framework became the trend thereafter in secondary and higher religious education. It was also part of a subtle competition between the ulama-controlled educational system and the state system. Eventually, however, the ulama realised that they could not turn the clock back and though they continued to adapt traditional education to the new situation, they now strove to become the supervisors of the development of 'modern' education as well.

The succession of Saud after his father's death in 1953 signalled the revival of the power of the conservatives, on the one hand, and the emergence of Saudi nationalists on the other. King Saud (r. 1953–64) is generally described as a reactionary who abrogated some of his father's reforms and even instructed all Saudis studying abroad to return home (in 1955). In this way he gained the cooperation of the ulama, who were suspicious of his heir (and Prime Minister) Faysal's reformist tendencies.[4] There were achievements, however. A Ministry of Education was created in 1953 to replace the Hijaz directorate and although study abroad was restricted to higher education, many students were sent to foreign universities. Indeed, the number of schools and students at all levels of education tripled or quadrupled during Saud's reign, and the budget for education — 2.8 million dollars in 1953 — grew to nearly 100 million dollars in 1964.[5] In 1957 King Saud established Riyadh University, the first secular university in the kingdom, and in 1958 adopted a three-cycle sequence of education: six years of elementary school, three years of intermediate, and three years of secondary school.

It would be misleading, of course, to attribute these achievements solely to Saud, because Faysal effectively ruled the country during 1958–60 and 1962–64. Although Saud was a conservative and weak ruler, he nevertheless helped to develop modern Saudi education; paradoxically, he even allied himself in 1960 with the Liberal Princes and the small new western-educated elite who were dissatisfied with Faysal's evolutionary reforms.

ULAMA, EDUCATION AND SOCIO-POLITICAL TRANSFORMATION, 1958–86

Modernisation, new elites and ulama under Faysal (1958–75)

The ulama joined Faysal's camp only in 1961. Their frustration with Saud's incompetence reached its peak when he stumbled into an alliance with the secular new elite and the Liberal Princes, whose reformist zeal they feared. Although he ignored the ulama's opposition to modernisation, Faysal followed his father's policy and tried to win their support for his reforms through concessions and compromises. For example, after pioneering girls' education in 1960 in the face of violent opposition (before he was replaced by Saud), Faysal placed the new General Directorate of Girls' Education under the Grand Mufti. Subsequently, ulama-controlled female education became completely segregated and male teachers communicated with women students only through closed-circuit television. The more conservative ulama continued to oppose girls' education altogether. Thus, only 50 per cent of Saudi girls attended elementary schools in the 1970s and an increasingly smaller proportion intermediate and secondary schools and universities.[6] In the 1980s, however, the number of females in the education system has become nearly equal to that of males; educated girls are more marriageable, it seems. But, to please the ulama, King Fahd halted the slow process of their integration in the kingdom's economy.

In return for ulama support in his struggle with his brother Saud in 1961–64, and for their acquiescence to his reforms, Faysal in effect granted them supervision of the modern education system. With the appointment of Shaykh Hassan Al al-Shaykh as Minister of Education in 1962, the ministry became a stronghold of conservative bureaucrats. Then in 1970 Faysal established the General Directorate of Religious Institutions and Colleges through which the government funded the religious system of education, and in 1975, when the government was reorganised by Prince Fahd and a Ministry of Higher Education created, Shaykh Hassan was appointed its head and a conservative technocrat replaced him as the Minister of Education.

Paradoxically, the ulama, who at first opposed modern education, under Faysal practically controlled it. The curriculum of Saudi schools came to be focused on Islamic and Arabic studies, to the point where mandatory Islamic courses constituted a third of the curriculum in elementary schools and nearly as much in the intermediate and secondary levels. Elementary school graduates could opt for a religious stream in separate intermediate and secondary schools, but even if they did not, **they would be constantly reminded of the organic relationship between the Saudi state and the Wahhabiyya.**[7] **Consequently, the younger Saudis, their minds conditioned by the educational system, become largely conservative in their outlook.** Hence, the ulama, though not unaware of the far-reaching social and cultural changes generated by Faysal's modernisation programme, continued to cooperate with the King, who was careful to preserve the kingdom's puritan Wahhabi framework and their privileged status within it.

Faysal, believing that the modernisation of Saudi Arabia was conditional on the emergence of a large educated elite, was determined to provide, eventually, a minimum level of education for every Saudi. Though he prudently slowed down the expansion of elementary education because of financial constraints in the mid-1960s and shifted the focus from quantity to quality, simultaneously he accelerated the development of secondary and higher education and the vocational system. The latter, however, failed to attract sufficient students (with the exception of Al-Hasa Province) notwithstanding a substantial investment in it in the 1960s, and even more so in the 1970s. This was due to the low prestige attached to manual work in Saudi society as well as to the availability of many other more attractive opportunities open to young Saudis after the late 1960s.[8]

In the 1970s and early 1980s the mammoth expansion of the Saudi educational system was facilitated by the enormous rise in state revenues from the sale of oil, and the planning — with American help — of further expansion of education. The kingdom's first five-year development plan (1970–75), prepared in 1969, had projected a substantial growth of the different levels of education, but no one envisaged the vast increase in the kingdom's oil revenues after 1973, or the subsequent huge budgets for the 'development of human resources'. Because of the economic recession, vocational education became more popular in the 1980s, but ironically, in addition to joining the civil service, many graduates of the system became in essence contractors, setting up with government loans workshops or small factories whose managers, foremen and workers were, in most cases, Asians.[9]

At the same time the rapid development of modern education necessitated more than ever the employment of foreign teachers and administrators. At first this dependence on foreigners (mainly

Egyptians) was nearly total, but in the late 1960s, after a major effort was made to expand and improve the training of teachers, an increasing number of them were employed in school administration and as teachers in the elementary schools. Today, it is claimed that elementary education is practically completely Saudi-ised but the intermediary and secondary levels remain largely dependent on foreigners.[10]

Possibly more serious is the poor quality of the Saudi education system itself. Two major reasons for this are the low standard of foreign teachers and the Egyptian model followed by the Saudis based on rote-learning, recitation and 'cramming'. Saudi teachers who replace foreigners in elementary and secondary schools are generally no better than their predecessors, which is why Faysal's government attempted to improve and expand the teacher training colleges in the late 1960s. The vast expansion of the Saudi education system in the 1970s, together with the accelerated development of the economy, however, completely undermined his efforts. As demand for the limited Saudi manpower constantly increased, educated Saudis were snapped up by the private and public sectors, while the lower levels of the teaching profession were not considered sufficiently prestigious or rewarding. Thus the poor quality of teaching in Saudi schools remains a problem to this day.[11]

Education and social change under Fahd (1975–86)

King Faysal was assassinated in 1975 and was succeeded by Prince Khalid (r. 1975–82). The true ruler of Saudi Arabia, however, was Prince Fahd, Khalid's heir and Prime Minister. Fahd's reformist enthusiasm had been restrained by Faysal, whose closest assistant Fahd was. Following Faysal's death in 1975, Prince Fahd, who held the reins of power while Khalid reigned, immediately stepped up the rapid industrialisation of the country which necessitated accelerated manpower training. As there was no shortage of funds, the education system was expanded to an unprecedented rate; by 1986, the total number of students in Saudi schools had risen to nearly two million (over 35 per cent of the population) compared to 33,000 in 1953. The fourth development plan (1985–90) anticipates for 1990 about 2,105,000 students, of whom 937,000 will be girls, assuming that education will become compulsory in addition to being free.[12]

The enormous expansion of modern education and the substantial decline of illiteracy in Saudi Arabia since the 1960s are impressive achievements. Yet Saudi statistics often conceal the low standard of the educational system and the social composition of its students. The quality of schools and students varies according to the geographical and social environment. Rural and urban lower-middle-class students (largely Bedouin) with traditional backgrounds, are often unprepared for the systematic approach and foreign philosophy of modern education. In the rural areas, especially the Southern, Northern and until recently the Eastern Regions, where the standard of teaching is even lower than in the cities,[13] the number of drop-outs and repeaters in the first years of elementary school is exceptionally high. Beyond these first years, education has no economic value for rural students who do not wish to change their way of life, or decide to go into business. The same is true, to a lesser degree, of many lower-middle-class students in the poorer sections of the big cities, largely populated by the newly urbanised who, despite generous grants, are incapable of, or are uninterested in, continuing their studies beyond the first grades.

An exceptional case is that of the Shi'ites of the Eastern Province, who until the 1980s were officially discriminated against by the Wahhabi kingdom. Their best chance to acquire education above the elementary level then was through the Aramco schools, and many Shi'ites who studied in Saudi or foreign universities until the late 1970s did so on Aramco scholarships.[14] Others were the sons of the new Shi'ite petty bourgeoisie, which began to emerge in the late 1960s. The Saudi regime became more sensitive to the Shi'ites' needs after the 1979–80 riots.

The standard of education in the urban centres catering to the Saudis of middle-class background is on the whole also relatively low. Memorising is still the backbone of the system, the standard of English and science teaching is uneven, often very poor, and cheating in exams is very common. Not surprisingly, only about one third of elementary school students reached the intermediate level in the 1970s and less than 6 per cent of those who had entered first grade reached secondary level.[15] Saudi statistics take no account of the middle and upper classes' disproportionate benefits from subsidised education and other government services. Middle- and upper-class children, especially from the major towns in the Hijaz, were better prepared for modern education and also had access to better schools with more qualified teachers. Children of the Najdi *hadr* and aristocracy were not far behind them. These groups also dominated secondary education and enrolment in Saudi or foreign universities in the 1960s and 1970s.

However, the government is not unaware that the first two development plans (1970–80) favoured the urban population, especially the middle and upper classes. One of the aims of the third and fourth development plans (1980–90) is to improve the standard of living in the rural areas, where traditional social differences were already polarised by modernisation, particularly modern education. Very large budgets were earmarked in the above plans for the expansion of education in the rural areas and in his budget speech for 1985/86, despite the decline in Saudi oil revenue, King Fahd announced 300 new projects in the field of education costing over one billion dollars. Such goals often remain unfulfilled. Nevertheless, the numerous successful 'lower-class'[16] entrepreneurs have not been constrained by minimal education or social background. They have largely been accepted in the last decade as part of the middle class, together with the increasing number of their brethren who are school and university graduates.

Since 1978, and especially after he succeeded King Khalid in 1982 Fahd progressively gave in to the ulama's demands in order to pacify the conservatives. Saudi Arabia, moreover, entered a period of recession and dissatisfaction with the regime was rising. Fahd was well aware of the ulama's contribution through indoctrination to the regime's stability and also needed their support in the power struggle within the ruling class. Hence, liberal trends which emerged in the 1960s and 1970s were reversed. Separation of sexes in schools and universities is strictly supervised by the religious establishment, the ratio of religious studies in the education system has risen markedly at the expense of 'secular studies', and additional funds have been allocated to the religious system.[17]

THE DEVELOPMENT OF HIGHER EDUCATION

The first stages of Saudi higher education (1949–57) were opened by Ibn Saud. Determined not to remain completely dependent on foreign higher education, he established in Mecca a college of Shari'a in 1949 and a teacher training college in 1952, with an extension in Taif.

The Grand Mufti, competing with the government system, also established in Riyadh a Shari'a college in 1953 and an Arabic language college in 1954, which offered more generous scholarships to attract students away from government institutions. Their growth was so rapid that by the early 1960s over 2000 students had graduated with 1000 more on the way, a development that helped prolong somewhat the conservatives' hegemony in education and in the Saudi administration.[18]

At this stage, both state and ulama-controlled colleges were still traditional institutions despite the use of modern terminology. The government, because of its growing need for trained bureaucrats, continued to send young Saudis to study in Egyptian and other Arab universities as well as to Europe and America. This costly — and to the Wahhabi ulama undesirable — solution was considered by the authorities an interim measure, and in 1957 King Saud founded in Riyadh the first western-type university.

The establishment of Riyadh University ushered in the second period in the development of Saudi higher education (1957–75). Older colleges were consolidated into, or merged with, full-scale universities, while new ones were opened elsewhere in the kingdom, in a rapid development of higher education intended to facilitate Saudi Arabia's modernisation and economic development. It was King Faysal's hope, apparently, to offset the tensions arising from rapid social change by enabling talented Saudis to acquire university education and to benefit from their country's prosperity.

As a result, numerous Egyptian, western and other professors and administrators were hired, and most new universities adopted an Egyptian model, itself based on the British system of higher education. Although the influence of the many US-trained bureaucrats caused the Egyptian–British format to be replaced in 1974/75 by an American one, Egyptians and other foreigners continue to dominate the faculties of most of Saudi universities. As in other aspects of the Faysal era, the path of modern educational development was facilitated by concessions to the ulama. In this case the state funded Islamic universities and schools, made religious courses mandatory in the curriculum of the 'secular' universities, and handed to the religious leadership the supervision of women's colleges.[19]

Riyadh University (in 1980 renamed King Saud University — KSU), the largest in Saudi Arabia, is the stronghold of the Najdi 'aristocracy' and is somewhat more conservative than other 'secular' universities. It grew from 21 students in 1958 to 5600 in 1975, and 30,000 in 1986/87, and has several campuses, including the original one in Riyadh for women with an additional 6000 students (1983), and one in Asir. Its four billion dollar facilities at the new male campus in Dar'iya were inaugurated in 1984/85.[20]

The Islamic University of al-Madina was established in 1961 following consultations between foreign fundamentalists (mainly

Egyptians), Wahhabi ulama, and the Saudi authorities. As it was designed to replace Al-Azhar (following the latter's reorganisation by Nasser in 1961) as an international Islamic university, 90 per cent of its staff and the majority of its students are foreign Muslims. Its traditional character, strong *salafi* influences and low admission requirements attract students of Bedouin origin and other Saudis with neo-fundamentalist tendencies.[21]

The University of Petroleum and Minerals (UPM; now King Fahd University) in Dhahran (Eastern Province) is, by western standards, the best and most prestigious university in the country. Established by Aramco in 1963 as the College of Petroleum and Minerals (P & M), it became a university in 1975. The UPM is an American enclave in Saudi higher education: its teaching language is English, its faculty is largely American, and it is the least constrained by Wahhabi custom. Unlike other Saudi universities, its students (1000 in 1974, 3000 in 1980 and 6000 in 1985) are admitted solely on merit and students' grants are 50 per cent higher than those of other universities. Here nearly all the textbooks are in English, despite the problem (common to all Saudi universities) of students' poor knowledge of English. In 1981 half of the students and some of the faculty of the UPM were said to be Shi'ites.[22]

Supported by Faysal since the mid-1960s, the ulama-controlled Riyadh colleges became (in 1974) The Imam Muhammad Ibn Saud Islamic University. A stronghold of Najdi-Wahhabi conservatism, this university in addition to producing jurists and teachers, was given the task of coordinating all Saudi religious schools and studies. In 1980 it established a branch in Abha, the capital of Asir, and had a total of about 6000 students, of whom 20 per cent were foreigners. Its intermediary and secondary schools, however, held approximately 15,000 students. In recent years it benefited from the large budgets allocated by King Fahd to the traditional schools system. The university also supervises schools established by the National Guard for the children of its personnel and the upgrading programme of the Morality Police. The number of its students in 1985 was estimated at about 9000.[23]

King Abd-al Aziz Ibn Saud University at Jedda was founded in 1967/68 by local philanthropists as a western-oriented business institution. In 1971, it became a state university ('secular') and the two Mecca colleges and their offshoot in Taif were temporarily affiliated with it (they became the nucleus of Umm al-Qura University in 1980). Thereafter, its orientation became more Arabic-Islamic and in 1977 it opened a new campus in Madina and one in

Abha (education). From 90 students in 1967/68, it grew to 2500 in 1974/75, 17,000 in 1980/81 and over 20,000 male students in 1985.[24]

King Faysal University (KFU), the fourth and latest 'secular' university, was established in 1974/75. Its main campus in Hufuf (Eastern Province) specialises in agriculture, veterinary science and medicine; while in Dammam the university's campus is devoted to a programme of medical science. After 1980, the university established a full range of faculties; and its student body grew from 1430 in 1980/81 to over 5000 in 1985. KFU was designed to provide for the special needs of the agricultural and Bedouin population of the Eastern Province and supply some of the technician-engineers required for Jubayl's new sophisticated industrial centre. Most of its faculty are westerners and courses in the sciences and medicine are still taught in English, a serious problem for the average Saudi student and another cause for tension between students and the foreign faculty and the administration. Since 1980, because of the regime's efforts to mitigate the traditional discrimination against the Shi'ite minority, the university has enrolled a growing number of Shi'ite students. The university rapidly grew after King Fahd succeeded to the throne and additional funds were allocated for its development.[25]

Umm al-Qura University (Mecca) was formed in 1980, its nucleus the colleges founded in 1949 and 1953. In so far as the Al-Madina University is an international Islamic institution, Umm al-Qura is apparently intended to serve the conservative population of the Hijaz. A synthesis of the traditional and the modern, Umm al-Qura's enrolment requirements and standards was said to be even lower than is usual in Saudi universities. In 1983 it had about 6000 students of whom one quarter were foreigners. Like other Islamic universities, its aim is to 'supply the judges [jurists], *imams* and teachers required throughout the country; in the government its graduates occupy posts in the ministries and committees concerned with education, justice, and the preservation of virtue'.[26]

By 1975 there were nearly 20,000 students in Saudi universities, and more than 5000 Saudis studying abroad, despite the intention of reducing the number of Saudis in foreign universities. While some (mainly the offspring of wealthy Hijazi and some Najdi merchants and aristocrats) studied at their own expense, many others, mostly of urban middle-class background, were given government grants throughout their graduate and postgraduate studies.[27] Upon their return to Saudi Arabia, foreign university graduates were often appointed to important positions in Faysal's new administration and even in his government. Graduates of 'secular' domestic universities (mostly of *ḥadr* or urban middle-class background), were appointed to lesser but still prestigious positions when they chose not to go into the private sector. Subsequently, bureaucrats of middle and upper-class background, largely Hijazis and to a lesser degree Najdis, came to dominate the Saudi administration (with the exception of the ulama-controlled ministries and the legal system, where the trainees of the Wahhabi ulama were preferred), at the expense of traditional bureaucrats and graduates of religious institutions.

The third period in the development of higher education in Saudi Arabia (1975–85) coincides with the rise to power of Prince Fahd and the second and third development plans. This was a period of almost uncontrolled growth in the existing universities. Unfortunately, it also saw the decline of quality and standards.[28] As the demand for educated Saudi manpower increased following the accelerated modernisation, budgets for the 'development of human resources' were comparatively increased and several multi-billion dollar campuses were built for the universities and for women's colleges. Thousands of foreigners — again, mainly Egyptians — were hired to teach in them. Many of the 'campus mercenaries', as foreign faculty are called by Saudi intellectuals, were not of the highest quality and even Saudis who opted for a university career were also, in many cases, poorly qualified. Research and publications by Saudi professors were rare. As in the past, teaching still focused on 'cramming' and memorising, rather than on evaluation and analysis. The transformation in 1974/75 from the Egyptian–British structure to the American one introduced the semester system and credit hours, but that was not enough to improve the universities' standards. The same Egyptian and other non-Saudi Arab professors remain the backbone of the faculty in most Saudi universities. Admission requirements to all the universities (the UPM excepted) were very low, on government instructions, and frequently overlooked altogether, and cheating in exams was an accepted norm.[29]

The rapid expansion of Saudi higher education after the 1960s was partly facilitated by the growth of secondary education, mainly in urban centres. In 1974, enrolment requirements in the 'secular' universities were noticeably lowered 'by order of the government' to provide higher education to more students,[30] who in addition to free education, housing, grants, book allowances, subsidised food and other privileges were assured (until recently) of government employment on graduation. Such concessions were obviously motivated by the regime's need to defuse socio-economic tensions. The majority of students normally opted for the less demanding humanities and social sciences where the teaching language and textbooks were mostly in Arabic; only a small minority chose engineering and sciences, which were badly needed in the kingdom's developing economy but where the teaching language and bibliography were often English and many of the professors were foreigners (the same applied to business administration and medicine).[31] Although the number of graduates rose quickly in the 1970s, it could not satisfy the demand. Nevertheless, women graduates were discouraged from seeking work and no more than 50,000 women were employed in the Saudi economy in 1980/81. As a result of King Fahd's political difficulties, when he succeeded to the throne (1982) the separation of sexes in institutes of higher education and the decline in employment opportunities for women, became even more pronounced than before.[32]

While some graduates of the local and foreign universities joined the private sector of the economy and the professions, the Saudi bureaucracy continued to absorb all the others. The great majority of the latter flocked to the ministries and government agencies in Riyadh, avoiding appointments in rural areas, and rejecting any connection with manual labour. By the early 1980s large sections of the administration had become over-inflated with university-trained bureaucrats, exacerbating the prevailing inefficiency.[33] However, as senior and even middle-rank positions were hard to come by, university graduates, including experienced bureaucrats, progressively opted for provincial offices of the ministries. Indeed, in the mid-1980s, as the economic recession in Saudi Arabia was exacerbated by the crisis in the oil market, the Bureau of Student Employment found it increasingly difficult to find suitable employment for school and university graduates and many businessmen and professionals found themselves in financial difficulties or went bankrupt. In 1986, it is alleged, government offices and agencies were instructed not to hire additional personnel and that unemployment among school and university graduates in the public and private sectors was on the increase.[34]

In 1985, Saudi Arabia's seven universities and fourteen women's colleges had 9000 professors of different ranks (of which only 7 per cent of the full professors, 16 per cent of associate professors and 28 per cent of assistant professors were Saudis) and a total student population of over 80,000. The number of Saudi students abroad, despite hopes that their number would decline as a result of the development of domestic universities, continues to rise and about 20,000 are believed to be attending American universities. New universities were to be opened, however, in Riyadh and Jedda (for women), in Taif, and Abha (Asir). Indeed, the total number of students in Saudi Arabia, according to the fourth development plan (1985–90) was projected to rise by 1990 to 108,000, with 20,000 graduates annually.[35]

In addition to Aramco, the growing American involvement in Saudi education arises from the strong ties developed by Faysal's reformist government with the United States since 1958. American influence in Saudi education was formalised through bilateral agreements, most important of which was the establishment of the United States–Saudi Arabia Joint Commission on Economic Cooperation in 1975, which, *inter alia*, deals with Saudi education.

American influence was absorbed and later spread by the increasing number of Saudi students enrolled in American universities, surpassing 15,000 by the early 1980s.[36] Subsequently, an office was set up in the Saudi Consulate-General in Houston (which moved to Washington in 1984 and is supervised by Ambassador Bandar ibn Sultan) to help Saudi students and coordinate and monitor their studies. Those who returned to Saudi Arabia in the 1960s and early 1970s, mainly with PhD and Masters degrees, were appointed to key positions in the government's bureaucracy and education system. The third wave of foreign-trained graduates returning home since the mid-1970s dominated most of the middle level of the civil service and government agencies, and increasingly the staff of the 'secular' universities. Besides their influence on the central government and its policy, although they did not improve the standards of the universities, their manners, ideas, and way of life have been copied by many others. Thus, the formal transformation of the universities from the Egyptian to the American system in 1975 seemed to the conservatives another aspect of the growing 'Americanisation' of Saudi Arabia.

Frustrated by what they perceived as the westernisation of the Wahhabi kingdom through uncontrolled modernisation involving numerous westerners, many conservatives accused the government and its US-educated technocrats of helping supplant Wahhabi puritanism and 'the Saudi way of life' with western culture and 'the American way of life'.[37] Even before the Mecca incident in 1979, Prince Fahd had come under growing pressure from the more extreme ulama and Saudi middle-class nationalists to reduce western influence in the kingdom. By the early 1980s, with the completion of the third development plan, even some American-trained Saudis, unhappy with the impact of rapid modernisation and western-influenced education on their society and culture, began to question western values and the aims of modern Saudi education which they had helped develop.[38] Indeed, after the Mecca incident, even Crown Prince Fahd found it necessary to restate his declared opposition to the westernisation of Saudi Arabia. The growing number of graduates of Saudi universities, who knew very little English and had little contact with the west, were largely conservative and increasingly anti-American. The ulama were given greater control of the education system and their influence seemed again to be on the rise.[39]

CONCLUSIONS

As in other fields, Riyadh tried to bridge over centuries of stagnation by allocating larger and larger budgets for education. Certainly, for a nation whose illiteracy rate was 95 per cent thirty years ago, the development of Saudi education is phenomenal. Yet its quality leaves much to be desired and **the low level of the Saudi education system and of its graduates is an accepted norm related to a great extent, to the kingdom's political realities**. Moreover, it seems an absurdity that Saudi Arabia, experiencing an acute shortage of manpower and needing to employ millions of foreigners, keeps, at an enormous cost to its Treasury, about 35 per cent of its population in school (some for indefinite periods) and excludes women graduates from the job market. Indeed, for a nation of this size, the number of its students in domestic and foreign universities seems excessive. This has become particularly evident since 1985, when the worsening economic recession curtailed the regime's ability to provide employment for an annually growing number of university and school graduates.

Saudi Arabia's oil revenue has declined from about 109 billion dollars in 1981 to (estimated) 16–18 billion dollars in 1986.[40] Consequently, Riyadh has been trimming its expenditures on the one hand, and drawing on its financial reserves on the other. For political reasons, the allocations to education, welfare services and subsidies, which benefit all Saudis, have been reduced only marginally until the end of 1986 (i.e. on the intervention of the royal family in view of the anger of the population when the government attempted to cut some of these). But Saudi Arabia will not be able to maintain its present level of expenditure and continue to drain its financial reserves for long. Thus, the education and manpower development budget, a significant proportion of the total (over 10 per cent of the kingdom's budget in 1984/85), could be noticeably reduced in the future unless the situation in the oil market was to change dramatically.[41]

Until recently the Saudi regime employed all the university and school graduates who chose to join the administration and thus hidden unemployment in the bureaucracy became a major cause of its inefficiency. By the mid-1980s, unless with a UPM degree or with a needed professional or vocational speciality, graduates had to be satisfied with whatever job they could get in the provinces. Indeed, students have begun progressively to adapt their studies to their country's needs and some, in addition to Al-Hasa and peripheral areas, are at last joining the science and engineering faculties and the vocational stream. The question, nevertheless, remains whether Saudi Arabia can afford its extensive, wasteful and inadequate educational system. Further economies by the government and the stagnation of the private sector already make it extremely difficult to provide suitable employment for over 100,000 school and 20,000 university graduates annually.[42] But this is a political and social rather than simply an economic issue of which the Sauds are well aware.

The relatively small but growing proportion of 'lower-class' students with secondary education in the last decade often chose the Islamic universities with their traditional character and curriculum, easy admission requirements, and higher stipends.[43] 'Lower-class' graduates from both Islamic and 'secular' universities, unless well connected, rarely reached high positions in the administration. This undoubtedly contributed to the involvement of some in fundamentalist (neo-Ikhwan) ideologies and, since the 1960s, to the tension between graduates of Saudi religious universities and of the 'secular' ones — and between both these groups and their western-trained colleagues, who have captured most of the key positions in the central government and its agencies.[44]

As the number of university graduates continued to grow in the 1980s, the three-sided competition for jobs, exacerbated by growing unemployment among the educated, has been extended to the lesser positions in the middle level of the provincial administration. With the economic recession reaching a peak in 1986 this competition and unemployment among the new elites are becoming a most serious socio-political problem and could dangerously escalate and threaten the country's stability, accompanied as it is by conflicting ideologies and socio-religious tension.[45]

As for the Shi'ites in Al-Hasa, their new intelligentsia and middle class were excluded until recently from government service and only a handful advanced to the upper level of the Aramco management. The frustration of students, university graduates and Aramco employees in particular made many of them receptive to fundamentalist Iranian propaganda and radical leftist ideologies to which they became exposed in the oilfields and in local and foreign universities.

The rise of the Saudi middle class has been ably discussed by William Rugh[46] in the early 1970s. However, the dramatic growth of Saudi oil revenues and the acceleration of the kingdom's modernisation in the 1970s on the one hand, and the dramatic rise in the number of educated Saudis on the other, have given new dimensions to this phenomenon. Faysal's policy in the 1960s and early 1970s, which enabled the new elites to participate in his government and share in the country's wealth. encouraged them to cooperate with his regime and, largely, to join its powerbase. Thus, notwithstanding two abortive *coups* in 1969 and another (alleged) in 1977, social unrest among the new middle class was avoided in the 1970s and early 1980s. Yet, despite the decisive role played by the new elites in their country's modernisation and the dramatic expansion of their ranks, it is the Saudi aristocracy which still monopolises the kingdom's decision- and policy-making. The following chapters will attempt to examine this phenomenon and how the new elites reacted to the changes in their country's economy and position in the world, and whether socio-political unrest is avoidable in the future. The continuous expansion of the Saudi education system, while the kingdom's economy is declining, is bound to exacerbate this problem.

Table 3.1: Number of students in the modern education system, 1953–1985

Year	No. of students	Level
1953	33,000	All[a]
1960	113,176	All[b]
1970/71	512,071	All[b,c]
1973/74	698,519	All[d,e]
1975/76	1,057,994	All[f]
	889,803	Primary, secondary & intermediate[g]
1979/80	1,452,856	All[f]
	1,201,038	Primary, secondary & intermediate[g]
1980/81	1,528,431	All[h]
	1,287,183	Primary, secondary & intermediate[g]
1982/83	1,600,000	Primary and secondary[i]
1984	2,100,000	All[a]
1985	2,200,000	All[j]

Notes:
a. King Fahd, *Sunday Times*, 2 December 1984. Number for 1984 probably including adult education.
b. H. Lackner, *A House Built on Sand. A Political Economy of Saudi Arabia* (London, 1978), pp. 67, 79.
c. M. Wenner, 'Saudi Arabia: Survival of Traditional Elites', in F. Tachau (ed.), *Political Elites and Political Development in the Middle East* (New York, 1975), p. 176.
d. Lackner, *House*, p. 79.
e. J.P. Entiles, 'Oil Wealth and the Prospects for Democratization in the Arabian Peninsula: The Case of Saudi Arabia', in N.A. Sherbiny and M.A. Tessur (eds), *Arab Oil: Impact on the Arab Countries and Global Implications* (New York, 1976), pp. 91–2.
f. *Statistical Year Book*, p. 40.
g. *Statistical Indicator*, pp. 175–7.
h. SAMA report 1981, p. 86.
i. King Fahd's budget speech, Foreign Broadcasting Information Service Daily Report (FBIS), 14 April 1983, Radio Riyadh, 13 April 1983.
j. IHT, 3 March 1986; FT, 21 April 1986, supplement, p. II (over 2.1 m).

Table 3.2: Number of students in institutions of higher education in Saudi Arabia, 1950–1990

Year	Students	Graduates	Source
1950/54		31	Rugh, 'Emergence of a new middle class in Saudi Arabia', *The Middle East Journal* (Winter 1973), p. 11.
1955/59		211	Rugh, 'Emergence', p. 11.
1960/61	1,300		A. McDermott, FT, 22 April 1985, supplement, p. XI.
1960/64		1,202	Rugh, 'Emergence', p. 11.
1969/70	6,942	488	Jan, 'Between Islamic and Western Education: Umm Al-Qura' (Michigan State University, 1983), p. 1; Rugh, 'Emergence', p. 11.
1974/75	18,966	1,885	*Third Development Plan*, p. 315.
1975/76	26,437		*Statistical Indicator*, p. 182.
	26,338	2,485	*Third Development Plan*, p. 315.
1978/79	44,101		*Statistical Indicator*, p. 182.
	36,112	3,779	*Third Development Plan*, p. 315.
1980/81	54,397	5,448	SAMA report 1981, p. 89.
	56,252		*Statistical Indicator*, p. 182.
	42,957		Faheem, 'Higher Education', pp. 115–16.
1982/83	63,000		King Fahd's budget speech, 13 April 1983, FBIS, 14 April 1983.
	68,892		*Al-Riyadh*, 22 June 1983, p. 11.
1983/84	75,000	7,500	King Fahd's budget speech, 1 April 1984, FBIS, 2 April 1984, Riyadh SPA in Arabic; A. Thomas, FT, 22 April 1985, supplement, p. II: 80,000 in 1984.
1984/85	95,000 (?)		A. McDermott, FT, 22 April 1985, supplement, p. XI.
1990	108,000	20,000	*Middle East Economic Digest* (MEED), 29 March 1985, p. 33, fourth development plan.

Table 3.3: Estimated number of Saudi students studying abroad*

Year	All countries	In the US	Source
1947		7	F.M. Al-Nassar, 'Saudi Arabian Educational Mission to the US', unpublished PhD thesis (University of Oklahoma, Norman, 1982), p. 44.
1953/54	43		Al-Nassar, 'Mission', p. 32.
1961		200 (B.A.)	A. Assah, *Miracle of the Desert Kingdom* (London, 1969), p. 311.
1963/64	1,058		Ibid.
1964/65	393		Al-Nassar, 'Mission', p. 32.
1973/74	944		Ibid.
1974/75	2,122		Ibid.
1975	5,108	2,003	Al-Farsy, *Saudi Arabia*, p. 160.
1976	approx. 8,000	4,350	Braibanti and Al-Farsy, 'Saudi Arabia', *The Journal of South Asian and Middle Eastern Studies*, No. 1 (1977), p. 19.
1979/80	10,035	6,896	*Statistical Year Book*, p. 107.
1980		13,000	WP, 22 July 1980.
		11,022	Al-Nassar, 'Mission', p. 70.
1981	18,000		*The Middle East* (July 1981), p. 63.
		14,000	*World Press Review* (July 1981), p. 70.
1982	over 15,000		Al-Nassar, 'Mission', p. 3.
		13,000	Faheem, 'Higher Education and Nation Building' (University of Illinois, 1982), p. 131.
1983	12,505		*Al-Riyadh*, 22 June 1983, p. 11.
1983/84		20,000	FT, 22 April 1985, supplement.

* Number of privately-financed students in the 1970s and 1980s is quite large but impossible to follow.

Table 3.4: Allocations for education in the kingdom's budgets[a] 1952/53–1985/86 (in million Saudi riyals)

Year	Ministry of Education		Women Education	Universities
1952/53	12.5	($2.8m)[b]		
1957		($33m)[c]		
1960	122.0		2.0[d] (less than $1m)[c]	
1963/64	301.0[c]	($78.7m)[f]	12.4[e]	
1965/66	473.0[c]			
1970	665.0	($148m)[b]		
1974/75				682.1[g]
1975/76		($597m)[h]		1,780.5[g]
1976/77		($3.3bn)[h]		2,666.7[g]
1979/80				5,471.8[g]
1981/82	9,835.0		4,867.0	8,333.0[i]
1982/83	13,239.0		6,738.0	9,003.0[i]
1984/85	11,535.0		6,535.0	9,840.0[j]
1985/86	10,427.0		5,916.0	6,145.0[k]

Notes:
a. US$ denomination when available or when exchange rate is known.
b. M. Wenner, 'Saudi Arabia', in F. Tachau (ed.), *Political Elites and Political Development in the Middle East* (New York, 1975), pp. 175–6.
c. A.H. Said, 'Saudi Arabia', (University of Missouri, 1979), p. 94.
d. Assah, *Miracle*, p. 313.
e. Ibid., p. 314.
f. J.P. Entiles, 'Oil Wealth', in *Arab Oil: Impact on the Arab Countries and Global Implications* (New York, 1976), pp. 91–2.
g. *Statistical Year Book*, p. 445.
h. Gh. Salameh, 'Political Power and the Saudi State', *Merip Reports*, No. 91 (October 1980), p. 15.
i. MEED, 30 April 1982.
j. FBIS, 4 April 1984.
k. MEED, 29 March 1985.

Table 3.5: Allocations for education in five-year development plans[1] (in US$ as well when rate of exchange known)

Plan	Total budget	For education	%
First plan, 1970–75	SR56,223.0 m.	SR10,007.7 m.	17.8
Second plan, 1975–80	SR498,230.2 m. $142 bn.	SR74,161.0 m. $22.7 bn.[2]	16
Third plan, 1980–85	SR782.8 bn. $285 bn. $268 bn.[4]	SR101,171.0 m. $54.15 bn.[3]	13 19
Fourth plan, 1985–90	SR1,000,000 m. $277 bn.	SR125,523.0 m. $34.8 bn.[5]	12.5 12.5

Notes:
1. Kingdom of Saudi Arabia, Ministry of Planning: *Second Development Plan 1395–1400 A.H.* − *1975–1980 A.D.*: Ibid., *Third Development Plan 1400–1405 A.H.* − *1980–1985 A.D.*; Ibid., *Fourth Development Plan 1405–1410 A.H.* − *1985–1990 A.D.* For first development plan see: M.M.A. Assad, 'Saudi Arabia's National Security: A Prospective Derived from Political, Economic and Defence Policies', unpublished PhD thesis (Claremont Graduate School, 1981), pp. 109–10.
2. Gh. Salameh, 'Saudi Arabia: Development and Dependence', JQ, No. 20 (Summer 1981), p. 113.
3. T.A. Sams, 'Education and training in Saudi Arabia', *Business America*, 13 July 1981, p. 12.
4. Al-Ibrahim, 'Regional and Urban Development in Saudi Arabia', PhD thesis (University of Colorado, 1982), p. 95.
5. FT, 29 March 1985.

NOTES

* This chapter is a revised and updated version of my chapter 'Modern Education and the Evolution of Saudi Arabia' (XIII), in Edward Ingram (ed.), *National and International Politics in the Middle East* (London, 1986).
1. H. Wahba, *Arabian Days* (London, 1964), p. 50; A.H. Said, 'Saudi Arabia', PhD thesis (University of Missouri, 1979), p. 75.
2. H. Lackner, *A House Built on Sand* (London, 1978), p. 74; O.Y. Al-Rawaf, 'The Concept of the Five Crises', PhD thesis (Duke University, 1981), p. 244; J.P. Entiles, 'Oil Wealth and the Prospects for Democratization in the Arabian Peninsula', in N.A. Sherbiny and M.A. Tessur (eds) *Arab Oil* (New York, 1976).
3. *Aramco Handbook* (Netherlands, 1960), p. 161; N.A. Jan, 'Between Islamic and Western Education: A Case Study of Umm Al-Qura University, Makkah, Saudi Arabia', unpublished PhD thesis (Michigan State

University, 1983), pp. 30, 33; M.E. Faheem, 'Higher Education and Nation Building', PhD thesis (University of Illinois, 1982), p. 3; Said, 'Saudi Arabia', p. 81; L. Mosley, *Power Play, The Tumultuous World of Middle East Oil 1890–1973* (Birkenhead, 1973), p. 327.

4. Buchan, 'Religious Opposition', p. 108; *Jerusalem Post* (JP. Israel), 1 July 1956; F.A. Shaker, 'Modernization of the Developing Nations'. PhD thesis (Purdue University, 1972), pp. 171, 222 (note 48).

5. See Table 3.4, p. 54. Also F.M. Zedan, 'Political Development of the Kingdom of Saudi Arabia', PhD thesis (Claremont Graduate School, 1981), pp. 73–6; Assah, *Miracle of the Desert Kingdom* (London, 1969), pp. 80, 298–307; Shaker, 'Modernization', pp. 170–1.

6. Kingdom of Saudi Arabia, Ministry of Planning: *Third Development Plan 1400–1405 A.H. — 1980–1985 A.D.* (Education), pp. 309–12. On projected number of girl students in fourth development plan: A. Thomas, FT, 22 April 1985, supplement, p. II. On women's position in society: FBIS, 29 March 1985, Radio Riyadh, 26 March 1985.

7. *Handbook* (1982), pp. 102–3, 105; also Said, 'Saudi Arabia', p. 111; Faheem, 'Higher Education', p. 77; Al-Farsy, *Saudi Arabia*, p. 166. On ulama control of education: D.P. Cole, *Nomads of the Nomads. The Al Murrah Bedouins of the Empty Quarter* (Chicago, 1975), pp. 141-2, 153; M. Katakura, *Bedouin Village, A Study of a Saudi Arabian People in Transition* (University of Tokyo Press, 1977), pp. 64, 115, 118, 157–9, 168–9.

8. M.M. Kinsawi, 'Attitude of Students and Fathers Towards Vocational Education in Economic Development in Saudi Arabia', unpublished PhD thesis (University of Colorado at Boulder, 1981), pp. 9–10, 90–1, 104; Said, 'Saudi Arabia', pp. 94–5; FT, 5 May 1981, supplement.

9. For instance, 22.8 billion dollars in the second five-year plan (1975–80). See Table 3.5, p. 55. On vocational schools in 1980s: *Saudi Gazette* (Saudi Arabia), 17 September 1986, p. 3. See also p. 181 below.

10. Sixty-three per cent in intermediate and 82 per cent in secondary in 1981/2: Faheem, 'Higher Education', p. 137 (note 56); *Handbook* (1982), p. 100.

11. *Handbook* (1982, pp. 100–1, 112. On Faysal's efforts to improve quality: Assah, *Miracle*, p. 298; Entiles, 'Oil Wealth', p. 91; Shaker, 'Modernization', p. 222 (note 48). On the Egyptian influence: Al-Farsy, *Saudi Arabia*, pp. 164-5; also M. Wenner, 'Saudi Arabia', in F. Tachau (ed.), *Political Elites* (New York, 1975), p. 176.

12. See Table 3.1, p. 51. Also King Fahd's speeches: 21 March 1985 (FBIS, 22 March 1985) and 26 March 1985 (Ibid., 29 March 1985); A. Thomas, FT, 22 April 1985, supplement, p. II; MEED, 13 July 1984.

13. On inferior schools in provinces: *The Middle East* (London), November 1984, p. 69. For conflicting figures for students: Kingdom of Saudi Arabia, Ministry of Finance and National Economy, Central Department of Statistics: *Statistical Year Book 1400 A.H. — 1980 A.D.;* Kingdom of Saudi Arabia, Ministry of Finance and National Economy, General Department of Statistics: *The Statistical Indicator, Sixth Issue 1401 A.H. — 1981 A.D.*; *Third Development Plan* (Education).

14. On Shi'ites see below, pp. 152-8, 190–1; also above, p. 44.

15. *Handbook* (1982), p. 105. See A.A. Al-Ibrahim 'Regional and Urban Development in Saudi Arabia', PhD thesis (University of Colorado,

1982), for instance, pp. 151, 153–5, 211; E.B. Gallagher, 'Medical Education in Saudi Arabia', *Journal of Asian and African Studies*, Vol. XX, No. 1-2 (1985), pp. 7–10; WP, 15 February 1987, p. A28.

16. The terms 'lower-class' or 'lower classes' used in this book for convenience sake, refer to most of the rural, and the lower-income urbanised (lower middle-class), population. A minor element in the 'lower class' supports, it is believed, ultra-fundamentalist ideologies. On development projects: see third and fourth five-year development plans (1980–90) and *Ukaz* (Saudi Arabia), 22 March 1985.

17. On King Abdul Aziz University developing a separate women's university: *Saudi Gazette*, 24 July 1986. Religious studies consist a third of the curriculum of 16-year-old Saudi students: Field, FT, 21 April 1986, supplement, p. VIII.

18. Kingdom of Saudi Arabia, Center for Statistical Data and Educational Documentation, *Development of Education in the Ministry of Education During 25 Years 1954–78* (Riyadh, 1978), pp. 13–15; A.L. Tibawi, *Islamic Education: Its Tradition and Modernization into the Arab National Systems* (London, 1972), p. 182; W. Rugh, 'Emergence of a New Middle Class', *The Middle East Journal* (Winter 1973), p. 11; N.A. Jan, 'Umm Al-Qura University, Makkah, Saudi Arabia', PhD thesis (Michigan State University, 1983), pp. 55–7.

19. Jan, 'Umm Al-Qura', pp. 58–9; A.L. Tibawi, *Islamic Education* (London, 1972), p. 183: on quality of education. On ulama and education: Al-Farsy, *Saudi Arabia*, pp. 166–7; Said, 'Saudi Arabia', p. 111; Faheem, 'Higher Education', p. 77; Tibawi, *Islamic Education*, pp. 182–3.

20. Jan, 'Umm Al-Qura', p. 59; *Statistical Year Book*, p. 87; Kingdom of Saudi Arabia, Saudi Arabian Monetary Agency (SAMA), Research and Statistics Department: *Annual Report 1401 (1981)*. (Riyadh, 1981) (henceforth, SAMA Report 1981), p. 89; *Christian Science Monitor* (CSM), 30 March 1983, p. B5; Kingdom of Saudi Arabia. Saudi Arabia: Education and Human Resources. A booklet prepared for 'Riyadh Yesterday and Today' exhibition, London 29 July to 8 August 1986; IHT, 20 February 1987, p. 2.

21. SAMA Report 1981, p. 92. Buchan, 'Religious Opposition', p. 123; Al-Farsy, *Saudi Arabia*, p. 156; I.M. Al-Khudair, 'Islamic University at Madina, the Kingdom of Saudi Arabia: A History and Evaluation', unpublished MA thesis (California State University, 1981); Jan, 'Umm Al-Qura', pp. 61–3.

22. F.S. Al-Hazzam, 'The College of Petroleum and Minerals, the Kingdom of Saudi Arabia', unpublished PhD thesis (Arizona State University, 1975): Jan, 'Umm Al-Qura', pp. 63–6; Shaw and Long, *Modernization*, pp. 81–3; B. Williams, FT, 5 May 1981; Gallagher, 'Medical', pp. 2–5, 7.

23. SAMA Report 1981, p. 89; Al-Farsy, *Saudi Arabia*, pp. 156–7; Ochsenwald, 'Islamic revival', pp. 281, 283; Al-Ibrahim, 'Urban Development'. p. 154; *Al-Jazira* (Saudi Arabia), 2 June 1983; *Al-Bilad* (Saudi Arabia), 12 May 1984; *Statistical Year Book*, pp. 92–5.

24. Huyette, *Adaptation*, p. 117; also Faheem, 'Higher Education', pp. 115–16, 141–51, 153–71, 180, 183; Jan, 'Umm Al-Qura', pp. 66–8, 77–80; *Statistical Year Book*, pp. 88–9; SAMA Report 1981, p. 91; *Saudi*

Gazette, 23 September 1986.

25. *Third Development Plan* (education), pp. 322–33; Jan, 'Umm al-Qura', p. 75; Al-Farsy, *Saudi Arabia*, p. 157; SAMA Report 1981, p. 89; Shaw and Long, *Modernization*, p. 81; *Mideast Business Exchange*, October 1982; *Al-Sharq al-Awsat* (London, Saudi), 29 March 1984; A. McDermott, FT, 22 April 1985, supplement, p. XI.

26. *Al-Nadwa* (Mecca), 25 March 1983, pp. 11–12; MEED, 29 March 1985; Jan, 'Umm Al-Qura', pp. 80–100, 105–8, 114–20; Gallagher, 'Medical', pp. 3–5, 7, 10.

27. The author's impression, based on the study of theses written by Saudis for American and European universities. Hijazi and later middle- and upper-class Najdis practically monopolised in the 1950s, 1960s and early 1970s Saudi secondary and higher education and were the first to return home with Masters and PhD degrees from western universities.

28. On standard of Saudi academics, little or no research and publications, use of recitation rather than analysis, and 'brain drain' due to low salaries: Faheem, 'Higher Education', pp. 125–6; *Ukaz*, 4 May 1984; *The Middle East*, November 1984, p. 69; McDermott, FT, 22 April 1985, supplement p. XI; Gallagher, 'Medical', pp. 7–10.

29. Faheem, 'Higher Education', p. 137 (note 56); also pp. 81, 124, 127, 167, 172–3, 177, 185–6; *Handbook* (1982), p. 112; *The Middle East*, November 1984; McDermott, FT, 22 April 1985, supplement, p. XI; WP, 15 February 1987, p. A23, A28; Gallagher, 'Medical', pp. 1–12, especially pp. 10–11.

30. Faheem, 'Higher Education', p. 159.

31. FT, 26 April 1982, supplement; *8 Days* (London), 16 May 1981; MEED, 12 October 1984, p. 47; Gallagher, 'Medical', pp. 2–5, 7–10. On 300 dollars a month pocket-money and other privileges enjoyed by students: WP, 15 February 1987. In 1986/87 70 per cent of KSU students were in humanities and social sciences. Of attempts to reduce this proportion to 50 per cent: IHT, 20 February 1987, p. 2.

32. CSM, 30 March 1983, p. B5; *Al-Jazira*, 2 June 1983; FBIS, 26 September 1985, Riyadh in Arabic, 22 September 1985. On diminishing employment opportunities for women: MEED, Special Report, July 1984, p. 2.

33. Faheem, 'Higher Education', p. 109; MEED, 30 April 1982; A.R.S. Islami and R. Kavoussi, *The Political Economy of Saudi Arabia* (Seattle, 1984), pp. 14–15; Holden and Johns, *House of Saud*, p. 459; Al-Rawaf, 'Five Crises', p. 494; 'Amr al-Faruq Sayyid Rajab, 'Nizam al-ta'lim wa-mutatalibat al-'umalah fi'l-Mamlaka al-'Arabiyya al-Sa'udiyya', *Dirasat al-Khalij wa'l-Jazira al-'Arabiyya* (January 1983), pp. 53–61.

34. On new students' attitude to career-oriented studies: Ottoway, WP, 27 November 1984. On graduates' unemployment: *Al-Thawra al-Islamiyya* (London), August 1986 (quoting *Al-Yamama* (weekly, Saudi Arabia), 20 June, 4 July 1986); also *Saudi Gazette*, 1 August 1986; IHT, 20 February 1987, p. 2.

35. Fourth development plan 1985–90. MEED, 29 March 1985, p. 33; FT, 22 April 1985, supplement, p. II; Faheem, 'Higher Education'. p. 4. On new women's university in Jedda: *Saudi Gazette*, 24 July 1986.

36. See Table 3.3, p. 53 above.

37. J. Buchan, *World Press Review* (July 1981), p. 30; P. Mansfield, FT, 15 May 1981, supplement, p. XX; Faheem, 'Higher Education', pp. 111–12.

38. Faheem, 'Higher Education', pp. 111–12, 117–18; Jan, 'Umm Al-Qura', p. 31; M.M. Marks, 'The American Influence on the Development of the Universities in the Kingdom of Saudi Arabia', unpublished PhD thesis (University of Oregon, 1980).

39. IHT, 22 November 1983, 6 August 1984, 16 April 1985; *Al-Madina*, 30 November 1983; *Ma'riv* (Israel), 22 March 1984; FT, 23 May 1984.

40. See Table 8.1, p. 180.

41. See Table 3.4, p. 54. Allocations for education in the 1985/86 budget were reduced by nearly one third compared to previous years. On intervention of the regime on behalf of students: IHT, 20 February 1987, p. 2.

42. A. Thomas, FT, 22 April 1985, supplement p. II.

43. N.N.M. Ayubi, 'Vulnerability of the Rich: The Political Economy of Defense and Development in Saudi Arabia and the Gulf' (Los Angeles, May 1982), a paper prepared for The Gulf Project, Center for Strategic and International Studies, Georgetown University, Washington, DC, p. 19; Buchan, 'Religious Opposition', p. 123; Holden and Johns, *House of Saud*, pp. 516–17; *Al-Mawqif al-Arabi*, 20 April 1981.

44. Ochsenwald, 'Islamic revival', pp. 278–9.

45. See below pp. 169–70, 181–2.

46. Rugh, 'Emergence'.

Part Two

Modernisation and Struggle for Political Reform

4

The Reign of Saud (1953–64): Struggle for Power and Nationalism

It is often assumed that the nationalist upheavals which had shaken the Middle East from the late 1940s to the early 1970s left Saudi Arabia's society relatively unaffected. Indeed, after the suppression of the Ikhwan uprising in 1929/30 the patriarchal Saudi regime seemed to rule the kingdom unchallenged at least until 1979. The uprising in Mecca in that year, moreover, was an outcome of a Wahhabi fundamentalist reaction to rapid modernisation and had nothing to do with the rather secular socio-politically-motivated opposition to the monarchy. Yet the changes which Saudi society has experienced in recent decades, the emergence of a new elite, of social ideologies, and the growing frustration of the Shi'ite minority, have produced in the kingdom a militant nationalist opposition to the Saud's authoritarian government. Despite its relatively limited following, this militant opposition had affected the kingdom's policies and, in certain instances, has threatened the regime's stability. Even more important, however, was the rise in the kingdom of new powerful middle-class elites whose struggle for political participation became a major issue in Saudi Arabia in the 1970s and 1980s.

The development of a militant nationalist (and Shi'ite) and middle-class opposition to the Saudi regime, the reason for its failure to gain power despite the dramatic expansion in the ranks of the new middle-class elites and the latter's partial incorporation into the ruling class's powerbase, will be discussed in the following chapters.

SOCIO-POLITICAL CHANGE IN THE POST-WORLD WAR II YEARS (TO 1958)

Authoritarianism and isolation

Largely nomadic in the past, Saudi society was traditionally democratic. Tribal shaykhs were elected on merit and considered *primus inter pares*. Policy decisions were usually adopted through deliberations with the tribal elders or regional notables rather than unilaterally by the shaykh (amir). Abd al-Aziz Ibn Saud, a strong leader, once his power was consolidated, often dispensed with this procedure. Yet in matters of outstanding importance, he did consult tribal and regional leaders and the ulama in addition to his closest associates, and appeared to follow the prevailing consensus. In the 1920s, as his power grew, the ruler increasingly made major policy decisions himself or consulted his unofficial *majlis al-shura* (Consultative Council) made up of his most senior kinsmen and devoted friends.

A milestone in this process was the collapse of the Ikhwan rebellion in 1929/30 and the dramatic rise of Ibn Saud's revenues — from about £100,000 in 1915 to about £5 million sterling in 1925 after the conquest of the Hijaz and following commercial exploitation of oil, to about 100 million in 1953/54. Ample funds not only enabled the ruler to begin building the kingdom's armed forces and dispensing with the military services of tribal and regional amirs but also, whenever possible, to buy off rather than fight the opposition — the Sauds' golden rule to this day.

The monarch still met tribesmen, merchants and ulama in his daily *majlis*. Such audiences largely served as a forum for petitions and complaints, while allowing the monarch to express opinions on different matters and listen to people's reactions. On rare occasions the King convened large gatherings of tribal shaykhs, notables and ulama. This was to obtain through *ijma'* (consensus) their formal sanction for a major policy decision which would have been reached previously after consulting senior members of *ahl al-ḥal wa'l-'aqd*.[1] Considering Ibn Saud's strong personality, his reluctance to delegate authority and tendency to identify the kingdom with himself (*l'état, c'êst moi*), his government after 1930 could be considered paternalistic and authoritarian rather than, as described by some authors, a 'desert democracy'.[2]

The Wahhabiyya, an islamic revivalist fundamentalist movement, preached a constant *jihad* again the infidels or polytheists (*mushrikun*). Ibn Saud's relations with the British were thus a major cause for the spilling over of the growing tension between the Ikhwan and the ruler in the 1920s. The Ikhwan rebellion, the last serious challenge to Ibn Saud's increasingly centralist government, was crushed by 1930. Notwithstanding, Saudi Arabia remained relatively insular until the end of World War II. Thanks to the Hajj and international trade, the traditional links which the Hijaz maintained with the Muslim world (particularly Egypt and Syria) served Ibn Saud as a channel for communication with the Arab countries. When appointed Viceroy of the Hijaz (in 1926) Prince Faysal was put in charge of relations with the outside world.[3]

Education and Arab nationalism — the Hijaz

Though they largely embraced the Wahhabiyya after 1926, most urban Hijazis, compared with their Najdi compatriots, remained tolerant and open-minded. Indeed modern education, the press, and broadcasting developed in the Hijaz faster than elsewhere in Saudi Arabia. In fact most of the reforms introduced under Ibn Saud, including the development of the kingdom's modern administrative and educational systems, were first tried out in the Hijaz, Saudi Arabia's most developed and populous province. At the same time, up to the 1970s, the growth of the foreign Arab community in the province outpaced that in the other regions in the kingdom.

A nascent educated elite had already emerged in the kingdom by the 1940s. Oil wealth, accelerated modernisation, and modern education helped its growth. The ranks of the new middle-class intelligentsia gradually expanded in proportion to the growing number of Saudis studying abroad. At this stage the majority of students attending institutions of higher education came from urban Hijazi families. Sons of merchant families, some Najdis and others from the Eastern Province, who had won Aramco scholarships also studied in foreign countries. Yet until the 1970s Hijazis remained the majority of those studying in Egyptian and Lebanese universities and then in European and American ones. On returning home they formed the backbone of the new middle class and the upper echelons of the modern administration.[4]

After World War II, the Hijaz was quick to respond to the rise of nationalism and anti-colonialism in the Middle East. These were reinforced by the strongly anti-western foreign Arab community living in the province. Accelerated modernisation and the 1948 war brought to the Hijaz many more Egyptians and Palestinians to join relatives who had already obtained employment there. The size of the foreign Arab communities was constantly growing through increased opportunities in the Saudi oil industry and the administrative and educational network. These communities were important in fostering nationalist agitation in Saudi Arabia as a whole. In the early 1950s, events in the Middle East and the growing foreign presence helped disseminate these sentiments which were reinforced by the press, particularly in the Hijaz, and by radio broadcasts from neighbouring countries. Aware of developments in the Arab world the nascent Hijazi urban middle class served as the vanguard of Arab nationalism in Saudi Arabia.

Rivalry in the royal house, 1953–58

Despite his uncontested succession to the throne in November 1953 King Saud (r. 1953–64) could not hope for the kind of authoritarian regime which his father had enjoyed. In addition to personal short-comings and serious health problems, his smooth succession was conditional on two factors: first sharing his power with Faysal his heir apparent who was to become Prime Minister, and second, sometimes consulting the informal *majlis al-shura* made up of the senior members of the royal family. Saud faced a variety of complex problems both within and outside the kingdom. The Middle East was in constant turmoil because of Nasser's militant nationalist leadership, while in Saudi Arabia oil wealth and modernisation were beginning to change the face of Saudi society.

Lacking the strength of character, finesse and *savoir-faire* of his brother and rival Faysal, Saud was unable to consolidate a power-base within the royal family. A conservative, he turned for support to the ulama and the tribal amirs but also tried to win favour with the emerging middle class. Unhappy at the loss of their power and the erosion of the traditional way of life, the old elite demanded an end to modernisation. Conversely, the new middle class, and some young princes, wished for constitutional reforms, faster develop-ment and limits on the power of the conservatives. Although he speeded up the modernisation of the government and expanded the educational system, Saud gave in on the whole to the demands of the traditionalists. He re-established the power of the ulama-controlled Committees of Public Morality and reinstated many of the harsh Wahhabi restrictions which had been relaxed in the last decade of Ibn Saud's government.

Although he established the Council of Ministers at the beginning of 1954 (decreed by Ibn Saud in October 1953) and later appointed Faysal to be its head, Saud did not delegate authority to this body but rather tried to rule the country with the help of unscrupulous advisers, in the same patriarchal style as his father. Though he was popular with members of the traditional government, and particularly with the Bedouin amirs, his management of the modern state apparatus frequently revealed his incompetence. There was no distinction between the king's privy purse and the kingdom's treasury. Saud ignored the Ministry of Finance and National Economy which Faysal set up. The kingdom's revenues from oil surpassed 230 million dollars in 1954; the larger the revenue from this source, the more Saud and his royal kinsmen managed to squander, and the kingdom's financial situation rapidly deteriorated. The widespread corruption in the government and the scandalous extravagance of the King and other members of the royal family were common knowledge in Saudi Arabia.

Matters were aggravated by the 1956 Suez War. Though Saudi oil installations were spared because of Saud's support of Nasser, the closure of the canal proved a setback to the kingdom's oil industry. But even though Saudi oil revenues continued to decline, this did not halt the extravagance of Saud and his kinsmen, and Saudi Arabia's debts continued to grow. By 1957 the kingdom was on the verge of bankruptcy and Saud was forced to turn to the International Monetary Fund for a loan, allowing its experts to examine Saudi Arabia's economic problems.[5]

The cohesiveness of the kingdom, which Ibn Saud had achieved through political marriages, proved to be its undoing after his death. His numerous sons, in what could be perceived a 'matrilineal system', represented rival power factions, and many wished to gain power and wealth, which meant more power. The young princes did not stand a chance because of the prevailing seniority system in the House of Saud.

Dissatisfaction with Saud's incompetence grew steadily in the royal family. In July 1956 a group of princes submitted to Saud a memorandum criticising his domestic and foreign policy. The King, however, ignored the memorandum and his Prime Minister, Faysal, and continued to mismanage the government of the country. Although Faysal considered himself far better suited to rule, he was not yet ready to challenge his father's succession arrangement and bided his time.

67

By the beginning of 1958, after Saud dramatically reversed his foreign policy and clashed with Nasser, it was clear that the country was heading towards political and financial crisis. By this time, the royal family was split into three camps. The first was made up of the King, the few princes who still supported him, Saud's numerous sons and most of the tribal amirs who admired the monarch and rejected the modernisation which eroded their power and income. The second consisted of most of the senior princes who supported Faysal's demands for financial reforms and evolutionary modernisation which would consolidate the power of the monarchy in the face of rising radical nationalism in the Middle East. The third consisted of a group of younger liberal princes, led by Talal who, until 1955, was Minister of Communications. Talal, who frequently visited Nasser between 1955 and 1958,[6] wished to turn Saudi Arabia into a constitutional monarchy and favoured more rapid modernisation of the kingdom.

When Saud's complicity in a plot against Nasser became public in March 1958, Faysal immediately resigned from his position as Prime Minister. Pro-Nasser and pan-Arab sentiments in the Middle East, including Saudi Arabia, reached an unprecedented peak following the establishment of Nasser's United Arab Republic in February 1958. The royal family, naturally, became exceedingly worried lest Saud's bungling would cause the overthrow of the regime. Subsequently, after consulting the senior ulama and some tribal amirs, the majority of the senior members of the House of Saud (*ahl al-ḥal wa'l-'aqd*) decided to divest Saud of most of his responsibilities and to request Faysal to assume the position of Prime Minister with full authority. Facing a *fait accompli*, Saud agreed to these demands and Faysal began his first term as *de facto* ruler of Saudi Arabia.[7]

Saudi inter-Arab politics and the West

The Middle East began to change rapidly in the last years of the reign of King Ibn Saud and especially after the 1948 war in Palestine. A new generation of Arab nationalists became increasingly impatient with the 'neo-colonial' presence in the region and with the traditional regimes and politics of their countries. The unrest in the Arab countries reached a climax with the 1952 officers' revolution in Egypt. The Middle East held a major part of the known oil reserves in the non-communist world, and this made the region a disputed zone between the superpowers. Together with its revenues from oil, the Arab nationalists considered Saudi strategic importance crucial for the achievement of their aspirations. As its expanding oil industry and fast modernisation were beginning to have an impact on its society, Saudi Arabia could no longer remain inward-looking.

In the 1940s and early 1950s Saudi inter-Arab policy was largely motivated by apprehension concerning Hashemite Arab unity plans, which were supported by the British. Pan-Arab and anti-British nationalist sentiments, prevalent in the Middle East at this time, were exploited by Ibn Saud with the help of his Syrian and Palestinian advisers, to undermine the Hashemite–British plans which he believed would threaten his kingdom's integrity.[8]

Ibn Saud's attempts, between 1949 and 1951, to persuade Washington to sign a defence agreement with Saudi Arabia failed, despite Aramco's support. However, they led to the expansion of Washington's military and financial aid to the kingdom and to the extension, for a further five years until 1956 of the agreement under which the US leased the Dhahran airbase (constructed by the US at the end of World War II). A training mission commanded by a USAF brigadier joined the military advisory group which had helped to organise the Saudi armed forces since 1946. Thus, military personnel further bolstered the American presence in the Eastern Province, which was constantly growing at this time because of the intensification of Aramco's activities in the region.

England, as was to be expected, was the main target of the Egyptian-led Arab nationalist propaganda. Anti-British sentiment in Saudi Arabia was further fomented in the late 1940s and early 1950s by the suspicion of British meddling in the Hijaz and/because of border disputes with Iraq, Abu Dhabi and Oman (Buraymi), which had been sparked off by Aramco's oil explorations. Following the 1952 revolution in Egypt and the undermining of Premier Musadeq's government in Iran by the CIA following the nationalisation of the Anglo-Persian Oil Company, sympathy for the United States in the Arab World gradually declined. The US, moreover, now the leader of the West, lent support to Israel and had initiated regional anti-Soviet defence pacts incompatible with Arab nationalist aspirations. However, motivated by traditional anti-colonialist principles, the United States not only welcomed the change of regime in Egypt in 1952 but also sympathised with the revolutionary officers' demands that the British evacuate Egyptian territories. Even earlier, the Americans tried to involve Egypt, the largest Arab country, in their defence alliances which were aimed at curbing Soviet expansionism. By 1953, when it became evident that such plans did not appeal to either the Egyptian officers or the Saudis, the Unites States fell back on its 'Northern Tier' plan comprising the non-Arab Middle Eastern countries bordering the Soviet Union. The British, however, wishing to promote their own interests, pressed forward with a Middle East defence plan (later the Baghdad Pact) which was to include the Arab periphery of the region. To Arab nationalists both plans were anathema and challenged their aspirations. As far as Saudi Arabia was concerned, the western defence pacts, which included the Hashemite kingdoms, were considered a threat to its existence.

Even before he came to power, the traditionally-minded Saud, heavily reliant on his father's Syrian and Palestinian political advisers, was believed to be unfriendly to the West.[9]

Immediately after his succession, King Saud declared that he was not favourably inclined to the proposed American–Middle East defence pact. He believed that the Arabs could ensure the region's defence without the participation of foreigners. He was apprehensive of the closer relations America was forging with Hashemite Iraq, critical of US support for Israel, and displeased with US policy in the whole region. In early 1954, Saud informed Washington that he wished to dispense with its Point Four aid and he instructed the Point Four Mission to leave the kingdom.[10]

A strange alliance emerged in 1954 between Saud and President Nasser. Each needed the other's help in fighting the western-sponsored regional defence pacts. Saudi oil and financial resources temporarily made Saud an ideal partner for Nasser who was leading the struggle against British and French colonialism in the Arab world. For his part, Saud hoped to capitalise on Nasser's popularity and prestige as a leader of Arab nationalism. Thus Saud rekindled the Buraymi dispute and supported subversion against the British-protected Sultan of Oman. In 1954 Saudi gold, combined with Nasserist propaganda, helped in the escalation of demonstrations and strikes against the British and their allies in southern Arabia, Jordan and Iraq. The expulsion of the Saudi *mujahhidun* from Buraymi by British-commanded Abu Dhabi levies and the launching of the Baghdad Pact in 1955 added to the deterioration of Saudi–British relations.

Aramco's relations with Saud were less amicable than they were during the reign of his father because of his political bias and his insatiable need for funds. Aware of the company's vital help in various fields, and with events in Iran unfolding before his eyes, Saud was careful not to antagonise Aramco. Saud, however, faced a difficult dilemma just before he came to power in November 1953 when confronted by growing unrest in the oilfields of the Eastern Province.

THE GROWTH OF OPPOSITION AND THE ISSUE OF POLITICAL REFORM (1953–58)

Aramco and the 1953 strike

Until the 1940s, the Eastern Province (*Al-Mantiqa al-Sharqiyya* or *Al-Hasa*), was generally considered backward and inhospitable in climate. Its population was largely made up of nomadic Sunni tribesmen, Shi'ite agriculturalists (mainly in the Al-Hasa and Qatif oases) and a mixed coastal population which engaged in trade, fishing and pearl diving. The discovery of oil in Al-Hasa in the 1930s, and its commercial exploitation from 1946 onwards, completely changed the character of the province.

Many American and other western oilmen came to live in 'Aramco towns' with their families. They maintained their own lifestyle as far as possible. In addition, Aramco employed thousands of Italian, Indian, Pakistani, Palestinian and Lebanese clerks and technicians. The expatriate Arab employees introduced to the province social, cultural and political values common in the Middle East but not compatible with those existing in the archaic Wahhabi kingdom. Thousands of Bedouins, who for social mores despised manual work, also settled temporarily on the peripheries of the 'oil towns' and provided the company with unskilled transient labour. Local Shi'ites (about one third and possibly one half of the province's Saudi population) formed the backbone of Aramco's permanent unskilled and semi-skilled workforce. Traditionally discriminated against by the authorities, their only chance of a better life was with Aramco, whose recruitment policy was 'colour-blind'.[11]

The growth of Aramco's operations triggered off fundamental changes in the Eastern Province. Its coastal 'oil towns' rapidly developed and economic activity in the region intensified.[12] The business of the oil company, the recruitments of its foreign employees and the wages earned by its Saudi workers caused the cost of living to rise sharply and the local population, including

71

Aramco's Saudi workers, experienced hardship. The proud Wahhabi Bedouin found it difficult to adjust to a western work regime. To their eyes they were being patronised and discriminated against in their own country by foreigners whom they had been taught to despise, and they resented this.[13]

Undoubtedly the Shi'ite community in Al-Hasa as a whole greatly benefited from Aramco's activity and its liberal employment policy and training programmes. Some qualified Shi'ite employees were even sent abroad by the company for further training and were later appointed to medium-level clerical and technical positions in the company.[14] As members of an oppressed minority with a tendency to extremism, many Shi'ites were attracted by radical anti-western Arab nationalism which held out the promise of social and political equality. The deep frustration of the Shi'ites of the Eastern Province with the Saudi-Wahhabi regime which oppressed them could find expression in the anti-western manifestation of unrest in Aramco.

At first Aramco's management was insensitive to the grievances of its Saudi workforce and disregarded the cultural, religious and political factors which fed these grievances.[15] Tension was increased by the nationalisation of the Anglo-Persian Oil Company by Prime Minister Musadeq in 1951 and the aftermath of this event. Although Saudi Arabia benefited from the decline of the Iranian oil industry, the intelligentsia and the non-Saudi Arab communities, not to mention Aramco's Shi'ite workforce, sympathised with Musadeq's struggle against the 'colonialist exploiters'.

In the early 1950s after Ibn Saud's health rapidly deteriorated, the kingdom was governed *de facto* by a Council of Regents. It was widely believed that when the old king died a struggle for power would break out in the royal family and that some tribal amirs and provincial governors might exploit the situation and rise up against the House of Saud.[16] Such an atmosphere of uncertainty, combined with the nationalist fervour which swept the region after the Egyptian revolution, increased the unrest in Al-Hasa and in the Hijaz.

Aramco began to experience labour difficulties in the first months of 1953. An American working for the company observed 'a new truculence among the Saudi employees', and reported 'anonymous manifestos and strike calls being circulated in the Saudi camps' and 'sudden demonstrations and walkouts on individual job sites'.[17] At the end of June a workers' committee, largely made up of Saudis trained abroad, who claimed to represent all native workers, handed the management a petition, demanding higher salaries, improved work conditions and facilities and the right to organise the workers.

A copy was also handed to the government.[18]

As the situation in the oil industry, which provided the government with its main source of revenue, continued to deteriorate, Amir Saud, the heir apparent, was asked to handle the crisis. He appointed a royal commission to look at the workers' grievances. The arrest of twelve members of the Workers' Committee, who became popular heroes overnight for their abusive treatment of the royal commissioners, sparked off a strike on 16 October. The strike involved 13,000 out of Aramco's total workforce of 15,000. The strike ended in the fourth week of October after National Guard reinforcements were rushed to Dhahran and other strike centres. The King ordered the workers to return to work and the strikers' leaders were released from jail.

On 9 November King Abd al-Aziz died and Saud succeeded him. The new king, striving to consolidate his authority, immediately issued a royal decree granting Aramco workers a 20 per cent pay rise and many other concessions. A new system for handling the grievances of Saudi employees was established. But there was no sign of jubilation in the Eastern Province and anti-western sentiments continued to grow.[19]

The 1953 Aramco strike is often described as a spontaneous protest of Saudi workers who were forbidden by law from organising to contest unsatisfactory pay and amenities. The purchasing power of Aramco's salaries were eroded by the high cost of living in the Aramco towns and by inflation. The Saudi workforce was incensed by the luxurious housing and other facilities enjoyed by the American employees.[20] However, another element — the strong xenophobic and anti-western sentiments of the domestic Aramco workforce — is frequently ignored. These were fomented by native and expatriate Arab (largely Palestinian) nationalist employees.

The fact that the strike was led by its Saudi trainees shocked Aramco's management. But in Beirut, the former had been exposed to Arab nationalist and socialist ideologies and in America to the western way of life and the occasional humiliation.[21] Back in Saudi Arabia, Aramco's trainees were expected to abide by the local norms and had to begin their apprenticeship, supervised by foreign technicians, at the bottom of the ladder. Naturally, they identified with the anti-western stance of Arab nationalism, led the strike against Aramco and were involved with later radical nationalist activities in the region.

The rise of a nationalist opposition and clandestine organisations

The scale of discontent and nationalist ferment in Saudi Arabia in the early 1950s is usually underestimated. Five centres of opposition to the Sauds' patriarchal regime emerged inside the kingdom during this period. The first was among the urban middle-class Hijazis; the second among the Shi'ites and the Aramco workforce; the third was among tribal and *hadr* elements in northern Najd and in the Eastern Province, who had resisted the rise of the House of Saud in the first decades of the century; the fourth emerged in Asir where some tribes were still not reconciled to the Saudi domination; the fifth was in the armed forces, largely among officers who had gone abroad for further training[22] or came into contact with their Egyptian and other Arab colleagues.

The sophisticated Hijazis were not only closely attuned to nationalist activity in the Arab world but, after 1924/25, found themselves governed by the Najdis whom they considered crude and uncouth. The Najdis, who looked down upon the Hijazis as being of mixed blood (due to the Hajj and concubinage) and religiously lax, imposed the restrictions of the Wahhabiyya upon them. To add insult to injury, King Saud, shortly after his succession, abolished the special status of the Hijaz, granted by his father and nourished by Faysal, which gave its population a degree of self-government.[23] He also ordered all government offices to be moved to Riyadh.

Although separatist tendencies were common in the province, it was inconceivable that the Hijazis would really wish to cut themselves off from Saudi oil revenue once the benefits became apparent.[24] The Hijazi intelligentsia, however, hoped that either a reform of the Najdi-dominated archaic regime, or its overthrow, would enable them to assume a more fitting role in the government of their country and *inter alia* abolish, or at least reduce, the ability of the Wahhabi ulama to constrain its development. In addition to a prolific nationalist-oriented press, several small, clandestine nationalist organisations were known to exist among the province's urban bourgeoisie in the early 1950s.

The Shi'ites and some of the Sunni tribes of the Eastern Province, who fought Ibn Saud and participated in the Ikhwan movement ('Ujman), had no reason to like the regime. The Shi'ites, subject to religious persecution and ill-treatment, and their Sunni neighbours, believed that their oil was enriching their oppressors while its benefits were denied to them.

The 1953 strike was an important milestone in the re-emergence of militant opposition to the Al Saud government. Anti-monarchical overtones surfaced in the later stages of the strike and the workers, despite the many concessions they had won, remained discontented and critical of the regime. In the following years, the Aramco workforce and the Eastern Province as a whole became the focus of nationalist and radical leftist activism.[25] Saudis, along with foreign Arab workers, most notably Palestinians, agitated against the Americans and the regime, and formed clandestine organisations demanding reforms, the right to unionise, the phasing-out of the US airbase in Dhahran and increasingly the ending of discrimination against the Shi'ites.

The Hijazi urban middle class had access to the whole of the Arab world, its press and radio broadcasts. Their opposition to the Sauds in this period reflected the Egyptian-led mainstream of Arab nationalism. It produced several small, clandestine nationalist groups, the most important of which was the Free Saudis. All such movements at this time demanded a constitutional-parliamentary regime and a faster pace of modernisation. Yet, although vociferous and with many sympathisers, the Hijazi opposition organisations were made up of only a small number of active members belonging largely to the educated well-to-do urban middle class.

Far more militant was the National Reform Front (NRF) which emerged at the end of 1953 or early in 1954. Founded by the leaders of the 1953 Aramco strike and of the small Najdi intelligentsia, it also claimed members in the Hijaz and the armed forces. The socialist and secular orientation of this organisation, a legacy of the early contacts in the Hijaz and in Al-Hasa with the Palestinian Arab Nationalists (*Qawmiyyun al-Arab*), was reflected in its pamphlets distributed in Al-Hasa, Hijaz and Riyadh. These called for social and political reforms and the abolition of the Committees of Public Morality.[26] As the NRF intensified its activities among the Aramco workforce and the military in 1954 and 1955, its more outspoken leaders were often imprisoned and some were forced to flee the country.[27]

In spite of persecution by the authorities, the NRF (renamed the National Liberation Front (NLF) in 1957/58) continued its activities as a socialist pro-Nasserite movement both in Saudi Arabia and abroad. Its leftist leanings, militancy and roots in the oil industry, the armed forces and among Najdis (mainly Shammar) inimical to the House of Saud, made the NLF exceptionally dangerous to the regime and a prime target for its security services.

The Saudi NLF moved further left from the Nasserite mainstream of Arab nationalism in the 1960s and was ideologically related to the Marxist South Yemeni NLF and Palestinian Liberation Fronts (especially the PDFP). Repeatedly splitting away from and regrouping with its mainstream Arab Nationalists and its left wing, the Popular Democratic Front (PDF), in the 1970s the NLF became the nucleus of the small Saudi Communist Party and other minor leftist organisations.[28]

A member of the Workers' Committee of the 1953 strike, Nassir Sa'id, the best-known Saudi opposition leader until the 1970s, was arrested and then released in October 1953. Two months later, after denouncing the authorities and their corruption in the presence of King Saud, he was exiled temporarily to his home town Ha'il (Jabal Shammar). Sa'id, a member of the newly established NRF, was the chief instigator of the 1956 disturbances in Al-Hasa, and was involved in an attempt to form an Arabian Trade Union Association. He was allegedly sentenced to death *in absentia* and escaped to Syria (in 1956). In 1958 in Damascus he founded the *Ittihad Shu'ub al-Jazira al-'Arabiyya* (Union of the Peoples of the Arabian Peninsula — UPAP), a pan-Arab pro-Nasserite organisation. In the same year he moved to Cairo and through radio broadcasts and pamphlets, called upon the Saudi population to overthrow their regime. By 1961 Nassir Sa'id's organisation was better known as *Ittihad Abna' al-Jazira al-'Arabiyya* (Union of the Sons of the Arabian Peninsula). In 1962, in Cairo, this organisation joined the Arab National Liberation Front (ANLF) incorporating the NLF and the Free Princes. In 1963 Nassir Sa'id moved to San'a. He later broke away from the ANLF and returned to Syria. In the 1960s his UPAP claimed responsibility for many acts of sabotage and for distributing pamphlets in Saudi Arabia.[29] Support for this organisation among Saudis seems to have been limited to the Aramco workforce and Jabal Shammar, and it was especially popular among the Yemenis and other foreign Arabs residing in the kingdom.

The Popular Democratic Front and the Organisation of the National Revolution, offshoots of the Arab Nationalists (*Qawmiyyun al-Arab*), also appeared in the 1960s. Their support in Saudi Arabia was highly marginal and shortlived.[30]

A Saudi branch of the Ba'th movement was founded in 1958, shortly after the emergence of the UAR. At first it looked to the Syrian Ba'th for guidance, and the little support it found in Saudi Arabia came mainly from townspeople in the Hijaz and Asir. After the early 1960s, with the rise in power of the Iraqi Ba'th, the small

Saudi Ba'th movement became largely Iraqi-oriented and its activities spread to the Eastern Province and the neighbouring principalities. Its most important contribution to opposition to the Saudi regime was probably its broadcasts on Radio Baghdad and the paper *Sawt al-Tali'a* (*Voice of the Vanguard*) which was published at irregular intervals. It first appeared in Baghdad and later in Europe and the US, where it became popular among Saudi students.[31]

In other Arab countries, discontented young nationalist army officers represented the most serious opposition to their regimes. In the 1950s the Saudi armed forces were still in an embryonic form. They lacked prestige and were easily counterbalanced by the tribal National Guard loyal to the Sauds. It seems that although suspected and discriminated against, educated Hijazi commoners reached key positions in its command. The threat of a 'Young Turks' revolution was somewhat exacerbated by King Saud's decision in 1954 to invite an Egyptian military mission to help the Americans train the new Saudi armed forces.[32] Thus he unwittingly facilitated the dissemination of Nasserite propaganda in his own army.

A movement called the Free Officers had already emerged in the armed forces by 1954. In the spring of 1955, after members of this group were arrested and their leaders executed, it was disclosed that it had planned a revolution similar to the one in Egypt and had plotted to assassinate Prince Faysal, the Prime Minister, and several other cabinet ministers as well as to force the King to abdicate.[33] However, the Free Officers Movement and members of the Arab Nationalists in the armed forces survived this setback and managed to participate in anti-monarchical activities in the following years. In 1957, 1958 and 1959, military personnel were occasionally arrested and even executed for subversion and mutiny. But such activities were of little consequence and only made Faysal more determined, in 1958, to freeze plans for the development of Saudi Arabia's army and air force by the United States — plans which Saud had agreed on at the beginning of 1957. Following the Egyptian intervention in Yemen, some members of the Free Officers Movement in the Saudi air force deserted to Egypt with their planes.[34] But the most serious, albeit amateurish, attempt by the military to overthrow the regime was to come, ironically, in 1969 after the *rapprochement* between Nasser and Saudi Arabia.

King Saud was not unaware of the discontent in the kingdom. Thus, paradoxically, while he courted pan-Arabism, he took steps to suppress the nationalist and radical opposition to his regime. A royal decree was published at the beginning of 1954 prohibiting strikes and demonstrations. New elite commando and National Guard units were stationed in the Eastern Province. A Directorate General of Broadcasting, Press and Publications was established: its duty was to tighten control on the media, especially in the Hijaz. The security services began to hunt down 'communists' and radical nationalists in Al-Hasa and the Hijaz. Foreign Arabs, particularly Palestinians, were accused of agitation or of membership in pan-Arab movements.[35]

The efforts of the regime to suppress the middle class and socialist-nationalist opposition were not very effective because of rivalry in the royal family between 1955 and 1961 and because the security services were inadequate. The bleeding of the country's economy by the royal family and Saud's pro-western and anti-Nasserite policy infuriated the nationalists. Agitation among the military, the intelligentsia and Aramco's workforce continued, and even intensified, in the years to come.

The 1956 strike and the collapse of the Egyptian–Saudi axis

Ironically, the intensification of anti-monarchical activities among the new elites and the Aramco workforce coincided with the climax of the Egyptian–Saudi cooperation. The Baghdad Pact was launched in February 1955. When finalised, it included Turkey, Iran, Pakistan, Iraq and Britain. Only the joint efforts of Egypt and Saudi Arabia prevented Jordan from joining as well. Saudi money was used to undermine the treaty and to help subvert the Hashemite regimes. Furthermore, King Saud visited Iran and Pakistan to persuade their rulers to withdraw from the pact. Yet Saud's anti-Hashemite and anti-western offensive could not offset the fact that his archaic, corrupt and reactionary regime was unacceptable to the new elites and the other nationalist elements in Saudi Arabia.

From 1955 anti-western and anti-American agitation, aimed, as well, against the regime, escalated in the Hijaz and the Eastern Province. At the same time Nasser was grappling with the West in a struggle which led to the nationalisation of the Suez Canal.

King Saud visited the Eastern Province in May 1956 to determine the future of the American base in Dhahran — its lease was about to expire. He was also preparing a summit meeting with President Nasser and President Shukri al-Kuwatly of Syria which was to take place in Dammam (the administrative capital of the Eastern Province) and which he hoped would contribute both to his prestige and to the stability of his regime. Yet when he reached Dhahran he was confronted by a hostile demonstration 'organised by nationalists and communists' demanding the phasing-out of the American base and the nationalisation of Aramco.[36]

At the beginning of June, Aramco was paralysed by a strike caused by granting private contractors the task of transporting the employees to the work-sites. There was little doubt that in addition to legitimate grievances the strike was politically motivated and was meant to be a popular protest directed against the regime and the West. This time the strike was quickly and brutally suppressed on Saud's orders by the Jiluwi Governor of the Eastern Province. A number of demonstrators and strike leaders were killed or executed, several were tortured to death, and others were imprisoned. Furthermore, a royal decree, published on 11 June, strictly forbade strikes and demonstrations of any kind.[37]

It should not be overlooked that modern education and the economic development of the Eastern Province had begun to make the Shi'ite population of the region more conscious of their disadvantages. Since 1953 Aramco gradually divested itself of different operations which it had carried out in the past by passing them on to local contractors. Because of this and the higher skill of its workforce and the termination of labour-intensive infrastructure projects, the company gradually reduced its workforce. At the same time, it was trying to increase the proportion of local employees and the number of Saudis in its administration and management, as can be seen in Table 4.1.

Table 4.1: Aramco manpower, 1949–72

Year	1949	1954	1959	1961	1964	1972
Saudis	15,311	21,858	11,682		10,000	8,630
Foreigners	5,288	7,676	4,575			1,423
Total	20,599	29,534	16,257	14,834		10,353

Source: Wenner, 'Saudi Arabia', p. 171; *Aramco Yearbook*, p. 161; *Hamizrah Hakhadash*, Vol. 12, No. 4 (November 1962), p. 418, according to Aramco's yearbook; Rugh, 'Emergence', p. 9; Mosley, *Power Play*, p. 327.

Coming as it did during a period of financial crisis in the kingdom, this reduction in manpower was especially painful for the Shi'ite population of the Eastern Province. Aramco's contribution to the development of the province was still substantial. This, and the increased security forces in the region, prevented another strike in the oil company. However, sporadic unrest in Aramco and demonstrations in the oil towns erupted occasionally in the next decade. To some extent Aramco became a focal point of radical anti-government and anti-American activity in the kingdom.[38]

President Nasser arrived in Dhahran in September for the meeting with King Saud and President Kuwatly. His nationalisation of the Suez Canal two months earlier and the humiliation of the West had aroused Arab pride and turned Nasser into the idol of the Arab masses. He was met in Al-Hasa by huge crowds who manifested their admiration for him with great emotion. Saud was not only ignored but, according to one source,[39] 'stones were thrown at the royal entourage and slogans denouncing the House of Saud were displayed by some of the demonstrators'. Shortly afterwards, when Nasser arrived in Riyadh, the whole population turned out to accord him a hero's welcome.

The disturbances in the Eastern Province in 1956 were an extension of the Arab nationalist struggle, led by Nasser, against western colonialism in the Middle East. The Aramco concession and the Dhahran airbase were viewed as a symbol of the 'neo-colonialist' presence in the region and constituted a challenge to Saudi pride and Arab independence. Understandably, the renewal of the airbase agreement by Saud, even for one year, together with the authorities' harsh suppression of the Al-Hasa demonstrations and strike, exacerbated the resentment of the population of the Eastern Province and Saudi nationalists towards their regime.

Nasser's visit to Saudi Arabia, it seems, was also a turning-point in the relationship between Saud and the Egyptian leader. Apprehensive of the universal empathy in the kingdom for Nasser and his policy, Saud ignored an Egyptian proposal for a Saudi–Syrian–Egyptian federation. Furthermore, due to the influence of his advisers, he became determined to resist Nasser's growing power in the Arab world.[40] When the Suez War broke out the following month, the King prudently severed Saudi Arabia's relations with Britain and France and imposed an oil embargo on them. He also agreed at the beginning of January 1957 to compensate King Hussein for the loss of a British subsidy which had occurred when, under Nasser's pressure, he withdrew the military facilities England enjoyed in Jordan and he pensioned off John Bagot Glubb, the Commander of the Arab Legion.

Despite the universal rejection of the Eisenhower Doctrine (January 1957) by Arab nationalists, Saud decided to visit the USA at the end of January. During his visit the Saudi monarch undertook to support the Doctrine and to help curb the rise of Nasserite power in the region. In exchange for an agreement to extend the lease of the Dhahran airbase for five more years Saud obtained from Washington an undertaking of economic and military assistance.

Relations between Saud and Nasser rapidly deteriorated in 1957, while the Egyptian media increased its attacks on the Saudi monarchy. In April a group of Palestinians who had arrived from Egypt attempted to assassinate the Saudi king.[41] For his part the Saudi monarch helped King Hussein of Jordan to rid himself of his pro-Nasserite government. Although the Saudis, it seems, were not involved in the American-sponsored attempt to overthrow the Syrian regime, King Saud nevertheless attempted to stop the unification of Syria and Egypt, in February 1958, which led to the establishment of the UAR. In March Colonel Sarraj, the head of the Syrian intelligence services, accused King Saud of financing a plot to assassinate President Nasser. As this happened when Arab euphoria at the establishment of the UAR was at its peak, the Egyptian and Syrian media exploited the affair for an all-out attack on the Saudi regime, and called upon the kingdom's population to rise against its corrupt rulers.

On the whole Faysal supported Saud's opposition to the western defence pacts and his anti-Hashemite policy. But he disagreed with Saud's anti-western extremism and his support for the subversion of Nasser in the Arab world. Always an advocate of a cautious and passive policy, Faysal was naturally unhappy with Saud's total change of attitude at the end of 1956 when he opted for an alliance with the US and active hostility to President Nasser and to pan-Arabism. It was obvious to him that overt opposition to the Egyptian leader was bound to cause Nasser and the nationalist camp to focus their efforts on undermining the Saudi regime. Although careful not to openly challenge his brother, Faysal took advantage of his mistakes practically to rule Saudi Arabia in his name.

POWER STRUGGLE IN THE ROYAL FAMILY AND THE NEW ELITES (1958–64)

Faysal's first cabinet, 1958–60

As soon as he assumed power Faysal adopted a policy of appeasement towards Nasser. His task was made more urgent by the overthrow of Iraq's monarchical regime in July 1958 and by the rise in nationalist fervour at home after the establishment of the UAR. Faysal, therefore, quickly declared his support for Nasser's positive neutralism, withdrew the Saudi troops from Jordan, and froze all the King's agreements with the USA, including the one concerning the expansion and modernisation of the Saudi armed forces. This agreement was not only in line with Faysal's wish to assure Nasser of his traditional opposition to America's Middle Eastern policy but also because he was convinced that the modernisation of the armed forces would exacerbate the regime's security problems.[42]

Although a wave of euphoria swept the whole of the Arab world in the period following 1958, relations between the traditionalist kingdom and its revolutionary neighbours were at best correct. By 1960, while Nasser was preaching socialism and militant pan-Arabism, Faysal began to experiment with a pan-Islamic policy meant to block the spread of radical ideologies. Earlier, the kingdom had become a haven for Syrian and Egyptian Muslim fundamentalists who were now permitted to use the media to criticise Egypt's secularisation and 'socialisation' of Islam.[43]

The period of Faysal's government in the late 1950s is marked by the success of his financial reforms, the reorganisation and modernisation of the cabinet and administration, and the rapid expansion of the educational system. Many Saudi graduates from foreign universities were given key positions in the administration.[44] Yet, ironically, Faysal's achievements caused him to lose many of his supporters. His austerity policy estranged the Hijazi merchant class because of its adverse effect on the province's economy. The substantially reduced allocations to the numerous princes and the tribal *umara* antagonised both, but the *umara* who were losing authority because of the centralisation of the government had an additional axe to grind. The Liberal Princes were disillusioned with Faysal's conservative measures designed to preserve the system rather than reform it. They considered the strong and capable Crown Prince a more serious obstacle to change and to their own aspirations than Saud had been. As for the nationalists, when they realised that Faysal's limited reforms were meant to perpetuate the Sauds' authoritarian regime they became more determined to transform Saudi Arabia into a constitutional monarchy or to get rid of the House of Saud altogether.

The nationalists at first thought that Faysal's rise to power in 1958 and the rivalry in the royal house constituted a turning-point in their struggle to modernise the kingdom's government. One of their leaders, Abdallah Tariki, is quoted as saying shortly after Faysal came to power: 'We in Saudi Arabia have just taken a step forward to a constitution. Eventually this country will become a constitutional monarchy.'[45]

Critical of Aramco for taking advantage of Saudi Arabia, in the mid-1950s Faysal was instrumental in the appointment of Tariki, a Najdi geology graduate of the University of Texas and covertly a leading member of the NRF, as the Director-General of Petroleum and Mineral Affairs in the new Ministry of Finance and National Economy.[46] A radical nationalist, and admirer of Nasser and his policy of advocating the use of Arab oil to advance the cause of the Arab revolution, Tariki would have liked to nationalise Aramco. But given the existing realities, his immediate targets were to gain greater control of the company and coerce Aramco into becoming an integrated company rather than just a producer of crude oil. In this way, Saudi Arabia would be able to share in the downstream profits of its parent companies. Tariki won Faysal's wholehearted support for this, for the involvement of other oil companies in the Saudi oil industry, and for the participation of Saudi Arabia in the formation of the Organisation of Petroleum Exporting Countries (OPEC) in 1960.[47]

Once it became apparent that Faysal had no intention of instituting a constitutional monarchy and as the Crown Prince and the King wished to win their sympathy, the nationalists skilfully manoeuvred between the two and in practice enjoyed the advantage of overt political activity. At the time the Saudi security services were extremely ineffective and the regime, attempting to appease Arab nationalism, did not wish to undermine its own efforts by persecuting the local progressives.[48]

Between 1958 and 1960 opposition organisations frequently distributed pamphlets in the Hijaz, Al-Hasa and in Riyadh, demanding a reform in the kingdom's political system and its policies. The Saudi press, dominated by Egyptians and the Hijazi intelligentsia, openly defied the strict censorship imposed by Ibn Saud and frequently published articles promoting the cause of Arab nationalism and indirectly attacking the regime.[49]

The establishment of the UAR caused many more Saudi officers and NCOs to join the Free Officers Movement and other Saudi clandestine organisations. On several occasions in 1958 cadets and officers demonstrated against the termination of the services of the Egyptian military mission in Saudi Arabia. Despite the improvement (for obvious reasons) in the salary scales for members of the armed forces in 1959, some officers — especially younger ones returning from courses abroad — still criticised Faysal's decision to reduce substantially the Saudi defence expenditures (1958–61) and to freeze the expansion and upgrading of the armed forces. Furthermore, they resented the priority given by the regime to the development of the tribal National Guard.[50] Yet the net result of Faysal's policy was that the armed forces remained weak and incapable of seriously threatening the regime.

Saudi Arabia suffered repeated droughts between 1958 and 1962. These, and the cuts in their subsidies, greatly increased hardship among the Bedouins. Later, the process of urbanisation was accelerated and unemployment in the kingdom's main cities increased. Economic-political-motivated tension in Aramco was also heightening. The government attempted to alleviate the situation by expelling foreign Arabs without work permits. But Saudis were incapable or unwilling to replace these workers and the Al-Hasa Shi'ites, whose situation was worsened by Faysal's austerity policy, did not benefit from the measures.[51]

By the beginning of 1960, Faysal's popularity was at a low ebb. Both conservatives and liberals, each for their own reasons, reached the conclusion that restoring the weak Saud to power would benefit them. Many members of the royal house also joined Saud's camp at this time, feeling that Faysal's stringent financial policy was no longer justified. So did the Hijazi merchant class which had suffered from the Crown Prince's economic policy. Pragmatically, the nationalists also began to support the monarch, whom they considered weak and easier to manipulate and who now appeared reconciled to constitutional and other reforms.[52]

A strange alliance thus emerged at the end of 1959 between Saud and his conservative supporters, the Liberal Princes and the intelligentsia. To force Faysal to resign, the King delayed the signing of decrees, legalising the government's decisions. He thus gradually brought to a standstill the government's operations, and exacerbated the recession resulting from Faysal's austerity policy.

In an effort to win the goodwill of the new elite, Faysal employed many in his administration, speeded up the process of modernisation, allocated greater funds to modern education, and abolished the censorship laws.[53] Yet when the Liberal Princes and the nationalist intelligentsia submitted a proposal to him in June for a constitutional monarchy and an elected body with legislative powers, Faysal, backed by most of the senior princes, rejected it out of hand. The nationalist-dominated press, which flourished under Faysal, no longer inhibited by censorship laws, openly attacked his conservative government and indirectly the Saudi regime.[54]

The rise and fall of Saud's 'progressive' government (1960–62)

By the last months of 1960 Saud felt sufficiently strong to oust Faysal. The opportunity came when the Crown Prince submitted the new budget; Saud refused to authorise it. This completely paralysed the activities of the government. A letter to this effect from Faysal was construed by Saud to be a letter of resignation, and on 21 December the King announced the formation of a new government which he would lead.

Saud's new 'progressive' government was probably the nearest that the nationalists and constitutionalists ever got to gaining power in Saudi Arabia. The new cabinet did not include any of the senior princes of the royal house. In addition to Saud's son Muhammad, appointed Minister of Defence and a junior member of the Sudayri clan, the cabinet included three Liberal Princes. Talal was granted a key position when appointed Minister of Finance and National Economy, as well as Deputy President of the Supreme Planning Council, and Abd al-Muhsin and Badr were given lesser ministries. Prince Nawwaf, Talal's full brother, was appointed head of the royal court.[55] Six out of eleven ministries in the cabinet were held by commoners, five of whom, mostly with university degrees, were moderate nationalists — one, a Hijazi merchant. Abdallah ibn Hamud Tariki, the exception, represented the militant element among the nationalists. His appointment as the head of the newly-created Ministry of Petroleum and Mineral Resources was appropriate. Two other radical nationalists, Abd al-Aziz al-Mu'ammar and Faysal bin Mubarak al-Hujaylan (a Hijazi diplomat who had served in Washington), both known for their strong left-wing views, were appointed royal advisers.[56]

The June 1960 programme for constitutional reforms which the Liberal Princes and the intelligentsia submitted to Faysal was strongly condemned by the ulama on the ground that it contravened the Shari'a. Even Saud dissociated himself from the document, declaring that the Koran was Saudi Arabia's constitution and the only source for its social principles. The King again distanced himself from the constitutional zeal of his progressive allies, when Talal and the nationalists handed him a proposal for a 'basic order for government' (*Al-Nizam al-Assasi li'l-Ḥukm*). This document, prepared with the help of Egyptian jurists, avoided terms offensive to the ulama such as 'constitution' (*dustur*). Immediately following the formation of the new cabinet, Radio Mecca announced in its name the promulgation of 'basic laws' and the establishment of a legislative council: two-thirds of the members were to be elected and a third appointed. The announcement was refuted by the King two days later in a radio broadcast and press interviews.[57]

Evidently the conservative King was opposed all along to his allies' constitutional reforms. Nevertheless, the Liberal Princes and the nationalist commoners in the government who 'rose to new heights of power, inspired by Nasser's revolutionary nationalism believed that the days of the Saudi monarchy were numbered and hoped that as champions of the constitution they would remain at the top.'[58] Indeed, as Finance Minister and Deputy President of the Supreme Planning Council, Talal frequently attempted to usurp the power of the Council of Ministers in order to achieve his aims, but he thereby alienated the King and the more moderate ministers.

Not unaware of the progressives' attempt to manipulate the weak King, the senior princes and the other conservatives in the Saudi ruling class exerted pressure on Saud to limit the influence of leftist nationalists in his court and government. The King dismissed his progressive advisers at the end of February 1961. In the next few months he began to strengthen the moderates in the government, ignoring the outraged protests of the Liberal Princes.

A harsh state security law was promulgated by the King in March 1961, paradoxically, while a 'liberal' government was ruling the country. It prescribed the death penalty or 25 years' imprisonment for any aggressive act against the royal family or the state (including treason, attempts to change the regime, or to spread disaffection among the armed forces). It also forbade the profession of any ideology other than Islam, or the formation of political parties.[59] This was necessitated by the rising tide of leftist-oriented clandestine activities aimed against the regime and the 'parasitic' royal family, which followed on the shelving of the constitutional reforms and the dismissal of Saud's progressive advisers. Pamphlets distributed by the NLF in February denounced the King's reactionary stance and called for a 'national' economic policy, a revision of the agreements with the foreign oil companies (Tariki), the adoption of positive neutralism, and the abrogation of the Dhahran airbase agreement with America.[60]

The American presence in Dhahran became a source of increasing embarrassment to King Saud who was accused of providing the imperialists with a base in Saudi Arabia. The Eastern Province, a centre of radical nationalism, did not benefit from government-sponsored development. Rather, partly due to the decline in the size of Aremco's workforce, suffered from growing unemployment. Thus, during a visit to the region in the first months of 1961, Saud was met by hostile demonstrators who demanded an improvement in the employment situation and government services and the annulment of the airbase agreement with the United States. Under pressure from Arab nationalists in the kingdom and abroad, the King, in mid-March, announced his decision not to renew the Dhahran agreement on its expiry in April 1962.[61]

However, Shi'ite and other radical nationalists in the Eastern Province remained restive, underlining the fact that, although Al-Hasa provided 90 per cent of the kingdom's revenues, its population did not benefit from them. Unrest was not confined to Sharqiyya. In the spring of 1961 nationalist ferment all over the kingdom was aggravated by economic problems, despite the growth in oil revenues, and by rising unemployment partly due to the fast urbanisation of the unskilled rural population. This unrest also reflected the growing tension in the Arab world.[62]

All the different ideologies prevalent at this time in the Arab world — communism, socialism, Ba'thism and Nasserism — were represented in Saudi Arabia although their actual following was limited in number. The Hijazi middle class generally supported the mainstream of pan-Arabism. The leftist NLF (Arab Nationalists), widely supported by the kingdom's intelligentsia, also had followers in this province and in Asir with its largely Yemeni population. Al-Hasa, the NLF's stronghold, with its Shi'ite community, many Palestinian and other Arab employees of Aramco, was also the centre of several small left-of-centre nationalist and Marxist organisations including the Ba'th. Nationalist activity in Najd and among descendants of the Ikhwan, although related to traditional dislike of the Sauds in Jabal Shammar, was focused largely on Riyadh, the site of government offices and the new university. Here, just as in the Eastern Province, the Nasserites and the NLF were dominant, but the Ba'th and the communists managed to establish a presence in the capital. All were united in their demands for constitutional reforms, for attuning Saudi foreign policy to pan-Arabism, and for faster development. Some even plotted to assassinate members of the royal family and to hasten the kingdom towards a popular revolution.[63]

Faysal's decision to freeze the development of the armed forces did not stop the activities of the Free Officers Movement, nor of other clandestine organisations among the military. Yet, the unrest in the armed forces following the outbreak of war in Yemen in the last months of 1962 rather demonstrated the wisdom of Faysal's decision and showed how weak the Free Officers were at this stage.

Tension between Nasser and King Saud surfaced again in 1961 because of the difficulties the former was encountering in Syria. Wahhabi ulama and Muslim Brothers, who found refuge in the kingdom, attacked the secularisation of the UAR and its relations with the Soviet atheists. The Saudi regime, exploiting pan-Islam to counter pan-Arabism, authorised non-Saudi fundamentalists to establish an Islamic University in Al-Madina to compete with the 'socialised' Al-Azhar. The Saudi government, claiming that the principle of Islamic solidarity supersedes foreign ideologies, also founded in 1962 the World Islamic League (*Rabitat al-'Alam al-Islami*) which later set up a permanent secretariat in Mecca.[64]

Inter-Arab relations after 1958 became increasingly polarised because of Nasser's militant pan-Arabism and the rivalry between the Egyptian and the Iraqi revolutionary regimes. Although the Saudis tried to maintain their distance from both, when Iraq attempted to annex Kuwait at the end of June 1961 shortly after its independence, they found themselves in the same camp with the UAR. Yet, when the UAR collapsed in September, the Egyptian media viciously attacked the Saudi regime. It alleged that the regime had funded the 'plot' against Arab unity and had encouraged Saudis to rise up against their reactionary rulers.[65]

The collapse of the UAR in September 1961 and Nasser's more radical policies towards the end of the year caused an escalation in Egypt's anti-Saudi rhetoric and subversive activities. Isolated in the royal family, and again facing a political and economic crisis, the ailing Saud sought reconciliation with Faysal, though he did not wish to relinquish the government to him. The shrewd Crown Prince agreed to cooperate on condition that Saud dismiss Talal and the other Liberal Princes from the cabinet. Earlier, Talal had again embarrassed the King by giving press interviews abroad about the Dhahran airbase and his proposed constitutional reforms. So, on 11 September, Talal and the other Liberal Princes were dismissed from the cabinet but Faysal's supporters were still excluded from it. Indeed, when he left the kingdom for medical treatment in November, Saud entrusted the premiership to Faysal on condition that the latter would not make any changes in the cabinet. Thus, from mid-November 1961 to the beginning of March 1962, Faysal deputised for his brother, presiding over a cabinet made up largely of nationalists and Saud's supporters, among them Abdallah Tariki.[66]

The usual cautious Faysal, abandoning his traditional appeasement policy, dismissed many of the Egyptian advisers employed by the Saudi administration, and recalled Saudi students studying in Egyptian universities. Because of allegations of Egyptian espionage, each government withdrew its ambassador from the other's capital. A special department to supervise foreigners was established at the Ministry of the Interior and the kingdom's security services were reorganised.[67]

Under the circumstances, Faysal was no longer willing to tolerate a hostile attitude on the part of the Saudi press. Although censorship was officially reinstated only at the end of 1962, the authorities began to dismiss Egyptian and local nationalist journalists and, from the beginning of 1961, replace the staff of some newspapers. The Office of Information was made into a ministry in 1962 in order to monitor the press and help counter the Egyptian media. A press law was promulgated in November 1963: all newspaper licences were revoked and the papers were brought under state control through appointed editorial boards. In 1962 Faysal obtained the consent of the ulama for the expansion of radio broadcasting to counter the vitriolic attacks of Egypt's *Sawt al-Arab* (the Voice of the Arabs). Despite the strong objections of the ulama, who had blocked the introduction of the television since 1959, a decision to introduce TV services was taken at the end of 1962, and a government decree, authorising the construction of TV stations in Jedda and Riyadh, was published at the end of 1963.[68]

Although he made no changes in the cabinet, Faysal gradually neutralised the nationalist element in it and consolidated his position. When Saud returned to the country in March 1962 he was coerced by a coalition of senior princes to surrender his responsibilities as Prime Minister to Faysal. Saud remained Prime Minister in name only, and Faysal deputised for him and acted once again as Minister of Foreign Affairs. Abdallah Tariki and several of Saud's commoner ministers were replaced by more moderate Hijazi notables and technocrats (the Hijazi, Zaki Yamani, replaced the Najdi Tariki as Minister of Petroleum). The exceptions were Saud's son, Muhammad, who remained Minister of Defence, and Amir Faysal ibn Turki, who continued as Minister of the Interior.[69]

Most important, Shaykh Hassan bin Abdallah Al al-Shaykh was appointed Minister of Education, thus ensuring the support of the ulama and its Al-Shaykhs leaders for Faysal, despite the modernisation of the kingdom and the rapid development of 'secular' education[70] and Musa'id ibn Abd al-Rahman, Faysal's uncle, became Minister of Finance. The latter ministry, always considered very important, was essential to the success of Faysal's modernisation policy and his intention to channel much of the kingdom's oil revenues to the population through government and welfare services. Musa'id's prestige, *inter alia*, enabled Faysal to reduce substantially the royal list and the amount of the stipends allocated to each prince who remained on it.[71]

Muzzling the press and purging the cabinet of radicals and the Liberal Princes, served as warning to the Saudi nationalists that a new era in their relations with the Sauds' regime had begun. Indeed, Abdallah Tariki, who was aware of Faysal's hostility towards him, slipped out of Saudi Arabia and, after visiting Egypt, settled in Beirut. He was later followed by Talal and some of his brothers. Yet the attraction of pan-Arabism was still considerable, and most of the moderate Hijazi nationalists in the cabinet did not hesitate to challenge Faysal's policy when it clashed with Nasserism. In August, for instance, they objected to a defence agreement signed with Jordan and in September they demanded that Saudi Arabia appease Nasser and recognise the republican regime in Yemen.[72]

The Saudi government became very alarmed when the Syrian Ba'thists followed by the Iraqis, began to negotiate a new unity plan with Egypt in 1962. This coincided with vicious attacks by Egypt and its allies in the 'revolutionary camp' on Faysal's Islamic entente and the *de facto* renewal of the leasing of the Dhahran base to America. The anti-Saudi propaganda offensive intensified in August after a military cooperation agreement between the kingdom and Jordan was signed.[73] But efforts to foment unrest in the Hijaz were generally unsuccessful although limited demonstrations and disturbances, focusing on the Dhahran airbase and Aramco, did break out in the Eastern Province. Indeed, during a visit to Aramco's headquarters in August, the King was confronted by a crowd carrying placards denouncing 'American imperialism' and 'exploitation'. The demonstrations, however, were harshly suppressed and their organisers were arrested.[74]

The overthrow of the monarchy in Yemen at the end of September 1962, and the Egyptian involvement there soon after, began a new era in active opposition to the Sauds' regime. While the

Sauds supported the Yemeni royalists, Egypt encouraged the Saudi opposition against the regime. Radical nationalist organisations, led by the NLF, Yemenis and Palestinians employed in Saudi Arabia, now turned increasingly to sabotage and acts of terrorism. Yet the Hijazi middle-class nationalists became less supportive of Nasser after his intervention in Yemen.[75]

The revolution in Yemen and the Egyptian involvement in it precipitated a new crisis in the Saudi government. The royal house could no longer afford to be led by an irresolute and incapable ruler and Saud, with the blessing of the ulama, was coerced into handing over the office of Prime Minister to Faysal and giving him unlimited authority. On 31 October, the Crown Prince formed a new government in which all the major power groups excluding Saud's royal and non-aristocratic supporters were represented. In addition to Faysal and Prince Musa'id, who continued to hold the foreign affairs and finance portfolios respectively, Prince Fahd (the leader of the 'Sudayri Seven'[76] and King in 1982), Faysal's staunchest ally and the leading reformer, became Minister of Interior, his full brother Sultan, replaced Saud's son, Muhammad as Minister of Defence and their older half-brother Khalid, Deputy Prime Minister. The *'alim*, Shaykh Hassan, Minister of Education, was joined by another *'alim* who became Minister of Pilgrimage and *awqaf*. Six Hijazis, most of whom were technocrats known for their moderation in internal and external affairs, were appointed to the remaining ministries.[77]

When Faysal assumed the premiership at the end of October 1962 the future of the Saudi regime looked quite grim. Nasser considered Yemen a springboard to the control of the enormous oil wealth of the Arabian Peninsula and he committed a large army and substantial resources to the war in Yemen. The Egyptian expeditionary force, supporting the republicans in Yemen, succeeded in defeating the royalists. At the beginning of November, Egyptian planes bombed the border towns of the southern province, Asir. These towns served as staging bases for Imam Badr's tribal army.

The Saudi armed forces at the time were small and poorly equipped, since Faysal had decided in 1958 that the US should not upgrade them. Moreover, it soon became apparent that many of the officers, especially in the air force, were sympathetic to the Yemeni revolution and to Nasser's aspirations. Saudi air force planes, despatched with supplies for the loyalists, were flown by their crews to Egypt, and rebellions erupted in remote garrisons. Several Jordanian pilots sent by King Hussein with their Hunter jets to boost Saudi morale also deserted to Egypt. Furthermore, the National Guard, theoretically numbering about 18,000, was incapable of waging a modern war and most of its traditional commanders (tribal amirs) were loyal to King Saud.[78]

Prince Talal, an exile in Lebanon, frequently visited Nasser. In August 1962 he gave several interviews to the Beirut press and published a number of pamphlets in which he discussed his proposed constitutional monarchy and 'socialism'. This aroused the anger of the royal family, which had Talal's property seized and his passport revoked. An embarrassment to the Lebanese government, Talal left for Egypt and there, with his brothers Abd al-Muhsin, Fawwaz and Badr, and his cousin Sa'd ibn Fahd, founded the Free Princes Movement in September and planned a government-in-exile. Following the revolution in Yemen it was widely believed that the days of the Saudi regime were numbered. So the Free Princes and the Saudi Nasserite and leftist organisations formed the Arab National Liberation Front (ANLF) in Cairo. Using its name, Egyptian, Syrian and Yemeni radio stations called upon the Saudis to overthrow their 'corrupt' regime, and Egyptian planes dropped consignments of arms on the mountains of the Hijaz. In propaganda broadcasts, the Liberal Princes encouraged the Saudi population and armed forces to coerce the regime into reforming itself and adopting a nationalist and socialist policy.[79] Their leftist partners, however, viciously attacked Al Saud and encouraged their countrymen to overthrow its 'reactionary archaic regime'.

When in the United States, in September and October 1962, Faysal realised that his policy had estranged America and that the kingdom could no longer count on Washington's support in relation to Yemen. Indeed, the Kennedy administration, enamoured of Nasser, was attempting to win his favour and was quick to recognise the republican regime in Yemen. But, contrary to his traditional policy of appeasement and caution, Faysal was now determined not to allow Nasser to have his way, and so he actively supported the Yemen royalists.

Faysal was not unaware of the rapid social change taking place in the country and of the growing strength of the new Saudi middle class. By 1962, for instance, the number of students profiting from the modern educational system had risen to more than 113,000, compared to 33,000 in 1953. Students in local colleges of higher education numbered several thousand while those studying abroad, with government or Aramco sponsorship, were conservatively estimated at about 1200. Many more — the offspring of well-to-do families — were attending foreign universities at their own expense.

Indeed, by the early 1960s the ranks of the educated middle class, especially in the Hijaz, had expanded to such an extent that they could support nineteen newspapers and periodicals compared to four in the early 1950s.[80]

In such circumstances it was of utmost importance for the regime to gain the support of the Saudi people as a whole and in particular that of the moderate nationalists, who were mainly from the Hijazi middle class and, to a lesser extent, of Najdi *hadr* origin. These nationalists mainly aspired to a constitutional monarchy and the development and modernisation of the kingdom, but were not fired by the idea of Nasser's new socialist radicalism, nor by the Palestinian-inspired militant socialism widespread in Al-Hasa.

Aware of the inherent weakness of the traditional conservative Wahhabi kingdom in a rapidly changing Middle East, Faysal, encouraged by Prince Fahd, was determined to modernise Saudi Arabia with the help of the new elites. Yet even though he was given a lot of latitude by *ahl al-hal wa'l-'aqd* to deal with the grave crisis threatening the regime, Faysal knew that there was a limit to the concessions that he could offer. He was aware that the majority of the ruling class would not agree to sharing decision-making with the new elites, a step which would begin the erosion of their power and privileges, nor did he himself truly wish for such a change. His experience with the Hijazi middle class led Faysal to believe that the moderate educated new elites would cooperate with him. All they needed were the right incentives: the chance to share in running the country's development and the hope of eventual participating in decision-making.

Civil war in Yemen and Faysal's ten-point 'reform' programme (1962)

On 6 November, the day that diplomatic relations with Egypt were broken off after the bombing of Saudi towns near the Yemen border and a week after he became Prime Minister, Faysal announced his ten-point programme; he promised a wide range of social and political reforms, rapid modernisation and economic development. They were the closest to constitutional monarchy ever promised officially and in detail by the regime. The following were the most important:

1. To promulgate a fundamental law, based on the Koran and the Sunna, that would allow for a National Consultative Assembly (*majlis al-shura al-watani*).
2. To regulate the provincial government and provide for provincial councils.
3. To guarantee freedom of expression (within the context of Islamic laws).
4. To preserve the independence of the judiciary and to create a Ministry of Justice.
5. As 'one of the government's most important functions is to raise the national social level', to establish welfare services that would take care of the needy and the unemployed.
6. To provide free education and medical services.
7. 'As the financial and economic development of the kingdom are of primary concern to the government' to enact laws to promote the above.[81]

The promised fundamental law incorporating a National Consultative Assembly (*majlis al-shura*) and the reorganisation of the provincial government with their councils have not yet materialised although the promises were reiterated by Saudi monarchs during the last 25 years following every crisis. Rather, shortly after undertaking to guarantee freedom of expression (within Islamic laws), Faysal launched a campaign to suppress the nationalist-oriented Saudi press. However, all the other points (some however substantially modified) were carried through immediately or in the next few years. Within a decade, they led to a rapid modernisation of the Saudi kingdom, an impressive rise in the standard of living and the involvement of its new elites in running the affairs of its government.

Free modern education and medical treatment, social security laws, welfare services and efforts to deal with unemployment were forthwith tackled by Faysal's governments. Together with modernisation and economic developments they were made easier by the growing revenue from oil.

Past experience had taught Faysal that the ulama would resist any attempt to undermine their control of institutions, such as education and justice traditionally within their jurisdiction. Yet, he also knew that determination to carry out the reforms seemingly resulting from *shura* and *ijma'* (consultation and consensus) would convince them to accept a compromise, especially if control of the modernised institutions was to be left in the hands of an *'alim*, particularly an

Al-Shaykh. Nevertheless, the promised independence of the judiciary and the creation of a Ministry of Justice met with strong opposition from the ulama and other conservatives from the ruling class.

As early as June 1963, Faysal attempted to reorganise his government and establish new ministries of Justice and Municipal Affairs. But the bitter opposition of Al al-Shaykh to this move, his uncle Musa'id's refusal to accept the Justice Ministry, and the hostility of the provincial and tribal *umara* to the proposed reorganisation of the rural government, caused Faysal to postpone this plan (only in 1970, following the death of the kingdom's powerful Grand Mufti, did Faysal establish the Ministry of Justice).[82] By the end of 1963, no longer worried about the Yemen war, Faysal published an edict for the formation of provincial government and councils but did nothing about it. Yet in later years, he systematically strengthened the authority of his central government at the expense of the power of the *umara*.

Faysal again avoided a confrontation in relation to his promise to establish a judiciary council. He opted for a compromise with the ulama by creating the Institute for the Issue of Religio-Legal Opinions and the Supervision of Religious Affairs (*Dar al-Ifta' wa 'l Ishraf 'ala 'l-Shu'un al-Diniyya*) and the Higher Council of *Qadis* (*Al Majlis al-A'la li 'l-Qada*) directed by, and composed of, senior jurists.[83] Another touchy problem was Faysal's undertaking to reform and restrict the authority of the ulama-controlled Committees of Public Morality. Their power, which Saud had re-established, and the zeal of their Morality Police was strongly resented by the new elites and the middle classes. Faysal, believing this extremist body to be a dangerous anachronism, re-established the status quo which had existed until 1953.[84]

Faysal's strategy proved most successful. The old elites accepted his policy because it enhanced both stability and the regime's ability to overcome the grave threat facing it. The ulama, as expected, were ready to compromise as long as the Wahhabi character of the kingdom was preserved and their role in it outwardly respected. The larger part of the middle-class intelligentsia, not drawn to socialist or Marxist ideologies, and somewhat apprehensive of Nasser's increasing radicalism, welcomed the ten-point programme.[85] Their main aim in any case was to achieve faster development in the country and constitutional reform granting them participation in decision-making, both of which Faysal appeared to promise.

Although it became evident later that the King had no intention of carrying out the promised constitutional reforms, the majority of the new elites, tempted by power, prestige and wealth, or induced by the cruel suppression of the militants, opted to continue cooperating with the regime. Their involvement in Faysal's government and administration continued to grow. Many even misled themselves into believing that Faysal's evolutionary reforms, the modernisation of the kingdom and their increasing involvement in it, would eventually lead to their participation in policy-making.[86] Some, however, felt that they had been misled by the ruler and apart from the leftist opposition that had rejected Faysal's evolutionary reform programme from the start, began to plot the overthrow of the regime.

The welfare benefits, government services and subsidies increased in the following years, in proportion to the country's rising oil revenue. This ensured the support of the rural population, the newly urbanised, and the middle class for the Al Saud regime. Most important was the fact that Faysal had publicly declared that the welfare of the population was the government's first concern and that the country's wealth was to be used to improve the population's standard of living.[87]

In his relations with the nationalist new elites Faysal adopted the carrot-and-stick principle. He differentiated between the moderate middle-class nationalists, mainly Hijazis who had been carried away by the early success of Nasser's anti-colonial struggle and the idea of pan-Arabism, and the hard-line militant leftists in the Eastern Province and elsewhere in the kingdom. Some of the latter came from Najd and Al-Hasa families traditionally unfriendly towards the Sauds. For this minority, the cadres of the different offshoots of the NLF (*Qawmiyyun al-Arab*), the Nasserites, socialists, Ba'thists and the communists, he had no compassion. They were mercilessly hunted and when caught, they were tortured and imprisoned for lengthy periods of time.[88]

Unwilling to subscribe to the extreme anti-Saud policies of their progressive partners, the Liberal Princes brought about the disintegration of the ANLF in September 1963. Nassir Sa'id and his pan-Arabist followers resumed the name Union of the Peoples of the Arabian Peninsula (UPAP), while the more leftist elements of the coalition once again called themselves NLF. Both were operating at this time from San'a and activating clandestine cells in the kingdom. Talal and the other princes, despairing of gaining support in Saudi Arabia and objecting to the use of their names in the vicious propaganda offensive unleashed by the Egyptians against Al Saud, begged Faysal's forgiveness. Their return to Saudi Arabia in 1964 signalled the demise of their quixotic movement and of open liberalism in the royal family.[89]

The outbreak of war in the Yemen, and the escalation in the activities of the clandestine opposition organisations, caused Faysal to expand and modernise the security services with the help of American experts. A Directorate of Internal Security was established by the Ministry of the Interior in 1964 (*Idarat al-Mabahith* later *Al-Mabahith al-'Amma*) as well as the Security Force College (in Riyahd). After the general mobilisation announced at the end of 1962, the National Guard, enjoying the favour of the royal house, was to be expanded from about 18,000 to about 30,000 men and with British help upgraded in quality. In 1963 it was put under the command of Prince Abdallah (now Crown Prince), the representative of the conservatives among the senior princes supporting Faysal, and its command structure was purged of King Saud's supporters.[90] All this helped combat the sharp rise in the Egyptians' encouraged activities of the militant opposition and convinced any waverers to accept Faysal's reforms.

Towards the end of 1962 the Kennedy administration agreed to restate its commitments to defend the territorial integrity of Saudi Arabia and a squadron of American fighters based in Dhahran occasionally overflew the towns of the Hijaz to underline this commitment.[91] By the latter part of 1963 it was already clear that the Egyptians were not going to win an easy victory in Yemen, and by the end of the year Syria succeeded in focusing Arab attention on the River Jordan project undertaken by Israel. This caused a temporary détente in inter-Arab relations and led to the Cairo summit of January 1964. But as Saud was still legally King and, with the help of his sons, occasionally attempted to regain his power in Riyadh, Faysal bided his time and still pretended to support his own proposed constitutional reforms.

Once enthroned in October 1964, and no longer apprehensive about the future of the Sauds' regime, Faysal gradually rescinded his promise to institute constitutional reforms. In an interview which immediately followed his succession to the throne in 1964, he declared that 'no political changes were to be expected or sought'. Shortly afterwards, in another interview, he stated, and has often repeated, that 'Saudi Arabia has no need for a constitution because it has the Koran, which is the oldest and most efficient constitution in the world.' Later he added, 'the only true criterion of a regime, monarchical or republican alike, is the degree of reciprocity between ruler and ruled and the extent to which it symbolizes prosperity, progress and healthy initiative . . .. The quality of a regime should be judged by its deeds and the integrity of its rulers not by its name.'[92]

By the second half of 1964, although Nasser realised that his Yemeni adventure had failed, he renewed his attacks on the Saudi regime. A major reason was the establishment of Faysal's World Islamic League, which represented a challenge to his pan-Arab policy.[93] The Saudi refusal to continue paying subsidies to their sister Arab counties and to the PLO also contributed to the renewed struggle. Saudi radical opposition movements enjoyed the support of Cairo, San'a and the Ba'th regimes of Damascus and Baghdad and were encouraged to escalate their operations in the kingdom. Apart from occasional bombing incidents and the distribution of anti-government pamphlets throughout the provinces, leftist organisations attempted to foment unrest in Al-Hasa and its oil industry. The College of Petroleum and Minerals (P & M), established by Aramco in 1963, with its partly Shi'ite student body, gradually emerged, it seems, as an additional focus of nationalist agitation.[94]

Faysal's hard-line policy towards the radical opposition was demonstrated immediately by the widespread arrests in the Southern Region (Asir) and the Eastern Province among the local intelligentsia and the Yemeni and Shi'ite workers. New anti-strike laws, announced in 1964, prescribed 10–15 years' imprisonment for incitement to strike compared to the 3–5 years in the past. After widespread arrests of opposition activists accused of communism, the Ministry of the Interior claimed in 1964 that it had crushed subversive activities in the province. Yet tension in Al-Hasa continued and demonstrations, rioting and even bombing incidents were reported in the following years.[95]

The struggle for power within the royal family between 1962 and 1964, which culminated with the deposition of Saud and the enthronement of Faysal in November 1964, is beyond the scope of this chapter. Suffice it to say that once free of Saud's intrigues and secure in his position as King, Faysal was better able to carry out his evolutionary reforms and modernisation plans and fight Nasser's pan-Arabism and the militant opposition at home.

CONCLUSIONS (1953–64)

The reign of Saud (1953–64) which coincided with the rise and continued success of Nasser's pan-Arabism, could be considered the golden age of Saudi nationalism. The weakness of the ruler and his ambivalent policies and the struggle for power within the royal family, presented the Saudi nationalist opposition with the opportunity to expand its activities practically unchecked. The potential threat to the power monopoly of the Saudi oligarchy by the largely bourgeois pan-Arab nationalists of the Hijaz, their socialist and even Marxist-oriented counterparts of northern Najd, Asir and Al-Hasa (including Shi'ites in the latter), and by frustrated pro-Nasserite officers,[96] was not underestimated by the rulers. Indeed, both Saud and Faysal, struggling for power, tried to win their favour, especially after 1958 when a wave of euphoria swept the Arab world following the establishment of the UAR.

In December 1960 when he ousted Faysal and established his 'progressive government', Saud valued the support of the nationalist intelligentsia to such an extent that they were strongly represented in his cabinet and among his advisers. When he again became Prime Minister in 1962, Faysal considered winning the sympathy of the nationalist public sufficiently important to merit his ten-point programme. This included promises of constitutional reforms and faster development. The very fact that once he had established his authority Faysal ruthlessly persecuted the radical nationalists who were either dissatisfied with his partial reforms or unwilling to join his camp, was a tribute to their estimated power. Indeed, the potential threat of the militant pan-Arabists to the conservative oil-rich Saudi monarchy was seriously exacerbated in the last months of 1962 by the establishment of a republican regime in Yemen and the presence of Egyptian expeditionary forces there.

The failure of the Saudi nationalists to oust the relatively weak and divided regime was the result of several factors. The Saudi armed forces were still in an embryonic state and were balanced by the tribal National Guard. **Most Saudis in the 1950s and early 1960s were still country people, backward and conservative. Their allegiance was to their tribes and traditional institutions, including the paternalistic Saud monarchy, rather than to the 'Saudi nation'.[97] The nationalists, moreover, were identified with the urban (ḥadr) middle class whom the Bedouins traditionally disliked. The socialists, even Najdis, were considered atheists or identified with the despised Shi'ites and their struggle for equality and improved living standards.** On its part, the regime increasingly channelled oil revenues to improve the standard of living of the population. Thus, notwithstanding the climax of pan-Arabism in the region, nationalism in Saudi Arabia failed to win popular support other than from the peripheral Hijazi new middle class, peripheral Najdi intelligentsia, Aramco's Shi'ite and expatriate Arab workforce and from the non-aristocratic officers in the inconsequential armed forces. Finally, **at the end of 1962, faced with a serious threat, the royal family and the ruling class overcame its differences and closed ranks behind Faysal.**

The Egyptian intervention in Yemen provided Saudi nationalists with what seemed their best chance ever to win a share in decision-making. Their clout was now combined with the threat of Nasser's all-powerful pan-Arabism in Yemen. Faysal's decision to abandon his appeasement policy signalled the end of the radical nationalists' overt political activity and their attempts to share in power and decision-making from within the establishment. It also led to the growing radicalisation and militancy of the small Saudi left. It was a milestone in the growing rift between the Saudi left and the largely Hijazi middle-class nationalists, many of whom were becoming disillusioned with Nasser's radical pan-Arabism which now threatened their country and attracted by new opportunities opened for them by Faysal. The majority opted, thereafter, to cooperate with the traditional elites and provided the numerous technocrats which Faysal's plans for speedy modernisation and his evolutionary reforms needed. Finally, it brought to the throne Faysal, a capable strong leader with political *savoir-faire* who mercilessly suppressed the elements of the opposition that he could not buy off (one of the golden rules of Ibn Saud's dynasty) or those he considered 'communist'.

NOTES

1. See above pp. 8–9, 10.
2. F.A. Shaker, 'Modernization of the Developing Nations', PhD thesis (Purdue University, 1972), p. 169, and D. Van Der Meulen, *The Wells of Ibn Sa'ud*, (London, 1957), p. 255. Ibn Saud frequently quoted to Philby (*Sa'udi Arabia*, p. 292) the following quotation from the Koran: 'Take counsel among yourselves, and if they agree with you, well and good: but if otherwise, then put your trust in God and do that which you deem best': also Craig's confidential report.
3. Jedda the town of the consuls: Van Den Meulen, *Ibn Sa'ud*, p. 16.
4. Of 1200 Saudi students abroad in 1953/54: *Mideast Mirror* (Beirut), 27 February 1954; also M. Cheney, *Big Oil Man From Arabia* (New York, 1958), pp. 224, 227; Lackner, *A House Built on Sand* (London, 1978), p. 188; R.H. Sanger, *The Arabian Peninsula* (New York, 1970), p. 108; F.H. Al-Nassar, 'Saudi Arabian Educational Mission', PhD thesis (University

of Oklahama, 1982), pp. 27–9. Of Abdallah Tariki and his Najdi nationalist comrades: S. Duguid, 'A bibliographical approach to the study of social change in the Middle East: Abdullah Tariki as a new man', IJMES, Vol. I, No. 3 (1970), p. 197; On the new middle class: W. Rugh, 'Emergence of a New Middle Class in Saudi Arabia', *The Middle East Journal* (1973). Al-Awaji (I.M. Al-Awaji, 'Bureaucracy and Society in Saudi Arabia', unpublished PhD thesis (University of Virginia, 1971), p. 176), a Deputy Minister of the Interior, stresses the Hijazis' dominance in the modern bureaucracy.

5. Inflation drove the cost of living up by 90 per cent. See: J. Listowel, quoting Anwar Ali, Governor of the Saudi Arabian Monetary Agency (SAMA), *The Listener*, 1 June 1967, pp. 705–6.

6. Talal, it is claimed, was 'exiled' in 1955 as Ambassador to France and Spain because of his association with the Saudi Free Officers. Of his visits to Nasser: A. Bligh, *Royal Succession in the House of Saud* (New York, 1984), p. 72.

7. The pro-Nasserite, *Al-Jarida* (Beirut) of 30 December 1960, claims that the Liberal Princes, the intelligentsia and most Hijazis at first supported Faysal, hoping for reform.

8. Of Faysal's support for pan-Arabism in the 1930s, probably anti-Hasemite motivated: A. Daghir, *Mudhakkirati 'ala Hamish al-Qadiyya al'Arabiyya* (Cairo, 1959), pp. 242–3. Of Arab nationalist counsellors and refugees: Van Der Meulen, *Ibn Sa'ud*, pp. 185–6, 232; also pp. 111, 133, 234; V. Sheean, *Faisal — The King and His Kingdom* (Tavistock, 1975), p. 106.

9. Saud's pro-Italian inclination in early 1940s and his Arab nationalist refugees and Nazi advisers in 1952: Bligh, *Succession*, pp. 41, 45, 61; Van Der Meulen, *Ibn Sa'ud*, pp. 111, 133, 232–4. Yusuf Yassin, Ibn Sa'ud's and Saud's chief political adviser, anti-western: Van Der Meulen, *Ibn Sa'ud*, p. 186.

10. NYT, 6 December 1953; *Mideast Mirror*, 2 January 1954; *Al-Hayat* (Beirut), 25 November 1953; *Hamizrah Hakhadash*, Vol. 6, No. 1 (1955), p. 67.

11. Buchan, 'Religious Opposition', p. 119. On the Shi'ites see below Chapter 6, pp. 152–8.

12. Van Der Meulen, *Ibn Sa'ud* p. 183 (1952); G. Anderson, 'Differential Urban Growth in the Eastern Province of Saudi Arabia', unpublished PhD thesis (The Johns Hopkins University, 1984).

13. On change and frustration, tension and inflation in 1952: Van Der Meulen, *Ibn Sa'ud*, pp. 200, 250–1. On frustration of Saudi employees with living standards of Aramco's foreign, and especially western, employees in 1953: *Al-Dustur* (London), 4 February 1979, p. 8.

14. Few Shi'ites, however, were promoted to key positions in Aramco.

15. Cheney, *Oil Man*, pp. 218–24; *Al-Dustur*, 4 February 1979, p. 8. On anti-American attitude of strikers and security forces: Cheney, *Oil Man*, pp. 230–1; *Al-Dustur*, 4 February 1979, p. 8.

16. H. Mejcher, 'Saudi Arabia's "vital link to the West": Some political, strategic and tribal aspects of the Transarabian Pipeline (TAP) in the stage of planning 1942–1950', MES, Vol. 18, No. 4 (October 1982); Cheney, *Oil Man*, p. 233.

17. Cheney, *Oil Man*, p. 227. Of a strike in 1952: *Al-Hadaf* (PFLP, Beirut), 7 March 1981, p. 27.

18. The petition was attributed to Palestinian and communist agitators: *The Times*, 19, 20 October 1953; *Al-Dustur*, 4 February 1979, p. 8.

19. Lackner, *House*, p. 96; Cheney, *Oil Man*, pp. 227–36; *The Times*, 19, 20 October 1953; *Al-Hayat*, 25 November 1953; Alyami, 'Modernization', p. 182; *Al-Dustur*, 4 February 1979, p. 8.

20. Labour and Workers Regulation Act of 10 October 1947: G.M. Baroody, 'The Practice of Law in Saudi Arabia', in W.A. Beling, *King Faisal and the Modernisation of Saudi Arabia* (London, 1980), pp. 121–2; Cheney, *Oil Man*, p. 221.

21. S. Duguid, 'Tariki', *IJMES*, Vol. I, No. 3 (1970), p. 197; Cheney, *Oil Man*, pp. 222–5.

22. A high proportion were educated Hijazis. The less prestigious armed forces did not attract Najdis, except to top command positions.

23. Consultative Assembly, Council of Deputies. F. Ḥamzah, *Al Bilad* (Mecca, 1937), pp. 90–1, 98–100; H. Wahba, *Arabian Days* (London, 1964), p. 73; C.W. Harrington, 'The Saudi Arabian Council of Ministers', MEJ, Vol. 12, No. 1 (1958), pp. 3, 12; Philby, *Sa'udi Arabia*, p. 292.

24. Of Hijazi separatism in late 1970s: Gh. Salameh, 'Political power and the Saudi state', *Merip Reports*, No. 91, (Oct. 1980), p. 21. In 1969: D. Holden and R. Johns, *House of Saud* (London, 1982), pp. 280–1, and below.

25. *Qaḍaya Sa'udiyya*, pp. 3–5; *Al-Dustur*, 4 February 1979, pp. 8–9. Educated Shi'ites are heavily represented in the small militant Saudi socialist and Marxist organisations.

26. *Al-Hayat*, 1 July, 3, 5 August, 17 September 1955; N. Safran, *Saudi Arabia: The Ceaseless Quest for Security* (Cambridge, Mass., 1985), p. 81.

27. Abd al-Aziz al Mu'ammar, a Najdi university graduate and strike leader (1953), appointed in December 1960 adviser to King Saud, but because of his leftist opinions was soon appointed Ambassador to Switzerland. Recalled in 1963, he was imprisoned for twelve years with many of his associates: Holden and Johns, *House of Saud*, p. 214; Blandford, *Oil Sheikhs*, p. 124.

28. *Al-Hurriyya* (PFLP, weekly, Beirut), 10, 17 June 1968, 19 January, 9 February 1970; Lackner, *House*, pp. 94–5, 98–104; *8 Days*, 23 May 1981; De Gaury, *Faisal*, p. 91; Salameh, 'Political power', p. 20. The NLF remnants formed The Communist Party of Saudi Arabia in a congress in Baghdad in 1975: Salameh, 'Political power', p. 20; Lateef, 'King Faisal', p. 124 (note 3).

29. *Al-Hadaf* (PDFP), 7 March 1981, p. 27; A.H. Alyami, 'The Impact of Modernization on the Stability of the Saudi Monarchy', p. 141; *Al-Hawadith* (Beirut), 23 November 1962, an interview with Nassir Sa'id; *Al-Nahar* (Beirut), 3 August 1963; De Gaury, *Faisal*, p. 91.

30. *Al-Hurriyya*, 9 February 1970; Salameh, 'Political power', pp. 21, 23.

31. Salameh, 'Political power', p. 23; N.N.M. Ayubi, 'Political Economy of Defense and Development in Saudi Arabia and the Gulf', The Gulf Project (Los Angelese, May 1982), pp. 17, 53 (note 26); Fred Halliday, 'The shifting sands beneath the House of Saud', *The Progressive*

(March 1980), p. 39. On *Tali'a* in the United States see: WP, 22 July 1980; M. Field, 'Society. The royal family and the military in Saudi Arabia', *Vierteljahresberichte*, No. 89 (September 1982), p. 223; Shaw and Long, *Modernization*, p. 101.

32. Holden and Johns, *House of Saud*, pp. 280–1; Alyami, 'Modernization', p. 201: officers arrested in 1969; also, N. Safran, *Saudi Arabia*, (Cambridge, Mass., 1985), p. 80.

33. NYT, 5 April 1955; *Daily Mail* (London), 26 May 1955. Holden and Johns (*House of Saud*, p. 209) ties Prince Talal to this group.

34. Alyami, 'Modernization', pp. 123–4; Holden and Johns, *House of Saud*, p. 208; Safran, *Saudi Arabia*, p. 105.

35. The media 'directorate' became a ministry: S.K. Al-Orabi Al-Harithi, 'The Mass Media in Saudi Arabia: Present Concept, Functions, Barriers and Selected Strategy For Effective Use in Nation Building and Social Awareness', unpublished PhD thesis (Ohio State University, 1983), p. 56. On deportation of Palestinian members of Arab Nationalists (*Qawmiyyun al-Arab*) and opposition suppression: *Al-Musawwar* (Egypt), 12 January 1954; *Al-Ahram* (Egypt), 23 March 1954; *Qaḍaya Sa'udiyya*, p. 4; Shaker, 'Modernization', pp. 166–70; *Al-Mustaqbal* (Iraqi-oriented. Beirut–Paris), pp. 9–10; *Al-Hawadith*, 23 November 1962, interview with Nassir Sa'id; Buchan, 'Religious Opposition', p. 112.

36. Alyami, 'Modernization', p. 182; *Al-Dustur*, 4 February 1979, p. 9; *Qaḍaya Sa'udiyya*, p. 5.

37. J. Arnold, *Golden Swords and Pots and Pans* (New York, 1963), p. 205; *Haaretz* (Israel), 27 June 1956; *Qaḍaya Sa'udiyya*, p. 5; *Al-Hawadith*, 23 November 1962, interview with Nassir Sa'id. The nationalisation of the Suez Canal by Nasser intensified demands in the Hijaz and Al-Hasa to nationalise Aramco and annul the Dhahran airbase agreement. *Al-Dustur*, 4 February 1979, p. 9.

38. On Shi'ites dissatisfaction: *Al-Bilad*, 13 September 1960; *Al-Hayat*, 17 November 1960. On opposition: *Qaḍaya Sa'udiyya*, pp. 5–7. Also below.

39. *Al-Dustur*, 4 February 1979, p. 9.

40. J. Arnold, *Golden Swords and Pots and Pans* (New York, 1963), p. 134; Safran, *Saudi Arabia*, p. 81.

41. Safran, *Saudi Arabia*, pp. 83–4.

42. Ibid., pp. 88–9.

43. Schulze, 'Ulama', pp. 10–14; N.O. Madani, 'The Islamic Content of the Foreign Policy of Saudi Arabia. King Faisal's Call for Islamic Solidarity 1965–1975', unpublished PhD thesis (The American University, Washington, DC, 1977).

44. Huyette, *Adaptation*, p. 75.

45. Holden and Johns, *House of Saud*, p. 210.

46. Tariki employed several radical university graduates. Holden and Johns, *House of Saud*, p. 210; Duguid, 'Tariki', pp. 201, 207 (note 2).

47. Duguid, 'Tariki'; Holden and Johns, *House of Saud*, p. 220. Although oil production rose between 1955 and 1960 by about 50 per cent, revenue from this source was in 1960 about 350 million dollars, only marginally over the revenue in 1955: Wenner, 'Saudi Arabia', p. 170.

48. Lackner, *House*, pp. 62, 99; Shaker, 'Modernization', pp. 167–70;

Duguid, 'Tariki', pp. 201, 207 (note 2), 210, 217; L. Mosley, *Power Play* (Birkenhead, 1973), pp. 317–18; F. Halliday, *Arabia Without Sultans* (Manchester, 1974), p. 55.

49. W.A. Rugh, 'Saudi Mass Media and Society in the Faisal Era', in Beling, *Faisal*, p. 133; Lackner, *House*, p. 99; Bligh, *Succession*, pp. 67–8.

50. Alyami, 'Modernization', pp. 123–4; Holden and Johns, *House of Saud*, pp. 207–9; Safran, *Saudi Arabia*, p. 105.

51. W.O. Lancaster, 'The Bedouin and "progress"', *Middle East International* (January 1978), p. 26; Halliday, *Arabia*, p. 55. Decline in Aramco's workforce, Table 4.1, p. 79. Also *Al-Bilad*, 10, 13 July, 13 September 1960. Of Shi'ite protesting against discriminatory laws excluding them from government employment: *Al-Hayat*, 17 November 1960; *Qaḍaya Sa'udiyya*, p. 5.

52. M. Field, *The Merchants. The Big Business Families of Arabia* (London, 1984), p. 37. Yusuf Tawwil a leading merchant and a Nasserite. He was among the leaders of the abortive 1969 *coup*: Holden and Johns, *House of Saud*, p. 280; also Bligh, 'Religious elite', p. 70.

53. On Saudi tactics: *Al-Hayat*, 1 January 1961; Holden and Johns, *House of Saud*, p. 112.

54. Niblock 'Political System', pp. 99–100; Buchan, 'Religious Opposition', p. 113; *Al-Jarida*, 30 December 1960. On development of press see p. 93 below.

55. Nawwaf maintained thereafter a neutral stance. Fawwaz, also a member of the Liberal Princes, and Majid, affiliated to them, were left out of the cabinet. On royal family rivalry: Bligh, *Succession*; also G.S. Samore, 'Royal Family Politics in Saudi Arabia (1953–1982)', unpublished PhD thesis (Harvard University, 1984).

56. Bligh, *Succession*, p. 69; Holden and Johns, *House of Saud*, p. 214; *Al-Hayat*, 22 February 1961, 1 September 1963.

57. *Al-Bilad*, 5 August 1961; *Al-Hayat*, 29 December 1960, 9 September 1961; *Al-Anwar* (Beirut), 23 December 1960; *Le Monde*, 28 December 1960; *Al-Jarida*, 30 December 1960; Lackner, *House*, p. 63.

58. Huyette, *Adaptation*, p. 70, quoting the Minister of Planning, Hisham Nazir (now Minister of Petroleum).

59. *Al-Haqa'iq* (Egypt), 16 March, 16 November 1961; *Al-Hawadith*, 5 May 1961; *Al-Hayat*, 14 March 1961; Holden and Johns, *House of Saud*, p. 214; Bligh, *Succession*, p. 70. On Saud's policy and repressive measures: *Al-Hayat*, 14 March, 10 June 1961; Lackner, *House*, p. 98; Salameh, 'Political power', p. 20.

60. *Al-Hayat*, 22 February 1961; *Afrique Action* (Tunis), 27 February 1961.

61. NYT, 17 March 1961. In line with his appeasement policy Faysal supported demands to rescind the Dhahran agreement: *Al-Hayat*, 18 March 1961; Lackner, *House*, p. 99; *The Times*, 18 March 1961.

62. *Umm al-Qura* (Saudi Arabia), 21 April 1961; *Al-Khalij al-'Arabi* (Saudi Arabia), 4 May 1961; *Al-Hayat*, 1 June, 17 May 1961. Of the new Ministry of Labour and Workers Affairs and attempts to Saudi-ise the workforce: *Al-Hayat*, 10 June 1961; *Al-bilad*, 31 August, 4 December 1961.

63. *Al-Hayat*, 1 September 1963; *Al-Nahar*, 2 April 1964; Salameh,

'Political power', pp. 20–3; Shaker, 'Modernization', pp. 309–13; Lackner, *House*, pp. 99–101.

64. Schulze, 'Ulama', pp. 11–12, 18; Ochsenwald, 'Islamic revival', p. 278; N.O. Madani, 'The Islamic Content of the Foreign Policy of Saudi Arabia (The American University, Washington, DC, 1977), pp. 78–9; also Holden and Johns, *House of Saud*, p. 215; *Al-Hayat*, 7 May 1961; *Akhir Sa'h* (Egypt), 3 May 1961; *Al-Anwar*, 7 June 1961; *Al-Hawadith*, 5 May 1961.

65. *Al-Ahram*, articles by Hasnayn Haykal, October 1961. On Saudi recognition of Syrian Republic: *Falastin* (Jordan), 11 November 1961.

66. *Kul Shay'* (Beirut), 14 October 1961; *Al-Hayat*, 15 August, 16 September, 17, 18 October 1961; NYT, 16 August 1981; *Al-Jihad* (Jordan), 13 September 1961; Bligh, *Succession*, p. 75; *Middle East Record*, Volume two: 1961 (Tel-Aviv University, Israel), p. 417.

67. *Al-Hayat*, 19 November 1961; *Al-Manar* (Jordan), 24 November, 31 December 1961.

68. *Akhir Sa'h*, 9 July 1961; *Haaretz*, 21 November 1961; *Al-Bilad*, 4 December 1961. On press: *Al-Haqa'iq*, 7 December 1961, 22 March 1962; *Al-Hayat*, 12 November, 3 December 1963; Rugh, 'Media', pp. 128–9, 133. On TV: A.T.M. Tash, 'A Profile of Professional Journalists', PhD thesis (Southern Illinois University, 1983), p. 52 (Faysal claimed that television would serve religion); M.T. Asad, 'Saudi Arabia: Administrative Aspects of Development', unpublished PhD thesis (Claremont Graduate School, 1978), p. 99; *Al-Musawwar*, 27 December 1962; *Falastin*, 26 December 1963. The TV stations eventually caused a confrontation with the Najdi fundamentalists who stormed the Riyadh station in 1965: Huyette, *Adaptation*, p. 74.

69. Huyette, *Adaptation*, pp. 70–1; Bligh, *Succession*, p. 76; *Al-Hawadith*, 12, 23 March 1962.

70. Huyette, *Adaptation*, p. 71. The Minister of Agriculture, Abdul Rahman Al al-Shaykh, was a nationalist technocrat and not an *'alim*: Bligh, 'Religious elite', pp. 39, 49 (note 3).

71. See p. 82 above; Al Saud, 'Permanence', pp. 136, 146 (note 26); Mosley, *Power Play*, p. 253.

72. *Al-Anwar*, 17 September 1963; Holden and Johns, *House of Saud*, p. 226.

73. F.A. Hafiz, 'Changes in Saudi Foreign Policy Behaviour 1964–75. A Study of the Underlying Factors and Determinates', unpublished PhD thesis (University of Nebraska-Lincoln, 1980), pp. 55, 60–1; *Akhir Sa'h*, 4 May 1962; *Akhbar al-Yawm* (Egypt), 11 August 1962; *Al-Hayat*, 21 August 1962.

74. *Qadaya Sa'udiyya*, p. 6; *Al-Masa'* (Egypt), 19 August 1962.

75. *Al-Hayat*, 1 September 1963. Also the case of Muhammad Alireza: Holden and Johns, *House of Saud*, p. 242; Field, *The Merchants*, p. 38.

76. This was the beginning of the rise of the 'Sudayri Seven' sons of Abd al-Aziz by Hassa bint Ahmad al-Sudayri, led by Fahd, the eldest. They formed (and still do) the most cohesive and powerful group within the senior sons of Ibn Saud. Next to Fahd is Sultan the Defence Minister and now second in line of succession, then comes Na'if the Interior Minister (1975), then Salman the Governor of Riyadh (1962), considered the most capable,

far-sighted and likeable. The fifth brother, Turki, was until the 1970s Sultan's deputy and was dismissed because of a marital scandal. The sixth, Ahmad became in 1975 Na'if's deputy and the last, Abd al-Rahman represents the family's business interests.

77. Huyette, *Adaptation*, p. 72.

78. Abir, 'Saudi security', p. 91; *Al-Gumhuriyya* (Egypt), 21 January 1963; Holden and Johns, *House of Saud*, p. 227; Lackner, *House*, pp. 99–100.

79. The Liberal Princes' supporters in the armed forces and the administration were arrested. Alyami, 'Modernization', pp. 123–4; Lackner, *House*, p. 66; Holden and Johns, *House of Saud*, p. 233.

80. *Mideast Mirror*, 27 February 1954. See Table 3.3, p. 53. On press: *Al-Hayat*, 12 November 1963.

81. *Faisal Speaks* (1 December 1963); De Gaury, *Faisal*, Appendix 1, according to Saudi Radio, 7 November 1962.

82. On *imarates*: Holden and Johns, *House of Saud*, p. 231.

83. Bligh, 'Religious elite', p. 42; Layish, "Ulama', p. 34. Both institutions were reorganised, became state supervised and funded in the early 1970s. See above Chapter 2, p. 23.

84. J.S. Bilmastis, 'Small States a Major Power: Case Study of Saudi Arabia', unpublished PhD thesis (George Washington University, 1980), p. 128; Layish, "Ulama', pp. 35–6.

85. Shaker, 'Modernization', pp. 313–15.

86. Ibid., pp. 312–14.

87. 'His [Faysal's] progressive policy in 1962 gave new hope to the people': Shaker, 'Modernization', p. 312.

88. Ibid., p. 227 (note 104); L. Blandford, *Oil Sheikhs* (London, 1973), pp. 123–4; FT, 22 April 1985, supplement, p. VI; Huyette, *Adaptation*, p. 77; Holden and Johns, *House of Saud*, p. 280.

89. Bligh, *Succession*, pp. 72–5; De Gaury, *Faisal*, pp. 103–9; Shaker, 'Modernization', p. 235 (note 244); Lackner, *House*, p. 91; *Al-Nahar*, 3 August 1963; *Al-Hayat*, 17 September 1963; *Al-Hadaf*, 7 March 1981, p. 27, interview with Nassir Sa'id's wife; *Al-Hawadith*, 23 November 1962.

90. W.A. Rugh, *Riyadh. History and Guide* (1969), p. 92; Safran, *Saudi Arabia*, pp. 108–9; Holden and Johns, *House of Saud*, p. 280. On National Guard: *Akhbar al-Usbu'* (weekly, Amman), 11 January 1963; De Gaury, *Faisal*, p. 100; Shaker, 'Modernization', pp. 306–7; *Al-Hayat*, 1 September 1963. On National Guard expansion after pro-Nasserite incidents in the armed forces: Holden and Johns, *House of Saud*, p. 244.

91. Safran, *Saudi Arabia*, p. 99. In 1964 Faysal claimed that the Dhahran base was being operated by a technically capable American company retained by the Defence Ministry: *Al-Manar*, 5 April 1964.

92. Shaker, 'Modernization', pp. 306–8, 311; *Faisal Speaks* (1963), p. 12; *Al-Hayat*, 7 November 1964; also *Le Monde*, 24 June 1966; Lackner, *House*, p. 65.

93. Hafiz, 'Foreign Policy', pp. 55, 60–4.

94. Holden and Johns, *House of Saud*, pp. 252, 280–1; Alyami, 'Modernization', pp. 182, 201. Alyami was an eye-witness to the 1967 rioting in Sharqiyya. Also B. Williams, FT, 5 May 1981.

95. *Qadaya Sa'udiyya*, pp. 6–7; Lackner, *House*, p. 188; *Al-Nahar*, 2

April 1964; *Kul Shay'*, 4 January 1964. Shaker ('Modernization', pp. 306–7) relates the intensification of anti-government activities to Faysal's failure to carry out the promised constitutional reforms.

96. Many of whom also Hijazis: Holden and Johns, *House of Saud*, p. 280; Alyami, 'Modernization', p. 201.

97. See Shaker's analysis ('Modernization', pp. 312–14), although referring to the 1969 abortive *coup*.

5

The Reign of Faysal (1964–75): New Elites, Oil and Rapid Development

MODERNISATION AND NEW ELITES: FROM CONFRONTATION TO COOPERATION (1964–70)

After he was enthroned in November 1964, Faysal continued to strengthen the central government and expand its responsibilities at the expense of the traditional socio-political institutions. With the exception of foreign relations, security and religious-oriented ministries, all cabinet positions were placed in the hands of commoners. Other ministries relating to social and economic development and modernisation, created in later years, naturally required the expertise of western-educated technocrats. Subsequently many more educated Saudis were incorporated into the administration, gradually replacing the officials with traditional background or establishing new government departments and services.

The ever-increasing need for an educated and skilled Saudi workforce necessitated the expansion of the kingdom's educational system and the establishment of additional 'secular' and Islamic universities, as discussed earlier. Together with the increased enrolment of Saudis in foreign universities, the growth of higher education swelled the ranks of the Saudi new elites.[1] However, the rapid urbanisation of the unskilled rural population, resulting from accelerated modernisation, presented Faysal's government with serious problems of unemployment, inadequate housing and welfare services and rising costs of living in the cities of the Hijaz, the Eastern Province and Riyadh. Paradoxically, modernisation necessitated the employment of large numbers of skilled and unskilled foreigners, most of them expatriate Arabs,[2] to do the jobs that Saudis could not, or were unwilling, to do.

On the whole, the bourgeois new elites were satisfied with Faysal's rate of modernisation and they reconciled themselves to the fact that some of his promised reforms seemed to take longer than expected to materialise. Indeed, even Saudi commoners who professed leftist ideologies during their studies abroad in this period were enticed into joining Faysal's service on their return home: the promise of high office, prestige and wealth soon facilitated their becoming part of the fold.[3] Yet, radical elements of the new elites and some graduates of foreign universities, as well as some Sunni and Shi'ite worker activists in the Eastern Province, remained sceptical about Faysal's reforms and were determined to bring down the 'reactionary' regime of Al Saud.

While rapidly expanding the responsibilities entrusted to the new elites in his government and the number of agencies involved in the modernisation project, Faysal also increased the central role of the royal family in policy decisions by consulting regularly with the informal *majlis al-shura*.[4]

By 1964 President Nasser was searching for a face-saving formula to extract himself from the Yemeni quagmire. This proved extremely difficult in the circumstances and damaged his prestige. The Syrian Ba'thist regime, by escalating the Jordan water conflict, succeeded in temporarily redirecting the focus of Arab interest onto the conflict with Israel (the Cairo and Alexandria summits in 1964). But Nasser's attention was again diverted to Arabia in the second half of 1964. The deterioration of the situation in Yemen in the following year culminated in Nasser's visit to Jedda in August 1965. He signed an accord with Faysal designed to enable him to terminate the costly adventure in Yemen. Yet shortly afterwards, it became clear that the Egyptian leader was unable to carry it out. In 1966 the British announced their intention of evacuating their forces from Aden by the beginning of 1968 and later from the Gulf by 1970. The vacuum which this step was bound to create rekindled Nasser's ambitions and his determination to replace the oil-rich traditional regimes of Arabia with progressive pan-Arab-oriented ones.

At the end of 1966 the Constituent Assembly of the World Islamic League in Jedda denounced the inter-Muslim war in Yemen and the persecution of the Muslim Brotherhood in Egypt. Faysal forged closer relations with the United States, bringing about the American–British military aid package in 1965, and renewed American guarantees for Saudi Arabia's territorial integrity in June 1966, as well as the military assistance agreement in September.[5] All this caused Nasser to pursue the war in Yemen with renewed vigour. The bombing of Saudi border towns and villages was resumed and anti-regime operations by Saudi and expatriate Arab clandestine organisations were escalated.

Unrest in the Eastern Province again erupted in 1965 and in 1966. This led to the detention of scores of nationalists and labour activists, nineteen of whom, labelled 'communists', were imprisoned for long periods.[6] At the end of 1966 rumours of attempted *coups* began to circulate in the country. Bombs were exploded in several places: in Riyadh's main post office, the Ministry of Defence, the office of the senior US adviser in Riyadh, near royal palaces including that of Prince Fahd, Minister of the Interior, at a Saudi airbase near the Yemen border, in the security forces' headquarters in Dammam, near the palace of the Jiluwi Governor of the Eastern Province, and at several sites along the Tapline.

The Arab Nationalist movement (*Qawmiyyun al-Arab*), originally pro-Nasserite and founded by Palestinians, gravitated towards the left and, by the mid-1960s, could be considered Marxist. Its success in South and North Yemen encouraged its offshoots in Saudi Arabia to escalate their operations in cooperation with Palestinian and Yemeni members of the movement both in the kingdom and in neighbouring countries. Not surprisingly, various Saudi groups identified with the *Qawmiyyun* became the primary target of the newly reorganised security services of the kingdom.

Although Nassir Sai'd's UPAP, the PDF and its sister offshoots of the Arab Nationalists claimed credit for the bombings, most of them, it seems, were carried out by Yemeni and Palestinian infiltrators and residents in Saudi Arabia. Seventeen Yemenis who were involved were beheaded in March 1967 in various towns of the kingdom, and many others, among them Saudis, were jailed. Hundreds of Shi'ites were arrested at the end of 1966 on suspicion of being members of the Ba'th and of participating in illegal activities (Aramco), and a large number of foreign Arabs were deported from the kingdom.[7]

During the Alexandria Arab summit of September 1964, Faysal realised that the era of inter-Arab détente was over. Faced with the expanding camp of hostile radical Arab regimes, he came to the conclusion that he must develop the Saudi armed forces. Furthermore, the Egyptians, fearing a *rapprochement* between the Saudis and the moderate Yemeni republicans in the first half of 1965, reinforced their troops in Yemen and launched a major offensive which threatened to spill over into Saudi territory. Faysal, overcoming strong opposition in the royal house, began to build up and modernise his armed forces. The Saudi defence budget which in 1964/65 was about 104 million dollars, rose to 335 million in 1966/67. By 1967 the Saudi armed forces numbered about 35,000 men compared to about 18,000 a few years earlier.[8]

Bearing in mind the kingdom's enormous territory and its sparse population, Faysal rightly gave priority to the development of the Saudi air force and air defence system. The inadequacy of this was underscored by the renewed Egyptian air strikes on Asir's towns and villages. Faysal requested and received in 1965 the assistance of the US Department of Defense in the form of an American–British military aid package (the outcome of the US desire to sell to the UK F-111 planes) worth several hundred million dollars. In addition to American-made Hercules transport planes and Hawk missiles, the Saudis purchased English-made Lightning fighters and SAM missiles. While some British and Pakistani mercenaries began to fly Saudi planes, ex-RAF pilots trained Saudi air and ground crews, many of whom were the better educated and more sophisticated Hijazis.[9]

Faysal's determination to build up the power of the armed forces was strengthened by the British decision to evacuate their forces from Aden (in January 1968) and the Persian Gulf (1970). The departure of the Egyptian forces from Yemen at the end of 1967, in Faysal's view, worsened the situation in the Arabian Peninsula. An NLF government[10] replaced the British in Aden (South Yemen) when they left in December. Marxist elements, benefiting from Soviet aid, attempted to take power in San'a and another *Qawmiyyun* offshoot began to operate in Dhofar and Oman in 1968. It called itself the Popular Front for the Liberation of Oman and the Arabian Gulf (PFLOAG). In response, Saudi efforts to develop their armed forces were further accelerated after 1967. Indeed the Saudi defence budget jumped to 2,331 million dollars in 1970/71 from 335 million dollars in 1966/67.[11]

The Six-Day War brought to a climax the anti-western sentiments among Saudi natives and expatriate Arabs. Anti-American demonstrations took place in the Hijaz and in Riyadh on 7 June. More serious incidents, with anti-regime overtones, erupted in the Eastern Province, climaxing with large-scale demonstrations organised by Nassir Sa'id's UPAP in Qatif, Dammam, Al-Khobar and Ras-Tanura. In Dhahran, mobs led by students of Aramco's College of Petroleum and Minerals and by leftist nationalists, attacked the company's installations, the American airbase and the US consulate. Only the intervention of the National Guard prevented more serious damage and bloodshed. Oil production was paralysed for a week by a strike of the Saudi workforce, despite the strict laws prohibiting strikes, and the Tapline was sabotaged in several places. Faysal prudently decided to stop the sale of oil to the West, a measure which had previously been demanded by radical Arab leaders and rejected. By the end of the year, however, following the Khartoum summit, the direct sale of oil to the West was resumed.[12]

ARAB NATIONALISM AND OPPOSITION IN THE SAUDI KINGDOM

Radicalisation in the Arab world and the suppression of Saudi militants

By 1968, the Nasser regime was no longer considered radical in the Arab camp. Egypt's relations with Saudi Arabia greatly improved, although they remained cool until the Egyptian leader's death in 1970. The Ba'th governments in Damascus and Baghdad now led the radical camp. They actively supported revolutionary pan-Arabism whether in Eritrea, San'a, the Persian Gulf or in Saudi Arabia. Damascus became the focal point for the activities of the Saudi leftist dissidents, while Baghdad hosted Saudi Ba'thists and other dissidents (including some Shi'ites) and allowed them to broadcast to Saudi Arabia and the Gulf on Radio Baghdad and to publish their journal *Sawt al-Tali'a*. This paper, which appeared intermittently, was popular among Saudi leftist intelligentsia and especially students abroad. Pamphlets smuggled out of Damascus in 1968 and the anti-Saudi broadcasts, complained about the ruthless persecution and arrest of 'progressives' by the Saudi authorities.[13] Apart from this, the radical Saudi opposition seemed relatively inactive.

The Iraqi Ba'th had a special axe to grind. It still laid claim to Kuwait, but more important, as Britain was preparing to evacuate its forces from the Persian Gulf, Baghdad became increasingly frustrated with the American–British plans that Iran, and to a lesser degree Saudi Arabia, should replace the UK as guardians of the region's stability. Baghdad therefore tried hard to undermine the British-sponsored arrangements and the pro-western conservative regimes of the Gulf, which were led by Saudi Arabia.

Although Saudi Arabia's income from oil was constantly growing, 1968/69 proved to be a period of increasing economic difficulties. Saudi revenues in 1969 were about one billion dollars. But, in addition to the aid promised to the 'confrontation countries' and the PLO (Khartoum Summit 1967), defence expenditures for the air force grew substantially.[14] The kingdom's involvement in the affairs of North Yemen and its active subversion of the Aden regime also proved very costly. Finally, Faysal's modernisation plans demanded ever-increasing funds. The Saudi government was forced to seek loans from Aramco and from commercial banks.[15]

The Central Planning Organisation, a most important tool for the kingdom's modernisation, was formed by Faysal in 1968. Another of his protégés, Hisham Nazir, a moderate, American-educated technocrat from a prominent Hijazi family, was appointed its head.[16] With American help, Nazir hastily prepared in 1969 an $8 billion five-year development plan (1970–75).

Aware of the hardships facing the masses of newly urbanised Saudis, Faysal, with the help of other technocrats, took steps to deal with the economic stagnation of the country. Following a decade of growing unemployment among Saudis, and with an atmosphere of tension at Aramco in spite of the many benefits the company's workforce now enjoyed, Faysal issued new Labour and Workers Regulations (1969). These were far more liberal and beneficial to the workers than the previous laws. The Shi'ites of Al-Hasa, always loathed by the regime and their fellow citizens, were still discriminated against, and had it not been for Aramco's liberal employment policy and other services, they would not have shared at all in their country's growing prosperity and rising standard of living. Yet, ironically, it was this community that produced the most radical anti-American elements in the kingdom.[17]

The 1969 abortive *coup* plots and their aftermath

By the late 1960s Faysal's handling of the kingdom's affairs had produced stability and a substantial reduction of tension, something it had not enjoyed since the time of Ibn Saud. Increasing oil wealth, and Faysal's development policies, helped speed a change in Saudi society. Urbanisation was greatly accelerated. The major towns in the Hijaz and the Eastern Province, and the capital, Riyadh, now held a greater proportion of the Saudi people, whereas the rural population, especially the Bedouin, rapidly fell in number. By 1970 the kingdom boasted 7000 students in its institutes of higher education and about half a million youngsters attending the modern schools — about 15 per cent of the kingdom's total population.[18] Saudi Arabia's prestige in the Arab and Muslim world was rising quickly. The Rabat (Morocco) Summit of the World Islamic League in September 1969 was attended by 25 Arab and non-Arab Muslim heads of state, with several radical ones among the participants; it adopted a decision to establish a permanent secretariat for the organisation in Jedda.[19]

1969 was a year of growing tension and upheaval in the whole of the Arab world. In addition to several abortive *coups*, the traditional regimes of Libya, Sudan and Somalia were overthrown by the military. After the decline of pan-Arabism, the 'Nasserites' were seeking a new ideology and leadership. The nationalist camp gradually radicalised its position and differences between it and the Arab conservatives were polarised. In the Gulf, the British had begun to evacuate their forces. This increased tension in the region as well as the activities of Marxist and Ba'thist-oriented organisations. Thus many believed that even the archaic conservative Saudi regime could be the target of a *coup d'état*.

Reacting to Saudi Arabia's undeclared war against it, the Marxist NLF government of the People's Republic of South Yemen (later People's Democratic Republic of Yemen — PDRY) retaliated by launching incursions into the Rub' al-Khali in the first half of 1969, while its Arab Nationalist allies in the kingdom and neighbouring countries escalated their clandestine operations against the Saudi regime. The Palestinian PLFP (led by George Habash), for instance, blew up the Saudi Tapline in the Golan Heights in May.[20] The Saudi security services arrested many Aramco oil workers in early June, especially Palestinians suspected of membership in the Arab Nationalists (*Qawmiyyun*) offshoots. Investigations uncovered a *Qawmiyyun* plot to overthrow the regime. This in turn led to the arrest of a large number of Saudis in the Eastern Province, in Riyadh and in the Hijaz. Among those arrested were army officers and government officials suspected of membership in the NLF.

Simultaneously (mainly in September) the National Guard and the security services rounded up about 200–300 officers, technocrats and other Saudis involved in another plot. About 100 were air force personnel. More than a score were senior officers — a few were even generals. The civilians were senior technocrats such as the head of the Institute of Public Administration, several of the directors of the Saudi Petroleum and Minerals Organization (Petromin) and other members of the new elites, largely Hijazis.[21]

It was estimated that by the end of 1969 the total of those arrested numbered about 2000. According to Dr Fatina Shaker, visiting the kingdom in 1970 in relation to her PhD thesis, there was a second wave of arrests at the end of the year and in 1970. She was told of 'a massive arrest of Saudi students who were recalled from the US on an alleged request on the part of these students to the UN to investigate the situation of the political prisoners in Saudi Arabia.' Also detained in the second wave was 'the liberal and popular' Dean of the College of Petroleum and Minerals in Dhahran, Dr. Salah Amba; his two radical brothers-in-law had previously been detained for involvement in the 1966 bomb outrages.[22]

Several hundred Shi'ites were also rounded up by the authorities at the end of 1970 on suspicion of membership in the Ba'th, but more likely in relation to the almost yearly disturbances in the Eastern Province. These were partly politically-religiously motivated, but clearly an outcome of the Shi'ites frustration resulting from the humiliation by the authorities and the lagging development of Al-Hasa province. It could also be that the disturbances were specifically triggered off in Al-Hasa by the detention of Shi'ite members of clandestine organisations which flourished in the Aramco workforce.[23]

As the Saudi government never disclosed the nature of the 1969–70 events, nor commented on the confused information published about them abroad, the story of the abortive *coups* remains unclear. However it is evident that the authorities dealt with four different and largely unrelated opposition groups in 1969 and 1970, that several thousands were detained for interrogation, of which about 2000 were jailed for longer periods.[24] It also appears that the 'plots' were blown out of proportion and led to disagreement between Faysal and the more liberal Fahd.

Among the first to be arrested, in April and May 1969, were Hadrami (PDRY) residents of the kingdom and Ghamid tribesmen from Asir suspected of sympathising with the leftist regimes in Aden and in San'a. More serious was the wave of arrests on 5–6 June when a large number of Saudis and non-Saudis suspected of membership in the different branches of the NLF were detained. It was alleged that, encouraged by the PDRY (South Yemen) and probably by the Ba'th regimes, they were planning the overthrow of the Saud government.[25] Although the Eastern Province was always the NLF's powerbase, its offshoots flourished among the Najdi and Hijazi new elites and its members were arrested as well.

The regime at first believed that the largely military conspiracy constituted the more serious threat to its existence. About a quarter of the air force officers, including several generals commanding air force bases and academies in the Hijaz and in the Eastern Province, and others holding, or who had once held, key positions in the general staff and the army technical services, as well as many technocrats, were involved. It was alleged that the Committee for the Liberation of Saudi Arabia, as they called themselves, were plotting the annihilation of the King and the senior princes by bombing their palaces and declaring Saudi Arabia a republic.

Many of the culprits were of Hijazi origin. To add to the confusion, Yusuf Tawwil, a prosperous Hijazi merchant, and an acquaintance of Prince Fahd, was believed to be central to this plot. Yet he and his family sympathised with the idea of Hijazi separatism. Others involved in this plot were Najdis[26] or Sunnis from the Eastern Province.

The high ranks of a large number of the officers — mainly air force — involved in the conspiracy indicate that the organisation may have been recruited by the pro-Nasserite pan-Arab Free Officers or Free Saudis movements in the 1950s and early 1960s. Probably in their forties, successful and well-to-do in 1969, it is unlikely that they would have been attracted by Marxist-Leninist ideologies.[27] To quote Holden and Johns,[28] 'There appears to have been no coherent ideology behind the conspicuous disloyalty . . . beyond dislike of the royal family and vague aspirations of an Arab nationalist nature.' Indeed, there were indications that relations between members of this group and the Egyptian secret services went back to the early 1960s. By 1969, however, such connections were no longer relevant to the amateurish *coup* plan.

The Saudi air force was grounded for several weeks, and when flying resumed, it was without munitions for some time. Some of the officers arrested during the first wave of detentions in June and July 1969 were tortured by the secret police and a few died in prison. Yet by the end of 1970, when the naive nature of the 'Hijazi–air force plot' was more fully comprehended, most of the 200–300 officers and civilians involved in it were moved to officers' quarters in military barracks or were held in an old palace on Prince Fahd's orders 'in reasonably civilised confinement': here, each had a room to himself, and their families received half-pay. Some were pardoned by Faysal in 1972 and most of the others were freed immediately after his assassination in 1975. All were able to share, thereafter, in the booming Saudi economy. Yet large-scale arrests of members of the opposition were still reported in 1971 and early in 1972.

The treatment of the members of the different parts of the radical NLF, especially those actually involved in the plot against the

Sauds' regime, was far harsher than that of the 'air force conspirators'. Horror-stories concerning their fate (probably exaggerated) circulated in Saudi Arabia until the mid-1970s. However, even the hard-core leftists arrested in 1969–70 were pardoned by King Khalid and Crown Prince Fahd in the years following Faysal's assassination,[29] and the Saudi state helped in their physical and financial rehabilitation. Indeed, by the mid-1970s circumstances were very different from the late 1960s and the Saudi regime did not feel threatened by the handful of home-bred radicals nor by its Marxist and Ba'thist neighbours. By then the oil boom had turned Saudi Arabia into a world economic power and a leader in the Arab camp.

Holden and Johns term the 1969 abortive *coups* 'half-baked', 'flamboyant' and lacking in determination and a clear plan. Yet, the dissidents, though coming from peripheral groups, had a strong powerbase in the armed forces. Moreover, successful revolutions in the Middle East were of similar character and their triumph was largely facilitated by the weakness of the traditional regimes which they overthrew and the alienation of their peoples. This was not the case in Saudi Arabia.

By 1969 the kingdom's security forces had been reorganised, expanded and trained by American experts and they enjoyed practically unlimited budgets.[30] The tribal-based National Guard, on whose loyalty the Sauds could count since the 1930s, had been strengthened in the 1950s and 1960s. The Saudi regime, moreover, did not depend on one person or small family but on a widely-based ruling oligarchy. Its head, King Faysal, a capable and strong monarch, preferred, whenever possible, to 'buy off' the opposition, and if unwilling to cooperate, he ruthlessly repressed it.

As a result of the 1969–7 abortive *coups*, the relatively small active opposition to the Sauds' regime was reduced to insignificance. The widespread arrests, repressive measures, and rumours about the fate of those imprisoned, demoralised the radical new elites and other dissident groups. Their activities within the kingdom were negligible and they no longer constituted a serious factor in the Saudi power equation. In the following years, as the kingdom became immensely rich and politically powerful, the Saudi opposition was further hindered by the seemingly endless funds at the disposal of the regime.

On her visit to the kingdom in 1970, Dr Shaker, whose sympathy for the radical new elites is obvious, conducted an informal survey of Saudi public opinion concerning the abortive *coups*. Her

117

conclusions correspond with the belief of this writer that the great majority of the kingdom's population, the intelligentsia and Shi'ites excepted, utterly condemned the conspirators. Part of the new elites 'with vested interest in the regime', and the older generation of the well-to-do urban middle class, were also unreservedly critical of the dissidents and glad that members of their families were not involved with them.

A most interesting finding of Shaker's survey was that the great majority of the technocrats, who became integrated into Faysal's government machinery, disapproved of the conspiracy because they were either worried about their personal achievements or apprehensive lest the abortive *coups* prove detrimental to the country's development, 'because the conservatives in the ruling class will have the upper hand in the government'. Though many were dissatisfied with different aspects of the traditional regime, they praised the progress achieved by Faysal's government, and were of the opinion that an attempt to change the system by force would be counter-productive.

Only a very small minority of those Shaker met, probably the educated young Saudis (some educated abroad) with a background similar to hers, supported the abortive *coups* fully, and said they were willing to participate in one, if it were the only way to bring about meaningful change in Saudi Arabia. An equally small percentage, though sympathetic to the conspirators and their aims, were disinclined to be involved in a similar conspiracy.[31]

Faysal's decision in 1958, but especially at the end of 1962, to allocate most of Saudi Arabia's increasing oil revenue to the kingdom's modernisation and to improve the population's standard of living, was fully vindicated by the events of 1969–70. So was his carrot-and-stick policy for dealing with the new elites. **Nearly all ordinary citizens were supportive of the Sauds' government (*hukuma*) in 1970 and most new elites, enticed by prestige, power and wealth and Faysal's modernisation and development programmes, identified with the regime, if not joined its powerbase.** Others in the new elites were frightened into accepting cooperation with Faysal's government as the second-best option in Saudi Arabia.

The 1969 abortive *coups* polarised the differences between the majority of the new elites of urban middle-class origin and the radical minority consisting of Hijazis, but largely made up of Najdi elements inimical to the Sauds and a mixture of leftist-nationalist Sunnis and Shi'ites from the Eastern Province (especially from Aramco's workforce) and to a lesser degree from Asir. The former tended to cooperate with the Sauds, although many were privately critical of their paternalistic archaic government, and their refusal to allow the new elites to participate in decision-making. The latter, mainly active abroad after 1970, with a growing Shi'ite membership, sympathised with or joined the small leftist opposition groups supported by the Ba'th regimes, the PDRY and communist parties universally. The débâcle of the PLO in Jordan during 'Black September' (1970), however, reduced the possibility of help for the beleaguered Saudi offshoots of the *Qawmiyyun* from their Palestinian associates.

A natural outcome of the events of 1969–70 was the stepping-up of the security measures in the kingdom. Screening of foreigners wishing to enter the kingdom became tighter, as did the supervision of those living in it. The ulama, a foreign visitor cynically observed, were cooperative with the authorities in matters of security: they sanctioned an edict in 1970 which required a photograph in the passports of Yemeni and other Arab women wishing to enter the kingdom.[32] Even more important was the decision of the Saudi rulers to replace expatriate Arabs working in the kingdom with non-Arab Muslim Asians or Non-Muslims whenever possible. The preference was to use short-term Asian contract labour. However, these Asian workers were not allowed to settle in the country or bring their families with them.[33]

The period from 1970 to 1975 (when Faysal was assassinated) saw a dramatic rise in Saudi Arabia's economic power and leadership in the Arab world. It coincided with the first five-year development plan which Faysal had launched and which at first looked unrealistic because of the 'enormous' funds it involved (8 billion dollars). This plan outgrew its original framework and budget, sparking off enormous changes in Saudi Arabia. These took place throughout the 1970s and accelerated the social revolution that the Saudi population was undergoing. Yet, inasmuch as the local opposition to the Sauds was practically paralysed, it was also a period of growing apprehension of foreign intervention.

The 1969 abortive *coups* aroused opposition to further modernisation and particularly to the development of the armed forces. It was found to be mostly among the conservatives in the ruling class, led by Prince Abdallah, the National Guard commander. Such a policy, they argued, was bound eventually to enable the 'Young Turks' in the armed forces to overthrow the Sauds. Purges slowed the development of the air force and army and the National Guard was given additional funds for expansion and modernisation. Yet King Faysal, supported by Prince Sultan, the Minister of Defence, and

Fahd, the Minister of the Interior (responsible for internal security), reached the conclusion that the 'air force conspiracy' was not serious enough to justify a total halt to the modernisation and expansion of the armed forces, just when the British were about to withdraw from the Gulf and Saudi Arabia was being threatened by radical forces in the region. The National Guard, moreover, vindicated at the time the claim that it remained an ineffective and anachronistic militia.[34]

In November 1969 PDRY's regular units conquered the Saudi southern outpost of Wadi'a. Only an air strike by Saudi planes flown by Pakistani pilots forced the South Yemenis to retreat after army and National Guard units had failed to dislodge them from the area. Threatened by the Ba'thist regimes in the north,[35] Riyadh feared the unification plans of the two Yemens initiated by the Marxist regime in Aden. Furthermore, by 1971 a Soviet flotilla appeared in the Arabian Sea shortly after the British evacuated their forces from the Gulf.

All the above, and the Iranian high-handedness in the region culminating with the forceful conquest of Abu Musa and Tumb Islands near Hormuz and claims to Bahrain, caused the Saudis to seek military aid in Europe and, when it was opportune, to turn again to the US for help (e.g. Peace-Hawk project, 1973). The kingdom's territorial size and manpower problem on the one hand, and the availability of funds on the other, again made the air force the natural choice for priority. In the next few years, thousands of educated youngsters, either of middle-class origin or Aramco-trained, were commissioned as officers and NCOs in the armed forces. Yet, they were counterbalanced by hundreds of aristocratic offspring who were encouraged to join the armed services, especially the air force, and thousands of foreign mercenaries, among them Pakistani, American, English and French pilots, technicians, instructors and advisers, who were hired by the Ministry of Defence.[36]

REGIME AND NEW ELITES — THE SHELVING OF POLITICAL REFORMS (1970–75)

Faysal, the technocrats and the central government

Having imprisoned most of the active opposition to the regime, King Faysal repeated his promise to establish a National Consultative Assembly at the beginning of 1970.[37] Despite the opposition of the conservative members of the ruling class, Faysal, supported by a majority of his informal *majlis al-shura*, continued the kingdom's course towards rapid modernisation, and increased the role of its central government at the expense of the traditional institutions (including the provincial amirs). The monarch expanded the authority and responsibilities of the cabinet, regularly attended its meetings, and encouraged discussion in it. He consulted his ministers daily before taking decisions, relying on their expertise to devise a strategy for modernisation.

Despite the involvement of some senior technocrats in the abortive *coups*, Faysal continued to appoint Hijazi, and when available Najdi graduates of foreign universities (some with known leftist leanings in their student days) to key positions in the government and its new agencies. Out of four new ministers appointed to his cabinet in July 1971, for instance, two were Hijazi graduates of western universities — Hisham Nazir, the head of the Central Planning Board (now Minister of Petroleum) and Abd al-Aziz al-Qurayshi, the head of Saudi Arabian Monetary Agency (SAMA). The other two (one Hijazi) were administrators from traditional backgrounds. In 1972 Muhammad Aba'l-Khayl (several members of whose family served the Sauds), the first foreign-educated commoner Najdi to be appointed Minister (without Portfolio and Finance Minister in 1975) since Tariki.[38] On the whole, graduates of the modern education system rapidly replaced the traditional bureaucrats in all ministries other than the religious-oriented ones.

However Faysal continued the paternalistic Saudi style of government. As he increased the proportion of technocrats in his cabinet and strengthened the authority of the modern central government, he only grudgingly delegated authority to the ministers who were commoners. Even then, he supervised them closely and frequently intervened in petty matters relating to the running of their ministries.[39] The repeated promise to establish a National Consultative Assembly was again ignored. Despite the growth of their numbers and their crucial role in governing and modernising the kingdom, the new elites were prevented from taking part in the decision-making process.

By the early 1970s Faysal no longer tolerated questions about a constitution (other than the Koran). He even insisted on the use of the term 'social development' rather than 'social change', and in his meeting with Shaker in 1970 told her: 'Revolutionary change is out of context with our traditional heritage and Islamic culture.'[40] The King, who was strongly opposed to the democratisation of the system, believed that the kingdom needed to modernise its patri-archal system which ensured the welfare of its population according to Islamic principles, rather than change to the 'corrupt material western democracy' or 'atheist communism'.

New elites and the modernisation of the bureaucracy

From the mid-1960s, increasing oil wealth facilitated the rapid modernisation of the kingdom and the consolidation of the Faysal regime. It provided endless opportunities of advancement for the educated Saudis who joined the government service and of pros-perity for the ones who opted for the private sector. As demand for trained Saudis in the 1960s and 1970s became almost insatiable, Faysal abandoned his attempt to improve the quality of the educa-tional system by slowing its growth, and allocated vast funds for its expansion. By the mid-1970s, **a million Saudis — more than 20 per cent of the kingdom's total population — were studying in the different levels of the educational system, about 25,000 students were registered in the kingdom's various universities, and more than 5000 were studying abroad.**[41] This, together with rapid urbanisation, totally changed the character of Saudi society, while the millions of foreign workers employed introduced cultural influences incompatible with the character of the conservative Saudi-Wahhabi kingdom.

The ranks of the new elites were now further swollen by the many graduates of Saudi and foreign institutes of higher education. The majority (Hijazis) chose to join the administration and rapidly changed its character by replacing or superseding the traditional civil servants (Najdis). Government appointments to high positions unrelated to security or religious affairs were increasingly deter-mined by education and ability, rather than by social status. The new government ministries, departments, agencies and institutions created to facilitate the country's development were, in most cases, run by bureaucrats with doctorates and masters degrees from univer-sities in the West, many with little or no practical experience, and often trained in other fields altogether. The majority owed their appointment to academic achievements, the recommendation of 'first-wave' senior technocrats, nepotism, or Faysal's relations with leading Hijazi merchant families. Although by the mid-1970s it was becoming apparent that academic excellence did not by itself provide administrative capability, only in the late 1970s, as the inefficiency in the government service became more apparent, did practical experience become a major criterion.[42]

As early as 1962, Faysal's government included several western-trained Hijazi technocrats besides traditionally-trained commoners. Yet, the heyday of the western-educated Hijazi new elites 'aristocracy' was the decade from the late 1960s to the late 1970s when many Hijazi graduates of western, particularly American, universities, were appointed to senior positions in the administration. This was not only due to Faysal's (and Fahd's) sympathy for the usually moderate and open-minded Hijazi middle-class elites (whom he befriended when Viceroy of the Hijaz), nor was it just an outcome of nepotism, but mostly because the more sophisticated and tolerant Hijazis were quicker than the conservative and xenophobic Najdis to take advantage of modern education and were not inhibited from enrolling in western universities. The Hijazi merchant community, and the middle class in general, could also afford to educate their offspring abroad, whenever necessary, without government or Aramco subsidies.

Nepotism, moreover, is a common and acceptable norm in Saudi society. Once established in a government ministry or agency, the Hijazi (or Najdi) technocrat helped his kinsmen graduating from the local schools or universities to obtain suitable positions in his ministry or the civil service in general, or prosper in business. Thus, the proportion of traditionally-educated Najdis in the civil service declined in the 1970s while that of modern-educated Hijazis and, to a far lesser degree, Najdis, grew.[43]

Some Najdis of *ḥadr* origin were also appointed by Faysal to senior positions in the government. A few merchant and Najdi notables' families, who had assisted Ibn Saud when the kingdom was formed, were far-sighted enough to help their sons to obtain modern education in the 1950s and to enrol in foreign universities.[44] Many more Najdis graduated from the Saudi modern educational system in the early 1970s and joined or replaced their traditionally-educated Najdi kinsmen who had joined the civil service under Abd al-Aziz and Saud. Najdis increasingly enrolled in local religious and secular universities or went abroad for further studies. By the 1960s, especially in the 1970s, tension and competition began to emerge between the Hijazi and traditional Najdi civil servants and by the mid-1970s between the former and the Najdi new elite bureaucrats and between both and graduates of the Islamic universities.[45]

In the years following Faysal's assassination it became increasingly clear that Najdis again enjoyed preferential treatment by the regime due to the dislike and suspicion in which the Hijazis were held by most of the senior princes. As the Saudi university system developed in the 1970s, a clear distinction also emerged between the western-educated senior technocrats, who, in most cases, joined the government service in the 1950s, 1960s and early 1970s and the numerous new elite bureaucrats, the product of the Saudi educational system or of foreign universities (BAs), who joined it in the mid- and late 1970s. The first, if they had proved capable, caught Faysal's attention in the 1950s or after he was back in power in 1962, and were appointed as heads of new or existing ministries, departments or agencies. This new commoner 'aristocracy' enjoyed enormous power, prestige and wealth by the early 1970s. Although it did not participate in decision-making proper, it could greatly influence it through membership in the cabinet, control of ministries and budgets and the fact that the King and his Consultative Council sought its advice. Indeed, as the government grew with the creation of specialised ministries, departments and agencies, the foreign-trained technocrats at their head had a better chance of influencing policy decisions relating to their particular field of expertise. For their part, the senior technocrats had a vested interest in the continuity of the Sauds' regime and closely identified with it. An aristocratic PhD student[46] visiting Saudi Arabia about 1980 wrote:

The [senior] technocrats seem to be content with the system; as one minister [Al-Gosaybi] observed 'the Royal Family command of the structure is not weakened because they have responded to the need for technocrats. They got them into the government to keep the system going; The [senior] technocrats are grateful for the stability this system provides'.

However, **in the final analysis, policy decisions were arrived at only in the royal** *majlis al-shura* **or by** *ahl al-ḥal wa'l 'aqd*, **to the exclusion of the senior technocrats**.

The rise of the foreign-educated technocratic 'aristocracy' was resented by the traditional non-royal elites whom they largely replaced and led to competition if not hostility between the two.[47] In addition to reform and modernisation which affected the 'Saudi way of life', their rise caused a noticeable erosion of the status and authority of the non-royal members of the ruling class. The decline of the ulama's power under Faysal has been discussed elsewhere in this book.[48] By 1970, for instance, a modern educational system, including a women's branch, radio stations and a television network, were established by Faysal despite their strong protest. Shortly after the kingdom's Grand Mufti and head of the ulama Shaykh Muhammad ibn Ibrahim Al al-Shaykh died (1969), Faysal established the Ministry of Justice and appointed Shaykh Muhammad 'Ali al-Harakan a distinguished Hijazi qadi, to its top post.[49] All these and the restrictions imposed upon the activity of their Committees of Public Morality, reduced the authority and prestige of the ulama's areas of activity. Even more noticeable was the eroding authority of the tribal and regional amirs. Many of their responsibilities had been taken over by the central government, their subsidies were substantially slashed, and Faysal hardly received them once a week in the 1970s, compared to his nearly daily meetings with them at the beginning of his reign.[50]

In the 1970s the number of rank-and-file new elite bureaucrats grew constantly. Opportunities for personal advancement, for achieving great wealth and for participation in the country's development, enticed the majority to join the service of the regime. This did not mean that the 'new men' were not critical of the paternalistic and archaic character of the Sauds' government and its refusal to allow them, and the middle class as a whole, to participate in the power system. Faysal's constitutional reforms were totally ignored and the frequently promised National Consultative Assembly did not take shape.[51] But inasmuch as such criticism existed, it did not mean that the successful new elites were ready actively to challenge the ruling class as it had in the 1950s and early 1960s. Only a minority sympathised with the clandestine radical organisations and a handful of those, remnants of the NLF and Nasserites, some students in foreign universities and members of the nascent Shi'ite intelligentsia actually joined them.

Elsewhere in this book[52] it has been pointed out that the expansion of the educational system largely benefited the traditional urban middle class until the 1970s, primarily the Hijazis, and, since the 1970s, Najdis of *hadr* origin. The city-dwellers, more than the rural population and the newly urbanised, also enjoyed the fruits of rapid modernisation and development in other fields. By the mid-1970s the middle class of *hadr* origin largely monopolised the technocratic 'aristocracy' (i.e. commoner ministers and high-ranking civil servants with university, largely foreign, degrees), the new elites' bureaucracy and new middle class as a whole.[53] The evidence indicates that the traditional tension between 'noble' Najdis and 'sophisticated' Hijazis still prevails, the historic aversion of the rural population for the *hadr* and vice versa, has now also been extended to the relationship between newly urbanised groups and the central government administration, controlled by the new middle-class elite of urban origin.[54] Social change in Saudi Arabia has thus far proceeded with only minimal national integration.

ARAB NATIONALISM AND SAUDI 'OIL POWER' (1970–75)

Wholesale arrests and harsh persecution virtually liquidated the whole spectrum of clandestine movements in the kingdom in 1969–70 and practically halted their activities within Saudi Arabia. Some radical members of the new elites who were still free in 1970 told Shaker with bravado: 'let them [the royal family] do as they please . . . repression will breed more hatred and frustration, which in turn will bring the existence of the monarchy to doom.'[55] Yet, the cruel suppression of the opposition brought stability and encouraged the majority of discontented intelligentsia to accept the Sauds' regime and the role which Faysal allocated to them. Faysal's biographer, Vincent Sheean,[56] a frequent visitor to Saudi Arabia, claimed in the early 1970s that 'The question of an alternative to Faisal's rule is, indeed, seldom considered . . . except in the youngest and most advanced circles of students returned from foreign countries . . . Few things seem solider than the present regime in Arabia.'

Inconsequential and rarely active in the kingdom, in the 1970s, the militant opposition to the Sauds' regime consisted of three groups. The first, the old NLF, now Marxist, was 'officially' renamed in Baghdad in 1975 the Saudi Communist Party. The second was Nassir Sai'd's UPAP, still ideologically Nasserite and pan-Arabist, with some supporters in the armed forces, in the northern parts of Najd (Shammar) and in the Aramco workforce. The last was the Popular Democratic Party (PDP) created by the amalgamation of the remnants of the Saudi Ba'th (both Iraqi and Syrian oriented) and a leftist Nasserite faction of the NLF after the 1969–70 abortive *coups*. The militant opposition remained inactive until the late 1970s. This was partly due to the prosperity enjoyed by nearly all the Saudis and partly because of Faysal's iron-fist policy until 1975 and Fahd's carrot-and-stick policy thereafter.[57] But the most important reason was the relative cohesion within the royal family under Faysal and immediately after his succession.

By 1970 the oil market had undergone a dramatic change. The United States had become a net oil importer and demand for oil in

Table 5.1: Saudi oil revenues 1959–74 (in $ millions)

1959	1963	1965	1970	1973	1974
315	607.3	655	1,214	4,340	22,574

Source: Duguid, 'Tariki', p. 201; Islami and Kavoussi, *Saudi Arabia*, p. 98; Abir, 'The Manpower', p. 1.

the industrial West was increasing at an average rate of about 10 per cent per annum. Not only was OPEC now able to flex its muscles but the balance of power in it had been changed, with Ghaddafi's Libya joining the militant camp of the organisation. Thus, the price of oil in the early 1970s began to rise dramatically compared with the 1960s.

Pressure had been building on Saudi Arabia since the 1960s both from its sister Arab countries and different circles in the kingdom to use its oil as political leverage against the West and the United States in particular because of the Arab-Israeli conflict. Faysal resisted this until 1970 on political and economic grounds; but then he reached the conclusion that confrontation with the United States over this issue was unavoidable. In 1972, therefore, Zaki Yamani informed Washington that Saudi Arabia was no longer willing or able to separate oil supply from Arab political interests and that unless the US were to take a more balanced (i.e. pro-Arab) stance in relation to the Arab-Israeli conflict, the kingdom might be forced to use oil as a weapon against the West.

Although there are conflicting reports about Riyadh's role in the preparation for the Yom Kippur War of 1973 it is evident that the use of the 'oil weapon' during and after the October War, and the embargo on oil exports to the United States and Holland, earned Faysal, at least temporarily, the respect and affection of most Arabs. As the kingdom's revenues from oil grew dramatically,[58] Saudi Arabia came to be the financier of the Arab and Muslim world, thus 'buying' her peace even with the more radical Arab countries. Egypt, now under President Sadat, became a close ally and even Syria, following a *coup* that brought Hafiz al-Assad to power in 1971 after he had overcome the leftist elements in the Syrian Ba'th, improved its relations with the 'reactionary' Saudis. Only Baghdad, with its dogmatic Ba'thist regime and interests in the Gulf, and the PDRY because of its NLF Marxist ideology, continued after 1973 the militant campaign against the Saudi regime, and gave shelter and support to the small leftist Saudi groups. With the ruling class united around Faysal and his succession arrangements accepted by all royal factions, the regime seemed to be stable and secure, notwithstanding the rapid change which the Saudi society was undergoing.

After a period of tension with Washington in the early 1970s, Faysal and Fahd felt confident enough in 1974 to improve their relations with the United States once again. These were considered essential to the security of the kingdom in view of the Soviet presence in Aden and the fact that the Gulf had become a focus of power politics. Following earlier arrangements, Prince Fahd visited Washington in June with a retinue which included the Petroleum, Finance and Planning Ministers (Zaki Yamani, Aba'l-Khayl and Hisham Nazir, respectively), the Deputy Minister of Foreign Affairs, and high-ranking officers. The result was a far-reaching understanding on economic, technical and military cooperation. Riyadh expressed its readiness to help maintain a regular supply of oil to the market and to curb the rise in oil prices. For its part, America undertook to help in finding a solution to the Arab-Israeli conflict acceptable to the Arabs, and enable the Saudis to build up their defence capabilities through the construction of a suitable military infrastructure, the sale of sophisticated weaponry and the training of suitable Saudi personnel. Close relations with the United States, cooperation concerning oil supply and pricing, and Saudi involvement in negotiations relating to the settlement of the Arab-Israeli conflict, became important strands in Fahd's government after the death of Faysal.

In March 1975, King Faysal was assassinated by a deranged nephew. The succession arrangements established by him after 1964 facilitated a smooth transfer of power. With the blessing of the ulama, Khalid was pronounced King, and Fahd Crown Prince and acting Prime Minister. Abdallah, Commander of the National Guard and a conservative with strong ties with the tribal leaders, known for his dislike of the West and for his relations with anti-American Arab nationalist leaders, became second in line of succession and second Deputy Prime Minister.

CONCLUSIONS (1964–75)

Faysal had been confronted with Nasser's pan-Arabism which established a foothold in Yemen and a rising tide of militant nationalism in the kingdom when he again became acting Prime Minister in 1962. Faysal believed the challenge to be so grave that at first he attempted to win the moderate new middle class by his 'ten-point programme', which included promises of constitutional reforms and participation in decision-making through a national *majlis al-shura*. At the same time, abandoning his traditional caution, he challenged Nasser's intervention in Yemen by supporting the loyalists, while suppressing with an iron hand the active opposition to his regime in this kingdom. While the militant nationalists were mercilessly persecuted, the moderate middle-class elite was practically 'bribed' by Faysal to participate in the government of the kingdom and its accelerated modernisation.

Faysal's reforms and the expansion of modern education in Saudi Arabia, made possible by increased revenue from oil, led to substantial growth in the new middle class and educated elite. Yet, although Faysal increasingly incorporated university graduates in his government and its agencies, enabling them to gain prestige and to share in the country's wealth, he conveniently forgot the constitutional reforms and participation in decision-making which he had promised them. **The ideological foundations of his (and his heirs') paternalistic regime rested on the premise that the Koran was the constitution of a Muslim state and that institutions of western democracies were incompatible with the principles of Islamic society** (in which the people are represented by *ahl al-ḥal wa'l-'aqd* and the rulers are obliged to safeguard the citizens' interests).

Faysal prudently channelled the major part of the kingdom's increasing wealth to modernisation and development and to improving the standard of living of the various classes of Saudis through a network of subsidies, welfare services and opportunities for advancement. Thus, the danger of social upheaval resulting from accelerated modernisation and rapid urbanisation was largely avoided. Notwithstanding the increasing power of the new, largely *ḥadr* elites-dominated central government, the Sauds' paternalistic regime continued to enjoy the loyalty of the newly urbanised masses and rural population, whose allegiance to their traditional institutions began to erode.

Following the 1969 abortive *coups* Faysal mercilessly crushed the vestiges of opposition to his regime which thus no longer constituted a serious threat to the Sauds' ruling class. Indeed, after Faysal's demise, when the struggle for power within the royal family re-emerged, the great majority of the intelligentsia neither opted for militant nationalism, nor attempted to challenge Al Saud's authority, as they had in the 1950s and 1960s. Even their half-hearted efforts to gain a share in the decision-making process through the often promised National Consultative Assembly was easily frustrated by the ruling class. With the exception of insignificant radical-nationalist leftist and Shi'ite opposition oganisations, largely based abroad, the disunited new elites on the whole preferred personal achievement, prestige and wealth to a confrontation with the regime and reconciled themselves to the existing situation.

NOTES

1. See above pp. 92–3. Also Tables 3.2 and 3.3, pp. 52, 53 above.
2. M. Abir, 'The Manpower Problem in Saudi Arabian Economic and Security Policy', Woodrow Wilson International Center for Scholars (Washington, DC, April, 1983), p. 32.
3. For instance, Dr Ghazi al-Gosaybi, a leading intellectual, who held several ministerial positions until 1984, Hasan al-Mishari (Minister of Agriculture under Faysal), Dr Abd al-Rahman al-Zamil (Deputy Minister of Commerce): A.R.S. Islami and R.M. Kavoussi, *The Political Economy of Saudi Arabia* (Seattle, 1984), p. 22; R. Lacey, *The Kingdom* (London, 1981), p. 55. Al Saud ('Permanence', p. 132) on Gosaybi: 'one of the new breed of technocrats who used to be critical of the system'. On radicals: Shaker, 'Modernization of the Developing Nations', PhD thesis (Purdue University, 1972), pp. 313–15, and below.
4. T.R. McHale 'The Saudi Arabian political system', *Virteljahresberichte* No. 89 (September 1982), p. 202; A. Bligh, *Royal Succession in the House of Saud* (New York, 1984), p. 88.
5. Schulze, 'The Saudi Arabian Ulama', The Hebrew University (Jerusalem, 1985), pp. 20–1; D. Holden and R. Johns, *House of Saud* (London, 1982), p. 249; N. Safran, *Saudi Arabia* (Cambridge, 1985), pp. 121–2.
6. *Qaḍaya Sa'udiyya*, p. 7; H. Lackner, *A House Built on Sand* (London, 1978), p. 100; Buchan, 'Religious Opposition', p. 114.
7. Holden and Johns, *House of Saud*, pp. 250, 278–80; *Qaḍaya Sa'udiyya*, p. 7; Buchan, 'Religious Opposition', pp. 114–15; Lackner, *House*, p. 101; Safran, *Saudi Arabia*, p. 121; *Sawt al-Tali'a* (Baghdad), No. 6, June 1974. See also above p. 98.
8. Abir, 'Manpower', Appendix A.
9. Ibid., pp. 44, 79 (note 73); Holden and Johns, *House of Saud*, pp. 244-5. Also above p. 116. The 'sponsorship system' related to defence contracts became common in this period: *Al-Jarida*, 2 December 1968.
10. Ideologically related to the Palestinian *Qawmiyyun al-Arab*, now unquestionably Marxist.
11. Abir, 'Manpower', Appendix A; also M. Abir, *Oil Power and Politics: Conflict in Arabia, the Persian Gulf and the Red Sea* (London, 1974), pp. 102–3.
12. Al-Rawaf, 'The Concept of the Five Crises' (Duke University, 1981), p. 368; Holden and Johns, *House of Saud*, pp. 252–3; *Qaḍaya Sa'udiyya*, p. 7; V. Sheean, *Faisal* (Tavistock, 1975), p. 97; Alyami, 'Modernization', pp. 181 (Table LI), 182.

13. Alyami, 'Modernization', p. 168; *Al-Akhbar* (Lebanon), 13 July 1969; also on Nassir Sa'id in Damascus: *Al-Hadaf*, 7 March 1981, p. 27; Bligh, *Succession*, p. 86; Salameh, 'Political power', p. 23 and note 20: on broadcasts from Baghdad and *Sawt al-Tali'a*.

14. On oil revenue: SAMA Report 1981, p. 140, Table 12. Defence allocations nearly quadrupled from 1962/63 to 1969/70. Abir, 'Manpower', Appendix A; Safran, *Saudi Arabia*, pp. 184–5

15. After unsuccessfully attempting to get Aramco's agreement to Saudi participation in it, Zaki Yamani got a 25 per cent participation in 1970 when he invited other companies to exploit the kingdom's oil: Mosley, *Power Play* (Birkenhead, 1973), p. 333.

16. A Berkeley graduate, Hisham Nazir (now Petroleum Minister) joined Tariki's Directorate of Petroleum in 1958. Like Yamani, whose deputy he became in 1962, he did not share Tariki's political views: S.S. Huyette, *Political Adaptation* (Boulder, 1985), p. 75.

17. Lackner, *House*, p. 190; For text and criticism of the 1969 labour law: *Qadaya Sa'udiyya*, p. 7 onward; also Baroody, 'Practice of Law', in W.A. Beling (ed.), *King Faisal and the Modernisation of Saudi Arabia* (London, 1980), p. 122; Holden and Johns, *House of Saud*, p. 271.

18. Abir, 'Manpower', p. 22.

19. F.A. Hafiz, 'Changes in Saudi Foreign Policy', PhD thesis (University of Nebraska — Lincoln, 1980), p. 63; N.O. Madani, 'The Islamic Content of the Foreign Policy of Saudi Arabia' (The American University, Washington, DC, 1977), p. 129.

20. Safran, *Saudi Arabia*, p. 129.

21. Shaker, 'Modernization'. p. 307. List of about 100 air force personnel arrested including 13 pilot lieutenant-colonels, 46 pilot majors, captains and lieutenants and the rest NCOs and technicians: *Sawt al Tali'a* (Baghdad, 1974, No. 6), pp. 11–27; also 'Political opposition in Saudi Arabia'. *Sawt al Tali'a* (California, 1980). pp. 15–16; Holden and Johns, *House of Saud*, pp. 277–81; *Al Hayat*, 18 June 1969; *Al-Akhbar*, 13 July 1969; *Al-Jarida*, 16 August 1969; *Al-Muharir* (Beirut), 9 February 1970; NYT, 9 September 1969. List of air force and army generals arrested: Safran, *Saudi Arabia*, pp. 124–5, 129; Abir, *Oil Power*, pp. 54–5, 73 (note 168).

22. Shaker, 'Modernization', p. 309; Holden and Johns, *House of Saud*, p. 280; Alyami, 'Modernization', p. 201, Appendix II.

23. Holden and Johns, *House of Saud*, p. 280; Halliday ('Shifting sands', p. 39) claims that the largely Shi'ite Al-Qatif was put under siege and of the many arrested some were brutally killed. According to Buchan ('Religious Opposition', p. 115) Shi'ite intellectuals, including Salah Amba, the Dean of the P & M, were arrested in the Shi'ite villages.

24. Shaker ('Modernization', p. 309), who seems to have been close to the 'progressives', claims that the figure was as high as 4000.

25. G.S. Samore, 'Royal Family Politics' (Harvard University, 1984), pp. 259–64. *Al-Hayat* (18 June 1969) claimed that PFLOAG and the Communist Party were behind this plot.

26. Many of the arrested were personally recruited by the Hijazi air force commander-in-chief (until 1972), General Hashim S. Hashim, not involved in the plot. A senior Najdi officer incarcerated was Abd al-Aziz al-Mu'ammar's brother, who following the latter's arrest (1964) was sent

abroad as a military attaché: Holden and Johns, *House of Saud*, p. 279.

27. Among the arrested were the Commanders of the Dhahran and Jedda air bases, the Director of Military Operations, the Director of the Office of the Chief of Staff, the Commander of the military garrison at Al-Hasa, the former Chief of Staff of the army, the former Commander of the Mecca garrison, the Director-General of the Maintenance Corps, the Director of Officers' Affairs of the Internal Security Academy, the Acting Commandant of the Staff College, a junior officer from the Sudayri family, and the Saudi military attaché in Tokyo, previously head of Prince Sultan's office: Safran, *Saudi Arabia*, p. 129; Holden and Johns, *House of Saud*, pp. 278–9. The Saudi intelligence attempted to assassinate Nassir Sa'id (head of the pan-Arab UPAP) at the end of 1970, according to his wife: *Al-Hadaf*, 7 March 1981, p. 27.

28. Holden and Johns, *House of Saud*, p. 278. Halliday (*Arabia*, p. 69), quoting Saudi exiles, estimated that about 2000 political prisoners were still in Faysal's jails in 1973; also Holden and Johns, *House of Saud*, pp. 280–1; FT, 22 April 1985, supplement, p. VI.

29. On arrests in 1971: Abir, *Oil Power*, p. 73 (note 168). On torture and assassinations of militants: Alyami, 'Modernization', pp. 124–5, 201; L. Blandford, *Oil Sheikhs* (London, 1976), p. 124; Holden and Johns, *House of Saud*, pp. 280–1. Remnants of the NLF and some of the released prisoners formed the Saudi Communist Party in the mid-1970s: *Handbook* (1984), p. 301. Also Chapter 4, note 28, above. Fahd was displeased with the indiscriminate arrests of the middle-class elites by Faysal: Field, FT, 22 April 1985, supplement, p. VI; R. Lacey, *The Kingdom* (London, 1981), p. 441.

30. *Sawt al-Tali'a*, No. 4 (Baghdad, 1974), p. 16. This biased source claimed that budgets for security activities were doubled between 1970 and 1972 and nearly tripled between 1968 and 1971/72. On 1950s and 1960s: Safran, *Saudi Arabia*, p. 70.

31. Shaker, 'Modernization', pp. 311–15.

32. Blandford, *Oil Sheikhs*, pp. 124–5; *Al-Hurriyya*, 18 May 1970; *Al-Ahrar* (Lebanon), 19 June 1970.

33. *Al-Ahrar*, 28 November 1969; also Abir, 'Manpower', pp. 33–6.

34. See Abir, 'Saudi security', p. 91.

35. In addition to Iraqi subversion in the Gulf, the Saudis were the target of a propaganda campaign from Damascus. Furthermore, the Syrians, who in 1970 sabotaged the Tapline, refused to permit its repair.

36. Abir, 'Manpower', p. 41: on armed forces and mercenaries in the 1970s; also *Al-Ahrar*, 28 November 1969. The less glorified transport command (C–130 Hercules) based in Jedda remained largely Hijazi. On different political considerations for upgrading of armed forces: Gh. Salameh, *Al-Siyassa al-Kharijiyya al-Sa'udiyya mundhu 1945* (Beirut, 1980), pp. 525, 532, 577.

37. But not to promulgate a constitution, Lacey, *The Kingdom*, p. 491.

38. Huyette, *Adaptation*, p. 76.

39. Ibid., pp. 75, 78, 80; Lackner, *House*, p. 73. Until 1975, Faysal personally authorised visas 'to Jews and journalists': Holden and Johns, *House of Saud*, pp. 379, 459.

40. Shaker, 'Modernization', p. 308.

41. See above pp. 38, 44. Also Tables 3.1, 3.2, 3.3, pp. 51–3.

42. Huyette, *Adaptation*, p. 96. On Fahd's derogatory words on ranking officials with PhDs: Holden and Johns, *House of Saud*, p. 460.

43. Until its modernisation in the late 1960s the administration was composed of 70 per cent offspring of traditional civil servants, merchants and other *hadr*. Of the total in 1970 over 60 per cent were still Najdis and less than 30 per cent Hijazis: Al-Awaji (Deputy Minister of the Interior), 'Bureaucracy', p. 179. This was partly due to the fact that many more traditionally-trained Najdis joined the civil service when King Saud moved the modern government from Hijaz to Riyadh. Najdis also dominated the religious institutions, the Hijaz included: Al-Nasser, 'Mission', pp. 47–8, 50; also Huyette, *Adaptation*, pp. 75, 95–6. Numerous Hijazis enrolled in foreign universities and the above proportion gradually changed from the late 1960s in favour of the Hijazi technocrats: I.M. Al-Awaji, 'Bureaucracy and Society in Saudi Arabia' (University of Virginia, 1971), pp. 176, 179–80; Said, 'Saudi Arabia', pp. 17, 76, 185. On nepotism: Al-Nassar, 'Saudi Arabian Educational Mission' (University of Oklahoma, 1982), p. 58; Al-Awaji, 'Bureaucracy', pp. 232, 236.

44. Muhammad Aba'l-Khayl was appointed a cabinet minister and Minister of Finance in 1975, Sulayman Solaym, Deputy Minister of Commerce 1974 and Minister of Commerce in 1975. Both Najdis from Qasim district. Ghazi al-Gosaybi, of Najdi origin from the Eastern Province, appointed Minister of Industry and Electricity 1975, was previously Dean of the Faculty of Commerce in Riyadh university and Faysal's adviser.

45. Al-Awaji, 'Bureaucracy', pp. 179–80; Huyette, *Adaptation*, pp. 95–6.

46. Al Saud, 'Permanence and Change' (Claremont Graduate School, 1982), p.116. A conservative, the writer is clearly jealous of the power and success of the technocratic upper-crust. Also Shaker, 'Modernization', p. 317. On Faysal's close relations with some of his Hijazi commoner ministers: Holden and Johns, *House of Saud*, pp. 378–9.

47. Al-Rawaf, 'Five Crises', pp. 341, 370–1; Huyette, *Adaptation*, pp. 96–7.

48. See above Chapter 2.

49. On Ministry of Justice: *Al-Hayat*, 21 June, 31 July 1963; Lackner, *House*, p. 199; Huyette, *Adaptation*, p. 76.

50. Al-Rawaf, 'Five Crises', pp. 341, 369. On erosion of *umara*'s authority by rise of central government: Said, 'Saudi Arabia', pp. 104–5; Al-Selfan, 'The Essence of Tribal Leaders' Participation' (Claremont Graduate School, 1981), p. 151.

51. Al-Rawaf, 'Five Crises', pp. 366–7.

52. See above Chapter 2.

53. 'All levels of technocrats tend to represent . . . the educated young of the major urban centres': Al Saud, 'Permanence', p. 116.

54. See Chapter 7, pp. 171–4. In this context the term Najdi refers also to 'noble' tribes who overspill into the nearby provinces.

55. Shaker, 'Modernization', p. 315. Cited as written. Also Lackner, *House*, p. 88.

56. Sheean, *Faisal*, p. 119. Cited as written.

57. F. Halliday, *Arabia without Sultans* (Manchester, 1974), p. 69; Salameh, 'Political power', p. 23; M. Field, 'Saudi Royal Family' *Euromoney*, (October 1981); *Al-Mawqif al-Arabi*, 20 April 1981.

58. See Table 5.1, p. 127 above.

6

Power Struggle, Modernisation and Reaction, 1975–80

OIL WEALTH AND DEVELOPMENT — NEW ELITES' POWER AND ROYAL HOUSE RIVALRY

King Khalid, a moderate conservative with little experience in administrative or political affairs, was in a very poor state of health when he came to power. From the outset, whether by design or necessity, he delegated much of his authority to Fahd, the Crown Prince and acting Prime Minister. The relationship between Khalid and Fahd resembled to some extent that between Saud and Faysal in the late 1950s. Then, the Crown Prince had almost complete authority, but the final power rested in the hands of the King. Like Faysal thirteen years earlier, Fahd used the Council of Ministers to fortify his own position in relation to Khalid. But the appointment of Prince Abdallah as next in line of succession and second Deputy Prime Minister limited somewhat the ability of Fahd and the modernist camp to act unilaterally and ensure the family's consensus in all major matters.

For six months after Fahd's accession to authority Faysal's appointed government continued to function almost unchanged. The only significant exceptions were the following: the appointment of Faysal's son, Saud al-Faysal, previously Deputy Minister of Petroleum, and a representative of the third generation royal family, as Foreign Minister. Prince Na'if, Fahd's full brother, replaced him as Minister of the Interior, and another of the 'Sudayri Seven', Ahmad, was appointed his deputy.[1]

Shortly after Faysal's assassination, in order to win the general support of the new middle-class elites whom he consistently befriended, Fadh, with Khalid's blessing, announced the regime's intention to establish a National Consultative Council (*majlis al-*

shura). This was to be composed of some 40 appointed 'young' representatives of the tribal leaders, technocrats, professionals and businessmen of the new middle class, as well as the ulama. Yet, once the regime consolidated its position and felt secure, the promise was again conveniently forgotten. The royal family was, however, aware of the need for some political reform, and in succeeding years a committee was established under Prince Na'if to study possible political and juridical reforms, foremost among which was the establishment of a national *majlis al-shura*. Indeed, when asked again about the National Consultative Council in April 1977, Fahd expressed an understanding of the need for it and for similar institutions, at the provincial level, stressing that the matter was under review.[2]

As Minister of the Interior responsible for security under Faysal, Fahd was considered far more lenient than the King in dealing with the opposition. Now that he was practically in power, Fahd quickly pardoned all those still imprisoned as a result of the 1969 abortive *coups* and ordered the authorities to help rehabilitate them. Censorship of the media was also relaxed and 'positive constructive criticism' of the administration, but not the Saudi regime, was permitted.[3]

At the same time Na'if, the new Minister of the Interior, reorganised and expanded the Internal Security Services, especially the feared *Al-Mabahith al-'Amma* (lit. The General Investigations Organisation, popularly known as *Mabahith*), enabling them closely to supervise foreigners and suspected radical elements.[4] Na'if also cultivated intelligence cooperation between Saudi Arabia and the nearby Gulf principalities, to counter subversion by Marxist and other radical organisations supported by the PDRY and Iraq. As an extension of such activities Na'if, rather than Saud al-Faysal, the new Foreign Minister, became responsible for relations with the Gulf mini-states. Thus, Na'if in 1976 initiated negotiations that eventually led to the establishment of the Gulf Cooperation Council (GCC) which excluded Iraq and Iran.[5]

Fahd was always considered the leading modernist in Faysal's camp. His enthusiasm was restrained, however, by the King, who was determined to preserve the balance of power between modernists and conservatives. Once in power, relying heavily on the technocratic upper-crust, the Crown Prince began to accelerate Saudi Arabia's development. The kingdom's second five-year development plan (1975–80) estimated at $142 billion (final cost over $180 billion) was, to a great extent, Fahd's responsibility. In addition to the enormous defence allocations (over 20 per cent of the total), the plan concentrated on building the kingdom's infrastructure, diversifying its economy and expanding its welfare and other services which benefited the citizenry. This necessitated a substantial increase in the workforce, at a time when Saudi manpower was already in short supply. It also necessitated that the central government administration and its specialised agencies be expanded. The employment demands of the late 1970s required, in addition to a large number of foreigners, many more educated Saudis in the government services and in managerial positions in the private sector.

In October, the cabinet was thoroughly reshuffled, showing more than ever the modernising trend of Crown Prince Fahd's regime. It now had 26 members, eight of whom were princes and the rest commoners, sixteen with university degrees. Yet to counter the Sudayris' power in the cabinet, two younger sons of Abd al-Aziz, Mit'ab and Majid (close to the Liberal Princes in his younger days), were appointed Minister of Public Works and Housing and of Municipal and Rural Affairs, respectively. Faysal's younger son Turki was also appointed shortly afterwards Director of the General (external) Intelligence Services (*Al-Istikhbarat al-'Amma*).[6]

Unlike Faysal, Fahd delegated real authority to his commoner ministers and encouraged them to take initiatives. Once a policy was decided upon by the royal *majlis al-shura*, it was the minister's responsibility to carry it out and thus, within their respective areas of responsibility, the non-aristocratic ministers enjoyed a measure of decision-making. Thus, according to a keen, but somewhat biased, American observer who had spent the 1970s and early 1980s in the kingdom, 'When Khalid and Fahd promoted the ambitious plans of the 1970s, they set in motion forces which necessitated the diffusion of power and the delegation of increasing responsibilities to the Council of Ministers.[7]

Another distinguishing feature of Fahd's cabinet of October 1975 was the assimilation to it of western-educated Najdi technocrats (the first after Tariki left the cabinet) such as Sulayman Sulaym, Minister of Commerce, Ghazi al-Gosaybi, Minister of Industry and Electricity, and later Muhammad Aba'l-Khayl as Minister of Finance (from 1972 Minister without Portfolio). This marked the beginning of the erosion of the Hijazi predominance and the re-establishment of Najdi hegemony in the Saudi government service and armed forces. The preference for their Najdi *hadr* 'constituency' was mainly an outcome of a royal family consensus, supported by King

Khalid, despite Fahd's ambivalence on this matter.[8]

The above trend was strongly resented by the Hijazi middle class also because of its economic ramifications. In the first place it undermined the advantage of the Hijazi businessmen and entrepreneurs to obtain fat commissions from foreign companies or win government contracts for themselves and their foreign partners. Furthermore, it also affected employment opportunities for Hijazi school-leavers and university graduates. As already mentioned, nepotism in Saudi society is a recognised norm which education and modernisation failed to undermine. Once in the government service the senior technocrat was expected to look after his own. If a Hijazi was appointed to head a ministry it was expected that he would favour applications for jobs who were members of his extended family, clan, tribe and region. Even the lowliest position in his unit of the administration went, in most cases, to a semi-literate client of the family of one of the important officials of this administrative unit.[9]

Faysal's appointment as Prime Minister in 1958 and his return to power in 1962–64 were facilitated to a great extent by a group of senior princes led by the 'Sudayri Seven' and Faysal's uncles (notably Abdallah). Among these princes, Fahd enthusiastically supported Faysal's reform plans even before he joined the Saudi government in 1954. A coalition, formed between the above group and other senior princes related to the Jiluwi branch of the royal family, led to the enthronement of Faysal in 1964. The more loosely connected Jiluwi group was led by Prince (later King) Khalid and his elder brother, Muhammad, Abd al-Aziz's sons by a Jiluwi wife. Prince Abdallah, another member of the group, was related to the Jiluwis through his mother who came from an eastern Shammar tribe and had married a Jiluwi. Another important member was the Jiluwi Governor of the Eastern Province. This group was considered conservative, as the Jiluwis were considered in general, and offset the modernising zeal of the Fahd-led Sudayris. In contrast, the Princeton graduate Prince Saud al-Faysal, and two other sons of Faysal by his Jiluwi wife Haya bint Turki, were modernists. Yet, Saud al-Faysal was considered by many a likely candidate for membership in the Jiluwi faction in the royal family.[10]

The strains between the Sudayri and the Jiluwi camps among the senior members of the royal family were exacerbated at the end of 1975, when the Sudayris pressed on with their demand that Prince

Abdallah, now second in line of succession and second Deputy Prime Minister, relinquish the command of the National Guard. Yet, the conservatives encouraged Abdallah to resist this demand because, at a time when the Saudi armed forces, under Sultan, were rapidly being upgraded and Prince Na'if as Minister of the Interior controlled the strengthened security services, the National Guard was their only powerbase. The conservatives and other members of the aristocracy also protested at the kingdom's pro-American policy revived by Faysal with Fahd's help, and now vigorously pursued.

Ironically, an important faction of the new elites supported the conservatives rather than Fahd's modernist camp, as had been the case with Saud and Faysal in the late 1950s. Although Fahd was always considered their patron, some of the graduates of the foreign and the 'secular' domestic universities were dissatisfied with his lukewarm position on political reform. Others were critical of his unbridled extravagant modernisation (one of these was the Planning Minister, Hisham Nazir, now Minister or Petroleum). Practically all of the expanding, domestically-trained, modernist and conservative intelligentsia was united in its criticism of Fahd's pro-American and oil policies.

Fahd's pro-Americanism, and the anachronistic character of the Saudi regime, became the target of a propaganda campaign directed by Iraq and Libya on one side and by the PDRY and its subversive affiliate organisations in the Gulf on the other. But in essence, anti-western sentiments were widely shared by the conservatives and by the new elites in Saudi Arabia. The regime, moreover, faced increasingly financial, as well as social, difficulties resulting from the rapid pace of change due to the second five-year development plan (1975–80) and the decline of oil revenues.

THE CRISIS OF 1977-79 AND ITS IMPACT

The kingdom's oil revenues declined in 1976/77 because of a decreasing demand for oil. Income no longer sufficed to finance the enormous expenditure relating to development and defence. American 'gold-plated' military projects concentrated on multi-billion dollar defence-related construction and, to a lesser degree, on the acquisition of very costly sophisticated weapons, rather than on upgrading the Saudi fighting capability. Building the country's communications infrastructure proved exceedingly costly, as did the enormous petrochemical complexes of Jubayl and Yanbu, meant to diversify the Saudi economy. All this necessitated the additional employment by 1977 of more than 2 million, mostly non-Arab, foreigners, including about 100,000 westerners. They all constituted a heavy burden on Saudi finances. The government, moreover, was also expanding the costly subsidies and network of welfare and other services which benefited the population.[11]

The first and second five-year development plans (1970–80) greatly accelerated changes in Saudi society underway since the 1940s. The expenditure of tens of billions of dollars on development, which in the 1970s largely benefited the urban population, further expedited rural migration into the towns, especially its five major cities. Thus, by the end of the 1970s, the proportion of urban to rural population was completely reversed. Indeed, by 1980 the percentage of true Bedouin, who had constituted the larger part of the population until the mid-century, declined to less than 10 per cent. City-dwellers and inhabitants of small towns made up about two-thirds of the population. Ironically, while Saudi Arabia was employing millions of foreign manual workers, technicians and experts of different kinds, unemployment among newly urbanised Saudis, whose social mores and lack of skills forwent manual labour in the cities and in the underdeveloped agricultural Southern Region (Asir), was a grave problem. At the same time, as the economy overheated, the cost of living and inflation in the kingdom were skyrocketing and the government was unable to provide sufficient housing and social services for the ever-growing urban 'proletariat'. For a time, the frustration of the 'lower class' was intensified by the increasing polarisation between rich and poor and by tales of corruption and scandals relating to the Sauds. Such infringements on Wahhabi puritanism, moreover, incensed the fundamentalists and especially the less sophisticated Najdis.[12]

Yet by the late 1970s, the Saudi government, with practically unlimited funds at its disposal, succeeded in overcoming most of the economic and some of the social problems which it faced. The kingdom's citizens now enjoyed adequate housing and a wide range of subsidies, free education and extensive welfare services. Guaranteed employment and advancement in government service, coupled with financial support to businessmen and entrepreneurs, enabled most Saudis to share in their country's wealth and facilitated the rapid rise of 'lower-class' Saudis, mainly of rural origin, to membership in the flourishing middle class. The threat to the traditional sympathy for the Saud regime of the rural and part of the urban population was thus averted.

The agent-sponsor system (an outcome of legislation in 1930 and 1977), and widespread corruption in the Saudi government, were nourished by the numerous multi-billion dollar defence, infrastructure and other development contracts. The kingdom's spending-spree and commissions generated at every level of economic activity enriched many Saudis, particularly ex-technocrats or Saudis related to the technocratic upper-crust, not to mention the members (especially senior ones) of the Saudi ruling class and their 'consti-tuencies'. That, and the fortunes which members of the royal family amassed as well through interference in the country's trade (fictitious partnerships and the like) and other economic activities since Faysal's period, enraged the Saudi intelligentsia and the business community.[13] A few commoner cabinet ministers and other senior technocrats refused commissions and bribes freely offered by foreign contractors and freely accepted by their associates and members of the royal family. The patronage and commission systems were in fact major means by which the regime channelled wealth to the new elites (and to the ruling class) and through them to all levels of the middle class. Indeed, in 1977 Crown Prince Fahd enacted the Tender Law by which, *inter alia*, no Saudi was allowed to represent more than ten foreign companies so as to enable many more technocrats and businessmen (and princes) to benefit from the sponsor and commission system.[14]

The ulama were also becoming increasingly frustrated with the impact of modernisation and the presence in the kingdom of large numbers of foreigners, especially western experts, whose alien cultural influences threatened the Wahhabi-Saudi 'way of life'. Some even began openly to criticise the Saudi ruling class for betraying the principles of (Wahhabi) Islam.

Rivalry in the royal family again broke out and endangered the Sauds' external common front in February 1977 when the ailing Khalid was rushed to London for urgent medical treatment. The Arab press published rumours that the King's health was rapidly failing. Such a possibility exacerbated the rivalry in the royal family and undermined the consensus essential for upholding the regime's stability. The Sudayris again demanded that Prince Abdallah, whose position was considered weak because he did not have any full brothers, surrender control of the National Guard. It was widely believed, moreover, that Fahd and his brothers wished to replace

Abdallah as second Deputy Prime Minister and second in line of succession with Sultan (Minister of Defence) and thus consolidate the Sudayris' hold on the government.[15]

The Sudayris' alleged attempt to monopolise all power in the royal family enraged many of the senior members of Al Saud but mostly the conservative ones. Led by Prince Muhammad, Khalid's elder (full) brother, and frustrated by the erosion of the kingdom's traditional character through modernisation and western influences, they rejected the new balance of power which the Sudayris wished to impose upon the ruling class. The conservatives considered the control of the National Guard essential to protect their interests and encouraged Abdallah to resist the Sudayris' demands to surrender its control to them. They also attributed the socio-economic difficulties facing the kingdom to Fahd's government and alleged that its pro-western oil and foreign policy served western interests rather than those of Saudi Arabia and other Arab states.[16]

By March 1977 the Arab press repeatedly reported that because of his deteriorating health, King Khalid was planning to abdicate in Fahd's favour. Subsequently, the rift in the royal family widened, and the conservatives attempted to form a coalition with elements of the new elites dissatisfied with Fahd and with the younger generation of princes, led by Faysal's university-educated sons. Despite blood-ties, the younger princes chose not to identify with any faction of their elder kinsmen and avoided as well the pitfall of allying themselves with the nationalist new elite with whom they shared some common interests.[17]

The complacent bourgeois new elites of the 1970s avoided a confrontation with the regime and did not seriously press the ruling class for constitutional reforms. Unlike in the 1950s and 1960s they operated, by and large, within the framework of the establishment and shunned the militant clandestine organisations. The officers of the modernised armed forces, who enjoyed high salaries and many privileges, were closely watched by the security services. More often than not, the ones appointed to key sensitive positions were the offspring of the aristocracy and of loyal Bedouin amirs. On the surface, it seemed that the Saudi officer corps no longer bred frustrated 'Young Turks' (see Chapter 8).

Responding to demands of the new middle class for political reform, Crown Prince Fahd said in April 1977:

I am for participation and we have declared our desire to

strengthen the provincial councils and the Consultative Council. . . . We believe that there must be popular participation within the proposed idea, namely, the Consultative Council and the provincial councils. Of course, these councils will include selected men in the country, men of opinion and expertise. I believe that any political, social or economic plan put before these selected men will be thoroughly studied. . . . The delay in achieving this is not because we do not want it but because we are a country that is advancing rapidly.[18]

Clearly Fahd was trying to win the support of the middle class at a time of crisis. The 1977 Tender Law, mentioned above, for instance, was meant to spread further the kingdom's oil wealth among the new elites; but, aware of the ruling family consensus, he was unwilling to grant the middle-class elites even the often promised *majlis al-shura*. Indeed, in the mid-1970s Fahd could be a benevolent ruler with regard to imprisoned opposition members and an ultra-modernist when it came to economic, technological and administrative development. Yet, when it came to political modernisation, although more liberal than Faysal and the other senior princes — his brother Salman excluded — Fahd was unwilling to jeopardise his position by granting the intelligentsia participation in decision-making. Such a step, his peers believed, was bound eventually to undermine the foundation of the Sauds' regime.

At the end of April King Khalid's health improved and he was able to return to Saudi Arabia. He immediately began an extensive tour of the various provinces and met tribal heads, local dignitaries and district and provincial governors. Thus, the conflict in the royal family was suppressed. In reality, fearing that the stability of the regime would be threatened by the inter-factional rivalry, the Sudayris accepted as final the existing arrangements by which Abdallah was to succeed Fahd as King. Nevertheless, they continued their efforts to reduce the power and efficiency of the National Guard and to turn it into a lightly armed gendarmerie.[19]

In mid-May 1977 in Riyadh, Fahd, in the presence of King Khalid met President Sadat and President Assad while he was preparing for a previously planned visit to Washington. Arriving in the United States on 20 May he discussed two major issues with President Carter: the supply of oil to the West and its price, and American policy relating to the settlement of the Arab-Israeli conflict. Although Fahd prudently coordinated the Saudi stance with the Egyptian and Syrian leaders,

143

the Crown Prince's pro-American policy again caused discord within the ruling class and antagonised a sizeable part of the nationalist (anti-American) new elites.

Earlier, opposing OPEC's decision to raise the price of oil by 15 per cent (in December 1976), the Saudi government increased its oil production and coerced the organisation into accepting its proposed 5 per cent rise in oil prices. The radical, mainly Palestinian-controlled, press in Beirut and the Gulf accused the Saudi regime of being an instrument of western imperialism and of US policy. Reports of unrest among Aramco workers were followed in May 1977 by two fires in the huge Abqaiq oil field, causing damage estimated at about 100 million dollars. Though the authorities claimed the fires were accidental, other sources alleged that they were the result of sabotage.[20]

A quixotic attempt at a *coup* against the regime involving thirteen Hijazi pilots of a squadron of the Saudi air force based in Tabuk and a number of civilians was also uncovered in mid-1977. Their 'plan' was to bombard and rocket government buildings and royal palaces in Jedda and Riyadh, and then proclaim the establishment of an Arabian Republic. Although the participants were, it seems, Ba'thists connected to Iraq, the plot was masterminded and financed by Libya. Ironically, the head of Libya's military intelligence involved in this affair was 'turned' by the Saudi security services (or the CIA) and Riyadh was aware of this naive plot from its inception. All those involved, with the exception of three pilots who escaped to Iraq, were arrested and for a time, all air force planes were forbidden to carry munitions and were restricted to enough fuel for only 30 minutes' flying time. Coincidentally, the salaries of all civil servants were doubled, as were those of soldiers and NCOs. Officers of different ranks also received salary rises, land grants and other benefits.[21]

A serious setback to Crown Prince Fahd's policy was President Sadat's visit to Jerusalem in November 1977. The kingdom's policy in OPEC and its stance concerning the American peace efforts, in addition to antagonising the Arab militants, caused growing dissatisfaction among the Saudi new elites and the conservatives. The latter were also increasingly critical of the unbridled modernisation pursued by Fahd which, they claimed, undermined the kingdom's religious and cultural foundations. Thus, discontent with Fahd's government tangibly intensified. The Crown Prince prudently dissociated himself from President Sadat's peace initiative and reduced the profile of Saudi relations with the United States. Britain and especially France subsequently benefited from military contracts meant to diversify the kingdom's sources of weapons and reduce its dependence on the USA.[22]

At the beginning of 1978, King Khalid was rushed to the United States for major heart surgery. The conservatives mobilised their supporters in case the Sudayris attempted to seize power in view of the King's failing health. The discontent with Fahd's pro-western policy and government in general among the new elites also became increasingly evident. Demands for political participation were openly aired by the intelligentsia and, when questioned on the matter, Fahd promised to review proposals for a Consultative Assembly. The Saudi press later published the text of a draft proposal for municipal elections, but by itself this awakened little enthusiasm among educated Saudis.[23]

The little anti-regime activity of the small leftist clandestine organisations in Saudi Arabia in the 1970s took place largely in the Eastern Province and to a lesser degree in Asir. In the former, the Shi'ite community increasingly protested against the discrimination practised against them by the government. The development and prosperity enjoyed by the kingdom's Sunni population, the Southern Region excepted,[24] resulting from the sale of 'their' oil, frustrated the Shi'ites of Al-Hasa and fuelled the growth of local radical and separatist organisations.

In the last months of 1978 it was alleged that tribal elements inimical to the Sauds (if true, probably the 'Ujman) staged an 'uprising' in the Eastern Province which coincided with labour unrest in Dhahran. Tension was also reported in Asir (especially in the Jizan district), historically an offshoot of Yemen, which was suffering badly from poverty and neglect. Pamphlets of regional separatist movements such as the Organisation for the Liberation of Al-Hasa, Asir and the Hijaz were circulated, it was reported, in various parts of the kingdom. At the beginning of 1979 the radical Arab press even alleged that Saudi Arabia was 'on the verge of an explosion'.[25]

The renewed unrest in Saudi Arabia emanated partly from the socio-cultural ramifications of hasty modernisation and the growing tension within the royal family related to the Arab radicals' consolidation of their power following the Camp David talks; but it was greatly enhanced by developments in Iran in 1978, the collapse of the Shah's regime and the decline of American credibility in the region. The success of the Iranian Revolution, although involving Shi'ite fundamentalism, fanned neo-Ikhwan sentiments among elements of the kingdom's Sunni population. It instilled, moreover, new pride among the Shi'ites and by 1979 the Organisation of the

Islamic Revolution for the Liberation of the Arabian Peninsula (*Munazamat al-Thawra al-Islamiyya litahrir al-Jazira al-'Arabiyya*), popularly called *Al-Thawra al-Islamiyya* — The Islamic Revolution (henceforth IRO) — began to operate in the Eastern Province.[26]

The Saudi ruling class was seriously shaken by the collapse of the Shah and the rise of the fundamentalist regime in Iran, prior to the Camp David agreement (March 1979). Fahd's pro-American policy was totally discredited and blamed for the grave situation which the kingdom faced. The Crown Prince prudently left the country in the spring for a long 'vacation'. Feeling exposed to Arab radicalism during the short-lived *rapprochement* between Syria and Iraq (September 1978 to July 1979) on the one hand and the rising tide of Shi'ite militant fundamentalism on the other, the royal *majlis al-shura*, presided over by Prince Abdallah, known for his friendly relations with Syria and anti-western sentiments, and Fahd's brother Sultan, hurriedly disengaged the kingdom from its 'special relations' with the United States. In contrast to the moderate policy they had followed in the past, the Saudis now supported the decisions of the militant Arab countries. At the Baghdad summit in March 1979 they supported the imposition of a boycott on Egypt, and a total rejection of the Camp David agreement and the US policy in the region. A humbled Zaki Yamani accepted a substantial raising of oil prices advocated by OPEC's 'hawks' and Saudi nationalists which caused the second 'oil crisis' in 1980. As he and Fahd expected, this led after 1981 to the collapse of oil prices with grave consequences for Saudi Arabia.

The Saudi rulers, in disarray, aimlessly followed in the coming months the radicals in the Arab camp. With the conservatives attempting to undermine the Sudayris' position and the middle-class new elites more vigorously pressing for power and participation in policy-making, the situation in the kingdom in the spring of 1979 somewhat resembled that of the early 1960s. The more radical among the new elites hoped and even believed that the end of the Sauds' regime was rapidly approaching.[27]

A strange coalition of conservatives and 'nationalists' in the ruling class, and the 'pan-Arab' anti-western elements among the new elites, endeavoured that spring to depose Fahd *in absentia*. Yet, by mid-1979, the Crown Prince was back in Saudi Arabia resuming his responsibilities. Although he temporarily dissociated himself from the United States and condemned its policy — specifically the Camp David agreement — his position remained precarious. Only the shock of the Mecca rebellion and the Shi'ite riots in the Eastern Province at the end of 1979 and the beginning of 1980 re-established solidarity within the ruling class and, paradoxically, helped consolidate the regime's stability.

Saudi Arabia's influence and prestige in the Arab world and the international arena continued to rise after the death of Faysal despite the struggle for power in the royal family. The kingdom with its enormous oil reserves and wealth was now considered by the international community a minor superpower. While Saudi relations with Egypt and Syria had improved under Faysal, Crown Prince Fahd, exploiting Iraq's resentment of the coerced 1975 (Algiers) border agreement with Iran, managed to smooth the differences between Riyadh and Baghdad and temporarily reduce the tension with the Marxist PDRY, largely the outcome of the Saudi efforts in the 1970s to prevent the unification of the two Yemens.

Despite its power, partly gained at the expense of the traditional institutions, the intelligentsia-dominated central government did not enjoy the sympathy of the newly urbanised and rural population.[28] The latter, as well as all classes of Saudis, shared in the country's prosperity through Fahd's accelerated development and the expanding network of welfare services and subsidies. The ruling class, with its wide powerbase, estimated that the fragmented new elites, corrupted by prestige and wealth, despite their expanding ranks, did not constitute a sufficiently serious challenge to merit special consideration. Thus, meaningful constitutional reform was rejected as being un-Islamic and the promised national (Islamic) *majlis al-shura*, resurfacing with every crisis, was again ignored.

In so far as the backbone of the leftist opposition was broken in the late 1960s and early 1970s,[29] the mainstream of the Saudi intelligentsia, enjoying prestige and economic prosperity, continued to serve the ruling class loyally. The tame, successful and deeply divided bourgeois new elites of the 1970s, half-heartedly attempted in 1977–79 to exploit the rift in the royal family to advance political reform in the kingdom and radicalise its oil and foreign policy. Yet it carefully avoided a confrontation with the regime over demands for meaningful constitutional reforms. The relatively conservative majority of the new elites were either satisfied with the status quo, or naively hoped that aware of their expanding ranks and role in the kingdom's government and economy, the ruling class would eventually agree to include them in some way in decision-making. In the meantime, the technocratic 'aristocracy' endeavoured to expand the measure of decision-making which it enjoyed in the central government and within the ministries by using its members' control of budgets and role in the cabinet. Their efforts, however, were usually blocked by the antagonism of the ulama and of the royal family. They were eventually more successful in pressing for a rise in oil prices following a reduction in the kingdom's production.

Even though the rival camps in the aristocracy occasionally courted the new middle class, its support was considered secondary to that of the ulama, the source of the Sauds' legitimacy. The eruption of the conflict in the royal family and the rising wave of fundamentalism in Iran and in the Muslim world as a whole, rather prompted Fahd to improve the Sudayris' image as guardians of the kingdom's Wahhabi character and to reverse Faysal's relatively liberal policy. Thereafter, the regime again increased the authority of the ulama and their Morality Police who supervised the piety of the citizens and curtailed the 'privileges' of westerners residing in the kingdom.[30]

NEO-IKHWAN AND THE MECCA REBELLION (1979)

Saudi Arabia's rapid modernisation since the late 1960s, and the socio-cultural changes which it induced, rekindled the fundamentalist sentiments which had been dormant after the suppression of the 1927-29 Ikhwan rebellion. The ulama, who strongly objected to innovations introduced by Ibn Saud and his heirs, reconciled themselves, in most cases, to the rulers' decisions. During Faysal's reign, when they were given control of the new religious institutions which he established and enjoyed the prestige and power which came with them, the ulama increasingly became part of the state establishment. Indeed, although some ulama bitterly criticised other Muslim rulers for introducing modernisation and foreign influences which were contrary to the principles of Islam, they were careful not to point an accusing finger at the Sauds' regime.

Even before the 1979 uprising, the Sauds and most new elites, not to mention the ulama, became increasingly concerned about the impact on their society of rapid modernisation, accompanied by westernisation. Traditional anti-western sentiments were enhanced in this period by the sense of power (from oil wealth) and the presence in Saudi Arabia of many foreigners. Hence, in the late 1970s, members of the ruling class and even part of the western-trained intelligentsia began to pay lip-service to the need to protect the 'Saudi way of life' from the corrupt western culture with its materialistic values and permissiveness,[31] in order to advance national solidarity.

To a simple but proud people whose oil has recently purchased their rapid modernisation and made them into a world (economic) power, **the 'Saudi way of life' has come to represent their unique-ness and has become their national ethos.** The 'Saudi way of life' is, in fact, a synthesis of customs of the pre-oil, impoverished Arabian society, symbols of the tribal-nomadic people (the camel, the tent, the dress) and aspects of Wahhabi asceticism and beliefs, many of these features are alien to the traditional urban factions, especially to the Hijazis who dominate the Saudi bureaucracy.[32]

The accelerated development and change, which Saudi society was experiencing under Fahd, exacerbated the discontent of the Najdi-led fundamentalists. The conservative ulama frequently felt threatened as well by the western-educated technocrats and bureaucrats, who often were critical, however discreetly, of the ulama.[33] During a visit to Riyadh's Islamic University in 1978 Prince Ahmad, the Deputy Minister of the Interior and Muhammad Abdu Yamani, the Minister of Information, faced a hostile audience of about 2000 students and faculty. Some felt that programmes broadcast by the state television were anti-Islamic and subversive of Wahhabi society. Abdu Yamani, who claimed that the programmes reflected modern times, was strongly reprimanded by Abd al-Aziz al-Baz, the Rector of Al-Madina Islamic University and the President of the Administration of Scientific Study, (religious) Legal Opinions, Islamic Propagation and Guidance. In the same year the furious ulama criticised the television for presenting the opinions of 'modernists' on the status of Saudi women — another sore point with the ulama — and described them as anti-Islamic. After Ghazi al-Gosaybi, the Minister of Industry and Electricity, considered the doyen of the Saudi intelligentsia, was quoted as having said in an interview that the kingdom's modernisation had 'bridged over three thousand years of sub-human existence', Abdul Aziz al-Baz, whose ultra-conservatism often embarrassed the rulers, condemned Al-Gosaybi for insulting Islam, and in an article published in a Kuwaiti periodical demanded that he rescind the words ascribed to him and beg Allah's forgiveness.[34]

The accelerated urbanisation which began during Faysal's reign brought to the towns many illiterate or semi-literate, yet deeply religious Bedouin, including offspring of Ikhwan who participated in the 1927–29 rebellion. Some newly urbanised young Saudis attended the Al-Madina University with its largely foreign student

149

body, very low admission requirements, and Islamic character and curriculum. This university, run by foreign *salafis* and some ultra-conservative Wahhabi ulama who often condemned the evils of modernisation and western culture, became the focus of Saudi neo-fundamentalism. A Najdi *'alim* discussing the Mecca incident in 1980 said: 'An atmosphere favourable to Islamic heresy sprang up at Medina because of the presence of large numbers of foreign students.' One group there called for the rejection of 'interpreted' doctrines in favour of a return to the Islamic sources. 'The authorities expelled the foreigners and rehabilitated the Saudis, but after the death of King Feisal the heresies started up again.'[35]

As the frustration of the conservatives rapidly grew after the mid-1970s, the wave of neo-fundamentalism began to spread from Al-Madina to the Imam Muhammad ibn Saud Islamic University (Riyadh) and to the theology faculty in Mecca and the one at Riyadh's 'secular' KSU. Many of the *'alims* and the students (a sizeable percentage of whom were foreigners) of the above were openly critical of many of the innovations and western influences introduced by the government.[36] Yet, the most outspoken critics of the regime, it seems, were offspring of the Ikhwan and drop-outs from the modern education system, mainly of Bedouin origin, overwhelmed by the revolutionary changes which their society was undergoing. Disillusioned with the establishment fundamentalists whom they considered hypocrites corrupted by the regime, some turned to a synthesis of militant 'neo-Ikhwan' and Muslim millenarianism.

A son of an Ikhwan warrior who fought Ibn Saud, Juhayman ibn Muhammad ibn Sayf al-'Utaybi, an ex-National Guard NCO, attended lectures by the Najdi ultra-conservative *'alim* Abd al-Aziz ibn Baz at Al-Madina University. In 1974 the disillusioned Juhayman left Al-Madina for his native Qasim (Najd) followed by a handful of Bedouin, largely 'Utayba, and foreign students. In the coming years he preached his version of neo-Ikhwan ideology in the towns and oases of the Najd where his kinsmen, many of whom Ikhwan descendants, had settled. During this period additional university drop-outs joined his group and he managed to link up with militant neo-fundamentalist organisations in nearby Arab and Muslim countries.[37]

By 1978 Juhayman and his followers moved to Riyadh where they began to preach in several mosques against the evils of modernisation, insinuating that the regime was responsible for the corruption of Islam by foreign influences. The Saudi secret services always kept an eye on the activities of extremist religious fanatics. Thus, in the summer of 1978, Juhayman and about 100 of his followers were arrested and interrogated by the *Mabahith*; but they were released from jail after Ibn Baz and other ultra-conservative ulama interceded on their behalf, declaring them harmless crackpots.[38]

With the help of local *salafis*, Juhayman printed in Kuwait four pamphlets in which he emulated the Ikhwan's philosophy, attire and criticism of the 'corruption of Islam' by the rulers through modernisation. 'For Juhaiman . . . ulema and state had combined in a truly unholy alliance.' In a pamphlet that appeared in 1978 Juhayman wrote that the 'Nejd ulema had been bought. . . . Where is it that the ulema and sheikhs find their money, except through corruption?' 'How could the religious authorities be so prosperous without active financial support from the Royal Family?'[39]

About this time Juhayman convinced Muhammad ibn Abdallah al-Qahtani, a Bedouin theology student at Riyadh, that he was the expected *Mahdi*. Indeed, in the pamphlets which he published and distributed at the end of 1978 and in 1979, Juhayman refers to the coming of a *Mahdi* from the tribe of Quraysh (the Prophet's tribe) who would redeem the Muslim world. Indirectly he was accusing the Sauds of being usurpers, and not of Quraysh origin.

After ordering his supporters to gather in Mecca on the night of 19 November, at the end of the Muslim fourteenth century, Juhayman and about 400–500 of his followers, including some of their women and children, entered the grounds of the Mecca mosque with an arsenal of weapons and food supplies. On the following morning, they seized the Ka'ba *haram*, denounced the corrupt government of the Sauds and especially the ulama who supported them, and declared Muhammad ibn Abdallah al-Qahtani the 'expected *Mahdi*'.

It took the regime two weeks to crush the rebellion and regain control of the Ka'ba. The rulers awaited at first a *fatwa* of the ulama permitting the seizure of the Mecca mosque by force; but the Sauds were also indecisive and apprehensive of the reaction of the population and of tribal elements in the armed forces to the events. For their part, the rebels bravely fought off the superior forces which surrounded them, expecting that all believers who rejected the corruption of Islam by the Sauds would rally to the flag of the 'expected *Mahdi*'.

When granted, after debates lasting several days, the *fatwa* proclaimed by the ulama did not denounce the rebels for heresy but rather for using weapons in the holy Ka'ba and rising against a legitimate regime. Among the thirty leading *'alims* who signed the *fatwa* were, ironically, leading Najdi ultra-fundamentalists known for their opposition to modernisation, such as Abd al-Aziz al-Baz, Shaykh

151

Abdallah ibn Humayd, Shaykh Abd al-Aziz ibn Nassir ibn Rashid, and Shaykh Salih ibn Muhammad ibn Lahidan.[40]

In the meantime the shocked population were for the most part angry at the rebels for defiling the holiest shrine of Islam. It became clear that by choosing the Ka'ba as the site of their uprising the Ikhwan rebellion misfired.[41]

Despite the enormous forces which the regime brought to Mecca, it took a great effort to overcome the rebels and the cost in human life was terrible. Only on 3 December did the exhausted remnants of the Ikhwan, including Juhayman, surrender to the authorities. Their execution in the different towns of the kingdom several months later was generally considered appropriate and did not seem to arouse any sympathy.

While the legitimacy of the Saudi regime was being challenged in Mecca the authority of the House of Saud was threatened from another quarter by the unrelated eruption on 28 November of serious violence in the Eastern Province. The Shi'ites in Al-Hasa had increasingly been protesting since the 1950s against their oppression and discrimination by the regime. The success of the Iranian Revolution gave them new pride and encouraged them to press their demands for equality. In addition, Teheran repeatedly called upon them to rise against their corrupt rulers. The above, and the Shi'ites' proportion among Aramco's workers and the population of Al-Hasa, whose oil provided the kingdom's wealth, made the unrest in Al-Sharqiyya seem extremely dangerous for the regime.

THE SHI'ITES AND THE AL-HASA RIOTS (1979–80)

In the early 1980s it was estimated that the Shi'ites in Saudi Arabia numbered about 500,000, or nearly 10 per cent of the population. Other than enclaves in the Southern Region (Asir), an offshoot of Yemen, and a small community in the Hijaz, nearly all Saudi Shi'ites (Twelvers) live in the Eastern Province, and are concentrated in the oases of Al-Hasa and Qatif.[42] The region's Shi'ites are closely related to their co-religionists in Bahrain and Kuwait (some are of Najdi origin) and relations between them and most of their Sunni neighbours are relatively good.

After the rise of the Wahhabiyya in the eighteenth century, the Al-Hasa Shi'ites, considered by the *muwahhidun* worse than infidels, were constantly persecuted. When Ibn Saud reconquered the region from the Turks in 1913 its Shi'ites unsuccessfully sought the protection of the British in Bahrayn. They renewed this attempt in 1927 when, under pressure from the Ikhwan, the Wahhabi ulama instructed Ibn Saud to increase their oppression. Even though the treatment of the Shi'ites improved after the collapse of the Ikhwan rebellion, they were despised by the Sunnis, and were considered at the bottom of the Saudi social stratification. They were officially discriminated against by the authorities in many matters including employment, and prohibited from having their own mosques and judicial system. Above all they were prevented from holding public religious ceremonies, especially the *Ashura* processions commemorating the assassination of Hussayn ibn Ali in *Muharram*, the last month of the Muslim year.[43]

The development of the Saudi oil industry has had a most beneficial impact on the oppressed, largely agricultural, Shi'ite community of the Eastern Province. Many Shi'ites from the rural areas of the large Al-Hasa oasis, seeking employment and a better life, moved to the peripheries of the coastal 'oil towns': Dammam, Al-Khobar, Ras Tanura and Dhahran. Originally small, poverty-stricken, villages, these towns prospered and rapidly grew in size.[44]

Aramco's 'colour-blind' employment policy was not an outcome of moral principles but of necessity. The Shi'ites composed more than one third and possibly one half of Al-Sharqiyya's population and their work ethics are quite different from those of most Sunni Saudis who consider manual labour demeaning. For the Shi'ites, employment in Aramco, in most cases, was the only way to earn a decent living and to advance in life. Thus, by 1978, Shi'ites were estimated to make up more than half of Aramco's workforce and while institutes of vocational training elsewhere in the kingdom failed to attract students, the ones in the Eastern Province had more candidates than they could handle. In the 1950s, moreover, Aramco encouraged its more enterprising employees to provide the company with supplies and services on a contractual basis. Thus, it was instrumental in the rise of a relatively sophisticated Shi'ite middle class and intelligentsia alongside a socially aware working class.[45]

Aramco not only provided employment but also education, which was partly the reason for Al-Hasa's having the lowest illiteracy rate in the kingdom. Many young Shi'ites trained by the company or in schools established by it found their way to domestic and foreign technical institutions and universities. Indeed, by 1980 half of the students of Saudi Arabia's most prestigious university, the UPM, and the majority of those of King Faysal University (with campuses in Dammam and Hufuf) were Shi'ites. A high percentage of the students sent to study abroad by Aramco, and some by the Saudi government, were also Shi'ites, not to mention the ones who were supported by their middle-class families.[46]

Notwithstanding the above, the Shi'ites remained a discriminated, if not a persecuted, minority. The Najdi establishment continued to distrust and abhor the Shi'ites and considered them, despite their achievements, backward if not mentally retarded. The testimony of Shi'ites, whose doctrines are viewed as heretical, was not admissible in Saudi courts of law and units of the Bedouin National Guard were stationed in the province's main towns. A foreign correspondent observed in 1980 that 'Cultural discrimination is perhaps the most bitter for them. Shi'ite literature is banned and Shi'ite history is not allowed to be taught in the local schools and university.' The teaching profession, one of the permitted areas of employment for Saudi women, is closed to Shi'ites who are virtually excluded from all but the lowest ranks of the civil service and prevented from serving in the army and the security forces. A young Shi'ite told the same reporter: 'there are Sunnis, below them are Christians and below them are Jews; we are below the Jews.'[47]

Not surprisingly, the educated Shi'ites and 'working class' have become involved in trade unionism and radical nationalist clandestine movements since the 1950s. The emergence of a new Shi'ite middle class and intelligentsia provided the community with the means to protest against their treatment and discrimination. Thus, as early as 1960, a Shi'ite delegation petitioned King Saud about a defamatory article published by a semi-official periodical and demanded an end to discrimination against them. Tension among the Shi'ites increased in the 1960s simultaneously with the rise of pan-Arabism in Saudi Arabia. Shi'ite workers and intellectuals joined offshoots of the *Qawmiyyun al-Arab* (mostly the PFLP), the UPAP and the Ba'th and were involved in different anti-government activities.[48]

Although the older generation and part of the new Shi'ite middle class were reconciled to the gradual improvement in their position, the young and better-educated Shi'ites became progressively more militant and anti-Najdi. Their frustration was enhanced by the fact that revenue from 'their oil' was used to finance the accelerated development of Saudi Arabia in the 1970s, yet only marginally benefited their province.[49]

When Khalid-Fahd came to power in 1975 and 'liberalised' Faysal's policy, the Shi'ites benefited, to some extent, as well. More funds were allocated for the building of communications and industrial infrastructure in Al-Sharqiyya and to expand the province's education system, including the new King Faysal University in Hufuf and Dammam. A few Shi'ites were advanced in the administration and one was appointed in 1976 the head of the Jubayl industrial complex. Many Shi'ites benefited indirectly as well from Aramco's and the government's development projects and joined the Saudi middle class, but not its upper levels which were composed solely of successful Sunni businessmen, industrialists and contractors.[50] Yet in the eyes of the Najdi establishment, the Shi'ites remained a despised minority. Despite the measure of liberalisation in regard to Shi'ite religious practices, their *Ashura* processions were still strictly prohibited, nor were they allowed to have their own religious courts. Shi'ite graduates of the education system and universities met with difficulties in finding suitable positions in the government and were rejected by the armed and security forces.[51]

The growing unrest in the Saudi kingdom and the revolution in Iran were bound to have an impact on the large Shi'ite communities of Al-Hasa and of the Gulf Emirates. The 1978 violence in Al-Sharqiyya was followed at the beginning of 1979 by labour unrest in the oilfields and the oil towns. Aramco had indeed been expecting trouble in the region following the victory of the Islamic revolution in Iran and the propaganda broadcasts from Teheran aimed at the Shi'ite population in Arabia. Bahrain, with its Shi'ite majority, a short distance from the Saudi oil towns, experienced very serious riots in September 1979 which led to massive repression of Shi'ite and other radical elements. By November the *mujtahids* of Qatif and the nearby Shi'ite villages announced their determination to hold the *Ashura* processions in defiance of the government's prohibition.[52] Several days before the event news of the rebellion in Mecca galvanised the Al-Hasa Shi'ites. When the police attempted to disperse the large crowds who participated in the *Ashura* procession in Qatif on 28 November, the Shi'ites went on the rampage. The British-Saudi Bank was attacked, buses were set on fire and shop windows were smashed. The trouble spread to Sayhat and other Shi'ite settlements in the region and oil installations near Ras Tanura and Dhahran were sabotaged.

The rioting lasted three days. Demonstrators carried pictures of Ayatollah Khomeini and placards denouncing the House of Saud and the American imperialists. **They chanted anti-American slogans, demanded that Saudi Arabia stop supplying the United States with oil and that it support the Iranian Islamic Revolution. Others demanded the establishment of an Islamic republic in Al-Hasa.** The reinforced units of the National Guard, who had no love for the Shi'ites, opened fire on the demonstrators on several occasions. A total of seventeen people were killed, many were wounded and hundreds arrested.[53]

Apprehensive of the impact of the ferment among the Shi'ites and the Iranian Revolution on the security of its oil industry, the Saudi government immediately despatched Prince Ahmad, the Deputy Minister of the Interior (a Sudayri) to the Eastern Province. Ahmad prudently admitted that the regime had neglected the Eastern Province and discriminated against its Shi'ite population and announced the beginning of a new era. He promised massive investments in the development of Al-Hasa's economic infrastructure, education system and other services. Yet simultaneously, he warned the Shi'ites that if they continued to undermine law and order they would be severely punished.[54]

In spite of this, tension among the younger Shi'ites continued to rise. A visitor to the Eastern Province reported that the walls of the old town of Qatif were covered with graffiti denouncing the Sauds' regime and praising the martyrs of the *Muharram* riots. A declaration by Prince Na'if, the Minister of the Interior, that the Shi'ite rioting was of inconsequential importance added fuel to the fire, as did the anti-Saudi propaganda from Teheran. More politicised and resentful of the Najdi establishment, the younger Shi'ites were more receptive to the Iranian incitement. Indeed, the Islamic Revolution Organisation (IRO) claimed (in 1981) that it had deliberately prepared the continuation of the *Ashura* demonstrations in order to bring about the release from prison of all those arrested following the November riots. Violent demonstrations again erupted in Qatif and Al-Hasa following the Friday prayers on the first of February, the anniversary of the return of Ayatollah Khomeini to Iran. Anti-Saudi and anti-American slogans were chanted and students from the UPM set buses and private cars on fire, but Saudi banks were the main target of the demonstrators this time. Four people were killed, and many arrested, during this spate of rioting which also lasted several days.[55]

The Shi'ite rioting caused the regime to realise that it could not continue blatantly to discriminate against the Shi'ites. Previously prepared, but shelved, plans for the development of Al-Sharqiyya were now quickly implemented. A modern vocational training centre was opened in Dammam at the beginning of 1980. It was designed to produce technicians for the huge Jubayl industrial complex which offered attractive job opportunities for the local population. New commercial centres were built and Shi'ite businessmen were helped expand their enterprises. Some traditional administrators in Al-Hasa were replaced by university-trained technocrats and additional faculties were opened in the KFU.[56]

The above and the change in the authorities' attitude notwithstanding, discrimination against the Shi'ite population was not eradicated. Rather, the appointment of two Shi'ite officials to high, yet secondary, positions in the administration, and the relatively modest success of several Shi'ite businessmen (in many cases related to Aramco) underscored the fact that on the whole Shi'ites were still excluded from the medium and upper levels of the Saudi administration and economy and totally from the security and armed forces. At the UPM Shi'ites composed about half the student body, yet they could not be elected as officers of the students' union. Shi'ite requests that they be allowed to settle personal judicial matters such as inheritance according to their customs were rejected out of hand. Even though the authorities legalised low-profile *Ashura* processions, the Shi'ite leaders were warned against exaggerated expressions of grief, typical of such processions, which anger Wahhabi puritans.[57]

In September 1980, following the eruption of the Iran-Iraq War, the Saudi government substantially bolstered its armed forces in the Eastern Province. Security in the oil installations, relatively lax in the past, was markedly tightened. A new Ministry of the Interior security force was established solely to protect essential installations, largely in the oil province. The Shi'ite community in Al-Hasa, constantly incited by the revolutionary regime in Iran, and especially discontented elements among the intelligentsia, fundamentalists and workers, were closely watched, if not harassed, by the authorities. The GCC was formally launched in 1981 but security cooperation between Saudi Arabia and its Gulf allies was promoted by Prince Na'if even earlier.

Simultaneously, the development of the Eastern Province supervised by Prince Ahmad was accelerated. Between 1980 and 1982, roads were paved, schools built, sewage systems constructed and a hospital was opened. When King Khalid visited the province in November 1980, ostensibly to inaugurate the Jubayl naval base, he announced that one billion dollars were being allocated for 'public service projects' in Al-Hasa. All those incarcerated during the November 1979 and February 1980 riots were pardoned and a general amnesty enabled political refugees to return to their homes. The legalised *Ashura* processions which took place shortly afterwards went off without incident, with the security forces keeping out of sight, yet ready to intervene if the processions got out of hand.[58]

The regime's carrot-and-stick policy in Al-Hasa proved quite successful. The efforts to develop the region and grant its Shi'ite population the nearest thing to equality in a Wahhabi state were appreciated by most of the community. This, in addition to the quantitative and qualitative upgrading of the security forces, prevented an outbreak of serious anti-government activity in Sharqiyya in the following years, despite Iran's vitriolic anti-Saudi propaganda and support of subversion in the Gulf, and the impact of the Iran-Iraq War.

Yet, the unrest among the young Shi'ites and other radical elements in the Eastern Province persisted under the surface. Anti-regime, separatist, radical socialist or fundamentalist sentiments were now fanned by Iranian militant propaganda. An Iranian plot to destabilise the regimes of Bahrayn and Saudi Arabia was uncovered at the end of 1981, when Shi'ites trained in Iran were detained in transit in the UAE. Large quantities of weapons were uncovered in Bahrayn, and among the many who were arrested were Saudi Shi'ites who had undergone training in Iran.[59]

The Islamic Revolution Organisation (IRO) which began to operate in 1979 joined in the 1980s existing small Shi'ite workers and intelligentsia-supported Marxist, Ba'thist and pro-Iranian organisations in their limited anti-regime activities at home and abroad. Subversive activities continued in the coming years in Al-Hasa's towns and villages. Although suppressed by the Saudi security services with an iron fist, they are still active and have, it seems, many followers among the students and other Shi'ite elements.[60]

CONCLUSIONS: THE EVENTS OF 1979–80 AND THEIR RAMIFICATIONS

The limited activity of the Saudi militant opposition in the early 1980s focused largely on Al-Hasa. There, in addition to the IRO, Shi'ites are an important component of the relatively inconsequential Saudi leftist clandestine movements. Undoubtedly, the rapidly growing Shi'ite intelligentsia and working class (the nearest thing to a proletariat in Saudi Arabia) would be among the first to join an anti-Saud nationalist-radical revolution if it were to erupt. Yet, a Shi'ite uprising in Al-Hasa is, ironically, likely to consolidate Sunni support for the regime because of the latter's nearly universal dislike of Shi'ites, fear of fundamentalist Iran, and concern about Sharqiyya's oil revenue. The frustrated and dissatisfied Shi'ite minority represents, nevertheless, a threat, even if not a major one, to the regime because it constitutes such a high proportion of Al-Hasa's population and of Aramco's workforce. The Iran-Iraq War and Teheran's subversive and propaganda activities in the Gulf underscored this danger. Thus, beside stepping up security measures since 1980, Riyadh has accelerated Al-Sharqiyya's development and strengthened and improved its administration. Progressively, the regime was able to pacify, if not win the goodwill, of most of Al-Hasa's population, including the majority of the Shi'ites.

In retrospect the failure of the Mecca rebellion and the little support that the 'Ikhwan' won rather demonstrated that, in contradiction to other Arab and Muslim countries, neo-fundamentalism in Saudi Arabia appeals only to marginal elements. Most Saudis, especially the religious and conservative 'lower classes', are quite happy with the synthesis of 'puritanism', modernism and material prosperity provided by Al Saud and legitimised by the ongoing alliance between the latter and the ulama. Tribal loyalties, which began to erode at the time of the Ikhwan rebellion, moreover, proved of little consequence fifty years later during the Mecca incident. Indeed, despite rumours to the contrary, nearly all the Bedouin and the newly urbanised masses, including 'Utayba elements in the population and the National Guard, remained absolutely loyal to the Sauds. Yet, it is also clear that such support is conditional on the continued prosperity of the population and their satisfaction with the regime's performance.[61] Lately, such satisfaction has been eroding due, among other factors, to the decline of the kingdom's oil revenue.

The damage caused by the Mecca affair to the prestige of the Saudi regime was considerable. The Sauds, who took upon themselves the role of 'protectors of the holy places' when they conquered the Hijaz, were widely criticised for their inability to prevent the Mecca rebellion and their mishandling of its suppression. The prestige of the National Guard and of its commander, Prince Abdallah, was also tarnished because of its poor performance during the incident and the fact that some of the rebels' leaders previously served in it. Juhayman's condemnation of the royal family's corruption, the scandalous behaviour of many of its members and their association with infidels, did not go unheeded as well. Prince Fawwaz, the Governor of Mecca, accused by Juhayman of indulging in alcoholic beverages, was removed from office, some senior officers in charge of the kingdom's internal security were retired, and restrictions concerning the possession of spirits and the behaviour of foreign residents were more strictly enforced. Aware of the grass-root apprehension concerning the kingdom's rapid development, King Khalid and Crown Prince Fahd expanded the ulama's authority in relation to the supervision of the kingdom's Wahhabi character, demonstrating whenever possible their own piety and devoutness. As long as the ulama did not interfere with the kingdom's modernisation and politics, Fahd, disregarding the reaction of his western-educated technocrats, was willing to grant the ulama's demands concerning a stricter observation of the Wahhabi edicts and feigned asceticism.[62] Thus Summer Scott Huyette who has lived in the kingdom since the 1970s and wrote her PhD on Saudi Arabia's 'political adaptation' observed:

> They [the graduates of the three religious universities] remain the mainstay of the legitimacy of the Al Saud and they do not hesitate to make their presence felt, enjoining the king to adhere to the tenets of ibn 'Abd al-Wahhab, but their impact is felt more in the social than in the political realm.[63]

Fahd's new policy of course outraged the intelligentsia, particularly its Hijazi members and most of the western-educated technocrats.

NOTES

1. On the 'Sudayri Seven' see Chapter 4, note 76. The powerful Sudayri Bedouin clan of northern Najd is intermarried with all of the main branches of Al Saud. When the term 'Sudayris' is used in this book by itself it refers to the 'Sudayri Seven' and their descendants, also called the 'Fahd clan', and their allies among the Al Sudayri. See also G.S. Samore, 'Royal Family Politics', (Harvard University, 1984), pp. 347–55.

2. H. Shaked and T. Yagnes, 'The Saudi Arabian Kingdom', in C. Legum (ed.), *Middle East Contemporary Survey* (New York, 1978), Vol. 1, p. 570; *Al-Hawadith*, 4 April 1975 (interview with Fahd); *Al-Usbu' al-'Arabi* (Lebanon), 12 May 1975; Gh. Salameh, 'Political power', *Merip Reports*, 91 (October 1980), p. 20; J. Shaw and D.E. Long, *Saudi Arabian Modernization, Washington Papers*, No. 89 (1982), pp. 64–5.

3. H. Lackner, *A House Built on Sand* (London, 1978), p. 88; *Qaḍaya Sa'udiyya*, pp. 5–6; L. Blandford, *Oil Sheikhs* (London, 1976), p. 123. Letters to the editor criticising irregularities in the administration and local government appeared in the press: Shaked and Yagnes, 'Saudi', p. 570.

4. Buchan, FT, 5 May 1981, supplement. On special security forces and US assistance to the above reorganisation in 1975: D. Holden and R. Johns, *House of Saud* (London, 1982), pp. 518, 522. On US: Lackner, *House*, p. 173. The different grade amirs in the rural areas and the *'umda* (plural *'umad* — the neighbourhood head in the towns, similar to the village shaykh) became part of the Interior Ministry's security apparatus, being required to supervise all foreigners and irregular activities: *Al-Yamama*, 4

January 1984; Al-Selfan, 'The Essence of Tribal Leaders' Participation', (Claremont Graduate School, 1981), p. 153.

5. Ostensibly an economic cooperation organisation the GCC coordinated the security activities of its members. Following the outbreak of the Gulf War (1980) it also became a mutual defence organisation.

6. A. Bligh, *Succession in the House of Saud* (New York, 1984), pp. 90–1. Majid resigned in 1979, in protest at his ministry's meagre budget, and in 1980 became Governor of Mecca: J. Buchan, FT, 5 May 1981, supplement. *Al-Istikhbarat al-'Amma* should not be confused with *Al-Istikhbarat al-Kharbiyya* — military intelligence.

7. S.S. Huyette, *Political Adaptation* (Boulder, 1985), p. 126, also pp. 78–80, 126; Lackner, *House*, p. 73; Holden and Johns, *House of Saud*, p. 459.

8. Huyette, *Adaptation*, pp. 44, 78–9, 97; M. Field, *The Merchants* (London, 1984), p. 40; M. Field, FT, 10 September 1982; M. Field, 'Society', *Vierteljahresberichte*, No. 82 (1982), p. 218. On armed forces and large number of officers in mid-1970s: Gh. Salameh, *Al-Siyassa*, (Beirut, 1980), pp. 319–20.

9. I.M. Al-Awaji, 'Bureaucracy and Society in Saudi Arabia', (University of Virginia, 1971), pp. 232, 236; I.F. Alghofaily, 'Saudi Youth Attitude Toward Work and Vocational Education: A Constraint on Economic Development', unpublished PhD thesis (The Florida State University, 1980), p. 77; R. Lacey, *The Kingdom* (London, 1981), p. 443.

10. Within the 'Sudayri Seven' Sultan and Na'if are known for their conservatism and are occasionally critical of Fahd's policy, whereas Salman is considered a modernist and the closest to Fahd. H. Shaked and T. Yagnes, 'The Saudi Arabian Kingdom', in *Middle East Contemporary Survey* (New York, 1978), p. 566; J.S. Bilmastis, 'Small States as Major Power' (George Washington University, 1980), pp. 119–20.

11. 'New king's unenviable mantle', FT, 14 June 1982. On involvement of US Corps of Engineers: Salameh, *Al-Siyassa*, pp. 320–3.

12. Farmers made up about 20–25 per cent and nomads less than 10 per cent of total population in 1981 (Kingdom of Saudi Arabia, Ministry of Planning, *Employment by Sector* (Riyadh, 1982)), compared to a total of 75 per cent in 1970 (Shaker 'Modernization', p. 186). Also A.A. Shamekh, *Spatial Patterns of Bedouin Settlement in Al-Qasim Region Saudi Arabia* (Louisville, 1975), p. 149; Abir, 'The Manpower Problem' (Washington, DC, 1983), pp. 22, 25.

13. King Khalid benefited from defence contracts with Northrop in the early 1970s and Fahd's son Muhammad earned hundreds of millions of dollars in commissions on a telecommunications contract granted to Ericsson (Sweden) and Phillips (Holland). O.Y. Al-Rawaf, 'The Concept of the Five Crises' (Duke University, 1981), pp. 332, 350, 487; WP, 15 September 1975; *The Times*, 23 May 1980; WSJ, 3 May 1981; Lackner, *House*, p. 205; Field, *The Merchants*, p. 40.

14. Chung In Moon, 'Korean Contractors', *Middle East Journal*, Vol. 40, No. 4 (1986), pp. 625–9; S.E. Ibrahim, *The New Arab Social Order. A Study of the Social Impact of Oil Wealth* (Boulder, 1982), pp. 8–13.

15. Holden and Johns, *House of Saud*, p. 465; Samore, 'Royal Family', pp. 367–82.

16. Lackner, *House*, p. 72; 'The Saudi royal family', *Arab Press Service*

161

(Beirut), June 1978; Salameh, 'Political power', p. 13. As promised to the US Fahd increased Saudi oil production and coerced OPEC to reduce the 15 per cent rise it adopted at Doha (Qatar) in December 1976.

17. Of tension among the 'third generation' princes: Al Saud, 'Permanence and Change' (Claremont Graduate School, 1982), p. 146 (note 20), p. 166 (note 24); J. Nevo, 'The Saudi royal family: The third generation', JQ, No. 31 (Spring 1984).

18. Shaked and Yagnes, 'Saudi', p. 570.

19. Ibid., p. 568. On Abdallah's recognition as second Deputy Premier and next in line of succession: J. Buchan, FT, 5 May 1981, R. Johns, 14 June 1982, supplement. On poor state of National Guard: Salameh, Al-Siyassa, pp. 324–5.

20. A. Alyami, 'The Impact of Modernization' (Claremont Graduate School, 1977), pp. 165–6; Shaked and Yagnes, 'Saudi', p. 571; Al-Dustur, 8 August 1977.

21. J. Keegan, World Armies (New York, 1979), pp. 617, 620; A. Dawisha, 'Saudi Arabia's search for security', Adelphi Papers, No. 158 (Winter 1979–80), p. 7; A.H. Cordesman, 'Saudi Arabia, AWACS and America's Search for Strategic Stability', paper No. 26A (The Wilson Center, Washington, DC, 1981), p. 14; Shaked and Yagnes, 'Saudi', p. 567.

22. Abir, 'Manpower', p. 46. On consequences of different weapons, tactics and instruction on armed forces' efficiency: Abir, 'Saudi security', pp. 85, 89.

23. A. McDermott, 'Politics', FT, 20 March 1978.

24. Al-Ibrahim, 'Regional and Urban Development' (University of Colorado, 1982).

25. Al-Dustur, 4 February 1979; Handbook (1984), p. 51; Buchan, The Middle East (September 1980); Ma'riv (Israel), 5 December 1978: of alleged high ranking Saudi officer who deserted to Iraq; also Salameh, 'Political power', p. 21; Halliday, 'The shifting sands beneath the House of Saud', p. 39.

26. Of claim that the IRO was founded in 1974/75 and began its operations in 1979: Merip Reports, February 1985. Its radical leftist orientation was demonstrated by its participation in Cyprus in 1980 in a conference of Middle Eastern Marxist organisations: 8 Days, 23 May 1981; Al-Mawqif al-Arabi, 20 April 1981.

27. M. Collins, 'Riyadh: the Saud balance', The Washington Quarterly (1981), p. 207; Bligh, Succession, p. 93. Criticism of Fahd's oil and pro-US policies: Al-Watan al-Arabi (Beirut–Paris), 28 March 1980. On the impact of the Camp David agreement and the fall of the Shah of Iran: Salameh, Al-Siyassa, pp. 603–11, 670–4.

28. See below pp. 172–3.

29. Of the enfeebled clandestine 'parties' in the 1970s and early 1980s: Merip Reports, February 1985.

30. Holden and Johns, House of Saud, pp. 464, 519; Lacey, The Kingdom, p. 436.

31. Faheem, 'Higher Education', pp. 111–19; Hisham, 'Saudi Arabia and the Role of the Imarates' (Claremont Graduate School, 1982), p. 197; A.A.F. Al-Moammar, 'The Manpower Dilemma of Saudi Arabia',

unpublished PhD thesis (University of California, Irvine, 1983), p. 176; Buchan, FT, 5 May 1981; Field, *The Merchants*, p. 339; Holden and Johns, *House of Saud*, p. 519.

32. Al-Farsy, *Saudi Arabia*, p. 172; Al Saud, 'Permanence and change' (Claremont Graduate School, 1982), p. 152; S.E. Ibrahim, *The New Arab Social Order* (Boulder, 1982), p. 7; M. Collins, 'Riyadh', *The Washington Quarterly* (1981), p. 202; M. Field, 'Why the royal family is more stable than the Shah', *Euromoney* (October 1981).

33. *Handbook* (1984), p. 113. Solaim (S.A. Solaim, 'Constitutional and Judicial Organization in Saudi Arabia', unpublished PhD thesis (Johns Hopkins University, 1970), p. 169), a Najdi PhD, cabinet minister since 1975, wrote in 1970: 'There exists today a communication gap between ulama on one hand and the technocrats and intelligentsia on the other.'

34. Al-Rawaf, 'Five Crises', p. 361; Ibid., pp. 359–60; *Al-Da'wa* (Riyadh), 5.3.98 (A.H.), p. 45; *Time* (magazine), April 1978.

35. Holden and Johns, *House of Saud*, p. 517; *Handbook* (1984), p. 113. On masses of ultra-orthodox illiterate new townspeople: Fahd's interview in *Al-Safir* (Pro-Libyan. Lebanon), 9 January 1980.

36. Al-Rawaf, 'Five Crisis', p. 356; *Al-Mawqif al-Arabi*, 20 April 1981.

37. Holden and Johns, *House of Saud*, pp. 517–18; Ayubi, 'Political Economy', pp. 19–20. Of Juhayman's kinship to one of the leaders of the Ikhwan and membership of *Al-Mushttarin* splinter of the Wahhabiyya: *Handbook* (1984), pp. 49, 112.

38. Interview with Crown Prince Fahd, *Al-Safir*, 9 January 1980; Holden and Johns, *House of Saud*, p. 518.

39. Holden and Johns, *House of Saud*, p. 515; J.A. Kechichian, 'The role of the ulama', *International Journal of Middle East Studies*, Vol. 18, No. 1 (February 1986), p. 59; Buchan, 'Religious Opposition', pp. 120–3. For full text of pamphlets: Abu Dhurr (pseud.), *Thawra fi Rihab Makka* (Dar Sawt at-Tali'a, Kuwait, 1980), pp. 265–73.

40. A. Layish, 'Ulama and Politics in Saudi Arabia', in *Islam and Politics in the Modern Middle East* (New York, 1984), p. 51; Bligh, 'Religious elite', pp. 47–8; Kechichian, 'ulama', p. 68. Only one of the signatories was an Al-Shaykh.

41. King Khalid admitted that had the Ikhwan attacked his palace, the outcome of their rebellion might have been far more serious. Fahd reportedly also said that had the rebellion erupted in Jedda, a town of one million people, many newly urbanised with complex problems, the government would have faced grave consequences: J.J.Malone, 'The Politics of Social Change in the Arabian Peninsula: Observations in Kuwait and Saudi Arabia', a paper published by Near East Center, University of Arizona (Tucson, 4 December 1981), p. 21; *Al-Mustaqbal*, 15 December 1979; *Handbook* (1984), p. 302.

42. Hufuf, the Al-Hasa oasis capital, had a population (largely Shi'ite) of over 100,000 already in 1974: Al-Ibrahim, 'Urban Development', p. 362; also Anderson, 'Differential Urban Growth in the Eastern Province' (Johns Hopkins University, 1984); Field, *The Merchants*, pp. 81–4. Typical of politically-motivated absence of statistics is a claim by P.T. Kilborn, a NYT correspondent, that the Shi'ites 'range between 500,000 and 1.5 million' out of a Saudi population of about 11 million (?!): NYT,

9 February 1987.

43. Field, *The Merchants*, pp. 226–7, 231; Field, 'Society', p. 219; Field, 'Royal family'; Wahba, *Arabian Days*, p. 86; Buchan, 'Religious Opposition', p. 118; *Handbook* (1984), pp. 113–14; NYT, 3 January 1980.

44. A.H. Said, 'Saudi Arabia' (University of Missouri, 1979), p. 85; T.R. McHale, 'A prospect of Saudi Arabia', *International Affairs* (1981), p. 635; *Handbook* (1984), p. 113; Field, 'Royal family'; Anderson 'Eastern Province'.

45. FT, 5 May 1981; Field, 'Royal family'; Said, 'Saudi Arabia', p. 81. Aramco employed 12 per cent of Al-Hasa's workforce: Al-Ibrahim, 'Urban Development', p. 146.

46. B. Williams, FT, 5 May 1981; J.S. Rossant, NYT, 3 January 1980; Al-Ibrahim, 'Urban Development', p. 150. Paradoxically, anti-American sentiments were common among Shi'ites.

47. NYT, 3 January 1980, p. A2; also Field, *The Merchants*, p. 82; *Handbook* (1984), pp. 113–14; McHale, 'A prospect', p. 635. Of National Guard in Hufuf: Cole, *Nomads of the Nomads. The Al Murrah Bedouins of the Empty Quarter* (Chicago, 1975), p. 111.

48. See above p. 111 and *Handbook* (1984), p. 51.

49. Field, 'Society', p. 219; *Handbook* (1984), pp. 113–14. On inferior administration, social benefits, education and health services: Al-Ibrahim, 'Urban Development', p. 154; Said, 'Saudi Arabia', pp. 165, 238; Al-Awaji, 'Bureaucracy', p. 236; *Statistical Year Book* (1980), p. 182.

50. Al-Ibrahim, 'Urban Development'; also Chapter 3 above, pp. 44, 50. On rise in standard of living: Buchan, 'Religious Opposition', pp. 118–19. On Fahd's carrot-and-stick policy: *Al-Mawqif al-Arabi*, 20 April 1981.

51. NYT, 3 January 1980; *The Economist* (London), 29 September 1979; Ayubi, 'Political Economy', p. 14; *Handbook* (1984), pp. 113–14; Field, *The Merchants*, p. 83.

52. Field, 'Society', pp. 217–18; NYT, 6 December 1979; Salameh, 'Political power', p. 21; *Handbook* (1984), p. 51; N. Maridi, 'State systems and revolutionary challenge: Nasser, Khomeini, and the Middle East', IJMES, Vol. 17, No. 4 (November 1985), pp. 507–27.

53. Salameh, 'Political power', p. 21; Safran, *Saudi Arabia*, pp. 357–8; NYT, 4, 6 December 1979. The IRO later claimed credit for preparing the 'uprising': *Al-Mawqif al-Arabi*, 20 April 1981. On separatist tendencies in Al-Hasa: *Merip Reports*, February 1985.

54. Field, 'Royal family'; Buchan, *The Middle East* (September 1980); *Al-Mawqif al-Arabi*, 20 April 1981; NYT, 3 January 1980; B. Williams, FT, 5 May 1981; Anderson, 'Eastern Province', part II.

55. Salameh, 'Political power', p. 21; *Al-Mawqif al-Arabi*, 20 April 1981; Field, 'Society', pp. 218–19; NYT, 3 January 1980.

56. See Chapter 3 above p. 44. B. Williams, FT, 5 May 1981; Field, FT, 17 September 1982; Field, 'Royal family'; Buchan, *The Middle East* (September 1980).

57. FT, 27 September 1980; *Al-Hadaf* (PFLP), 18 April 1981, pp. 30–1, according to *Al-Masira* (publication of Saudi Workers Socialist Party). On a police circular (November 1980) on expected demonstrations on 'Jerusalem Day' following incitement by Teheran radio: *Al-Thawra al-Islamiyya*, October 1984, p. 38.

58. Field, FT, 17 September 1982; B. Williams, FT, 5 May 1981. On Saudi (Shi'ites?) anti-regime demonstrations in London and Washington: *Al-Mawqif al-Arabi*, 20 April 1981.

59. *Al-Yamama*, 2 April 1982, interview with Amir Na'if; NYT, 17–19 December 1981; FT, 21 January 1982 (quoting *Ittihad* — UAE); also FT, 29 March 1980, 17 September 1982.

60. See Chapter 8, p. 195, also note 45, p. 209.

61. Al Saud, 'Permanence', p. 114; Field, 'Society', p. 218. On marginal support for neo-Ikhwan among Bedouin students and government employees in November 1980: *Al-Mawqif al-Arabi*, 20 April 1981; Fahd's interview, *Al-Safir*, 9 January 1980. Of King Khalid's frequent visits to Bedouins in different provinces: *Al-Watan al-Arabi*, 28 March 1980. By the beginning of 1987 participants in the Mecca rebellion, among them 34 Egyptians who were jailed, were pardoned. The Egyptians were deported to their country: *Al-Ahrar*, 1 February 1987; *Al-Akhbar*, 1 February 1987.

62. On this subject: Crown Prince Fahd to *Al-Safir*, 9 January 1980; also *Al-Watan al-Arabi*, 28 March 1980.

63. Huyette, *Adaptation*, p. 117.

7

The Zenith of the New Elites' Power: A False Dawn (1979–83)

THE MIDDLE-CLASS ELITES' STRUGGLE FOR POLITICAL PARTICIPATION

By 1980 the Saudi school population was about 1½ million strong. As noted earlier, the number of students in Saudi universities exceeded 50,000 and an additional 15,000 were studying abroad.[1] Nearly 11,000 Saudis graduated that year from local and foreign institutions of higher education, the majority of whom joined the civil service, considered a prestigious employment. In addition to sixteen cabinet ministers, 2000 senior technocrats held a PhD or an MA (out of 1500 PhDs and 3000 MAs in the kingdom). Many other university and high school graduates joined the private sector of the economy and became members of the professions, businessmen, industrialists and contractors or are employed in their families' enterprises or by members of the above group in managerial positions.[2]

By the early 1980s it seemed that the new middle class, led by the technocratic 'aristocracy', had reached the zenith of its power. Although the ruling class did not grant them political participation, the 'new men' were largely absorbed into the system and formed a non-royal elite which exerted enormous power and competed for authority with the traditional non-royal elite. The technocratic upper crust shared indirectly in policy-making, by controlling the huge government budgets, by participating in cabinet discussions, or by acting as advisers to the informal royal *majlis al-shura*, not to mention their active role in their respective ministries. A frustrated Al Saud PhD student wrote in 1982:

With the influx of wealth and the necessity to administer

166

development plans, the role of the technocrats is expanding and their influence and power increases. Their administration of government tenders of billions of dollars make up their power base. Power among the technocrats tends to be concentrated in the hands of the ministers.[3]

The technocratic elite seemed to enjoy wealth and prestige in addition to enormous power and some, such as Zaki Yamani, were considered all-powerful in the West. They had gradually replaced the non-royal traditional elite as a source of influence since the mid-1960s as the central government had eroded the traditional socio-political institutions. Their role in the internal power struggle was often exaggerated by the foreign press. Their impact on the kingdom's foreign and oil policies, which manifested itself in 1979–80 crisis, was believed by some to be also a reflection of the technocrats' growing power. By the early 1980s many foreign observers and scholars believed that in view of their expanding ranks it was only a matter of time before the new elites would gain full political participation, or even replace altogether the Sauds' regime.

In reality, the technocrats, notwithstanding the honours and authority they enjoyed, remained senior executives and advisers to the King and the royal *majlis al-shura*, their power being totally dependent on the goodwill of those who appointed them. The *ahl al-hal wa'l-'aqd* jealously guarded the ruling class's monopoly of decision-making and retained the key positions in the cabinet essential for safeguarding its supreme authority. Although occasionally disagreeing with their mentors, aware of the limitations of their power, members of the technocratic upper-crust, especially the new Najdi executives, reconciled themselves to the situation. When the Minister of Finance and National Economy, Muhammad Aba'l-Khayl, for instance, was asked by a journalist in 1983 about the monarch's oft-repeated promises of constitutional reform, he directed him to 'someone higher up than a minister' — most probably meaning a member of *ahl al-hal wa'l-'aqd*.[4]

The rise of fundamentalism in Teheran and the 1979 neo-Ikhwan rebellion did not strengthen the intelligentsia's position but rather forced it further into the arms of the regime. With the example of Iran fresh in their minds, the new elites now feared a fundamentalist backlash aimed against modernisation and the secular (especially western-educated), middle class. Indeed, despite the constant expansion of their ranks, the importance of the Hijazi-led secular bureaucrats suffered a grave blow when Crown Prince Fahd decided to abort his relatively liberal policy and seek, whenever possible, the ulama's blessing for his modernisation programme. Although he still needed their cooperation to govern and develop the kingdom and to resist the conservative opposition within the ruling class, when it came to a choice between the new elites and the ulama, Fahd, considering the circumstances, chose the latter.[5]

Moreover, the new elites' growing criticism of the royal family's corrupt practices and extravagance, while many of the former benefited far more from the commission system and kickbacks, hardened the ruling class's opposition to 'democratise' the regime. It also accelerated the previously mentioned trend to prefer 'loyal' Najdi technocrats and civil servants to the jealous, politically sophisticated and conscious and religiously 'liberal' Hijazi bourgeois elite.[6]

Even before the Mecca rebellion was over, the rulers revived the committee charged with exploring ways and means of involving the new middle class in the political process.[7] On 10 January 1980, Crown Prince Fahd announced the government's intention to promulgate a basic law (based on the *Shari'a*), to establish a national *majlis al-shura* 'that would share with the cabinet the responsibilities of government' and to reorganise the provincial government. An eight-member committee made of ulama and conservative ministers headed by Prince Na'if was appointed by King Khalid on 18 March to study and propose a basic law (*Nizam Asasi li'l-Hukm*), a framework for a National Consultative Assembly and a Provincial Government Act *Nizam li'l-Muqata't*), with the aim of modernising the latter.

The new *majlis al-shura* of 50–70 members, it was claimed, was to represent the different powers in the kingdom: the royal family and the ruling class as a whole, the ulama, the technocrats and other educated elements. Yet the members of this 'National Assembly' were to be appointed and not elected. Their role in the government was limited to participation in the legislative process but they lacked authority to veto the King's decisions. The new *Nizam li'l-Muqata't* was to redefine the kingdom's provinces (and towns), their status and the authority of the provincial amir and his subordinate governors in all matters relating to their administrative unit not in the purlieu of the central government. On the day following King Khalid's previous edict, the King also appointed new amirs for the provinces of Mecca, Al-Qasim, Tabuk and Ha'il, all of whom were younger and capable sons of Abd al-Aziz. This was the beginning of a trend to strengthen the provincial government and expand the authority of its amirs, including some from the cadet branches of Al Saud, to some degree at the expense of the central government, reversing Faysal's policy in the 1960s and early 1970s.[8]

It was evident from the start that, even if carried out, this reform would not turn Saudi Arabia into a 'constitutional democracy'; indeed members of the *majlis al-shura* were to be largely appointed from among the old and new elites. This, Crown Prince Fahd stressed, was in line with the Islamic mode of government (*ahl al-hal wa'l-'aqd*), 'as the Koran was the country's constitution' and, Fahd claimed, 'when the government allowed voting in the local councils, the rich were always the winners.'[9]

In the spring of 1980, when questioned about the progress made by their 'constitutional' committee, Princes Na'if and Salman responded that it was still meeting regularly but underscored the fact that the committee was not preparing a constitution because 'the Koran is Saudi Arabia's constitution'. They hinted that an elective system of a sort might be recommended within the Provincial Government Regulation, but that it would not apply to the National Consultative Council. Fadh claimed in a press interview in March 1982 that the recommendations concerning the promised *majlis al-shura* would be implemented in a matter of months, although the committee's report was still not ready.[10]

Quite obviously, once the storm was over, the Saudi ruling class had no intention of enabling the new elites to share in decision-making. This policy was vindicated by the difficulties experienced by the Kuwaiti and Bahrayni rulers, who had experimented with a parliamentary system, including nationalistic but unwieldy members.[11]

Yet Fahd, who sympathised with the numerous middle-class elites, felt compelled at least to reassure them that he still intended to grant them some participation in decision-making, especially since he needed their cooperation. By reiterating previous promises of limited political reforms, the Crown Prince, in addition to responding to popular demands for participation in decision-making, wished to appease the new elites, especially the Hijazi middle class. This was also necessary because the ulama had won concessions which led to a more vigorous enforcement of Wahhabi laws and customs in the Hijaz and the Eastern Province.

The Saudi bourgeoisie — strength or weakness

As mentioned before, it appeared that the Saudi new elites were steadily becoming a power that could no longer be ignored because of its sheer size. By the early 1980s the technocrat-bureaucrats and the other components of the middle-class elites probably numbered hundreds of thousands.[12] Yet the new elites of the early 1980s were even less monolithic than in the 1950s and the 1960s. Rather, the differences that had emerged in the past, besides the Najdi-Hijazi cleavage, were now exacerbated. The new intelligentsia, especially of Najdi origin, was not necessarily socially liberal and supportive of reform. Most remained deeply committed to Islam and the Saudi way of life and critical of western life-styles. While a large number became very wealthy, the majority were well off and a minority just got by.

Western-educated technocrats who dominated the key positions in the government and its agencies and professionals were largely the ones most anxious to modernise the kingdom and generally impatient with its traditional institutions, including the quality of the domestic universities and their 'product'; but graduates of Saudi 'secular' universities, jealous of the former, though they supported modernisation and reform in principle, were more traditionally-oriented and introverted and therefore more concerned about the impact of modernisation on their society and culture. Graduates of religious universities and institutions, some of rural origin, were, as expected, the most conservative in their outlook and critical of many aspects of modernisation. They resented, moreover, the preference given by the government in the employment and advancement of their 'secular' (ḥadr), particularly the Hijazi middle class, counterparts and accused the foreign-educated intelligentsia of introducing westernisation into the kingdom which 'corrupted the principles of the Wahhabi state'. A foreign professor who had spent several years in Saudi universities described the cleavage in the following way: 'English and Arabic are forces which have powerful symbolic valence in Saudi Arabia; they stand for modern/traditional; secular/sacred; alien/comfortable.'[13]

The new elites were also polarised by social status determined by position, income, level of education, origin, and connections with the ruling class.[14] According to a source with access to official material, the number of 'technocrats' (bureaucrats) employed in the government administration and its agencies in 1980, was 173,290.[15] Only a tiny fraction (0.77 per cent) received the highest grade's monthly salary (SR 6491–11,460) of the civil service pay scale and belonged to the technocratic upper-crust, largely composed of graduates of western universities with masters or doctoral degrees.[16] About 21 per cent receiving upper-medium and medium grade salaries (SR 3076–6490) were mostly university-educated technocrats. Over 78 per cent of the civil servants received the lower grade of the monthly pay scale (SR 1610–3075) and were probably largely traditional civil servants, graduates of religious institutions and of the different levels of the modern educational system. The standard of living of the last group could be considered relatively low in the Saudi context, especially when compared to the other two groups of bureaucrats, or to their counterparts who opted for the less prestigious and more lucrative private sector. They thus belonged to the middle and lower rungs of the middle class. Clearly the interests and sympathies of such varied components of the 'new elites' were very diverse, adding to its weakness.[17]

It would be wrong to think of the middle-class elites as being synonymous with technocrats and bureaucrats. It was mentioned above that many graduates of domestic and foreign universities, especially the ones whose studies were financed by their families, became professionals, businessmen or entrepreneurs. Some of the most successful Saudi businessmen entrepreneurs, however, did not acquire a university degree or even a secondary or an intermediary school certificate. The many members of the lower middle class who run petty business enterprises such as small trucking and taxi ventures, petrol stations, shops, or who became paid sponsors (kafil) of foreign workers, often of Bedouin origin, obtained only a minimal education, if any. Obviously, in addition to the gap in wealth and standard of living between the latter and the middle-class elites, their interests and sympathies are also different and often opposed to the members of the intelligentsia and the upper-crust technocrats and wealthy businessmen enterpreneurs.

The 'lower class' Saudis between *dawla* and *ḥukuma*

The Saudi 'lower classes', with the exception of an insignificant element, faithfully support the regime, its policy and the conservative Wahhabi character of the Saudi kingdom. Their allegiance to the government of the Sauds (*ḥukuma*) goes back to the pre-kingdom era and has been maintained through the network of traditional socio-political institutions. Even after the establishment of the modern Saudi kingdom in 1932, townspeople, nomads and agriculturalists were still governed through their respective hierarchy of village, town, district and provincial amirs, tribal shaykhs (amirs)

171

and *'umad*. The leadership of the rural population was integrated in the regime's powerbase through numerous matrimonial arrangements and managed to somewhat preserve their influence in the rural areas and provincial government system.[18] The Saudi patriarchal system, moreover, provided for the needs of the largely nomadic rural society through the *majalis* system, welfare services, stipends, subsidies and employment in the National Guard, the armed and the internal security forces.

The accelerated development of the kingdom since the 1960s and through the first and second five-year development plans (1970–80), mainly benefited the townspeople though it sparked off rapid changes in the rural society. By creating attractive employment opportunities in the cities, moreover, it accelerated the urbanisation of the Bedouin and settled rural population. This, and the development of a centralised government administration, eroded the traditional socio-political institutions of the tribal society. Yet, the newly urbanised, on the whole, maintained their contacts with their tribes, villages and amirs. The third five-year plan (1980–85) gave the highest priority to the rural population with the aim of raising their standard of living to that of the townspeople and curbing the process of urbanisation. Indeed, the development of the rural areas is one of the major goals of the fourth development plan (1985–90), yet due to the economic recession by the mid-1980s circumstances had changed somewhat.[19]

Oil wealth and its distribution to all levels of Saudis through welfare services, subsidies and the like, and by the senior princes directly to their constituencies, helped maintain the links between the regime and the people. Al Saud continues to exercise its patriarchal rule based on patronage, marital ties with the important tribes and families, and personal relationship between the rulers and the ruled. Such contacts with the tribal rural and newly urbanised population are maintained through the hierarchy of amirs and other traditional institutions. Most important are the *majalis* held by the King, all the senior princes and their offspring, the leaders of the aristocratic families and the provincial and district amirs. The royal family up to the monarch is thus, at least in theory, accessible to the lowliest citizen. He can petition for, and receive, financial and other help, or may bring before the ruler for consideration any grievance or injustice which has been done to him. Individuals and groups also use the *majalis* to lobby for 'worthy' public and regional causes.[20]

Despite the erosion of tribal or regional loyalties through the extension of the central government services and urbanisation, the tribal

172

fraternity still eased the settlement of the individual *badu* or villager in the towns by providing financial support and/or the necessary connections in the new and foreign environments. Thus, although the authority of the traditional socio-political institutions of the rural population was often replaced by the bureaucrats of the central government (*dawla*) who now provide services and subsidies to the newly urbanised masses, the latter's allegiance (if not affection) is still largely reserved for the Sauds' regime (*hukuma*) and its representatives. The deeply religious new townspeople, who regularly attend the Friday sermons in the different mosques may occasionally hear the *imam*'s criticisms of foreign Muslim rulers, the *dawla* and the technocrats but, if anything, only praise of the Sauds' *hukuma*.

The distinction made by the Saudi 'lower class' between *hukuma* and *dawla* (both of which literally mean government) is quite significant. To the simple Saudi, *dawla* means the modern central government and its agencies, largely controlled by western-educated bureaucrats of urban origin. The central government, the expansion of its services and rapid urbanisation, brought the Saudi 'lower and lower middle classes', both largely of Bedouin origin, into daily contact with the *dawla* and made them dependent on services and subsidies provided by it. Nevertheless, the new townspeople usually dislike the bureaucrats who they considered inferior and crafty, and who in turn despise them. In contrast, the Sauds' paternalistic *hukuma*, which retains personal contact with them, they believe, respects them, understands their problems, and as befits a (paternalistic) government provides all their requirements whenever the need arises.[21]

Some authors espousing radical ideologies lament the fact that the Saudi 'lower class' are not really a lower class *per se* because the poorer Saudis have already elevated themselves to the middle class, or are in the process of doing so, and hence are not proper 'revolutionary material'.[22] The rapid expansion of modern education among the rural and recently urbanised Saudis, and the rise in their standard of living, may gradually bridge the differences between the Saudi 'lower class' and the new elite. But at present the new elites, mainly of urban middle-class origin, can expect little sympathy or support from the lower and lower middle-class Saudis in the former's bid to penetrate or overthrow the Saudi ruling class.

After the Mecca rebellion, Crown Prince Fahd was determined to reinforce, reorganise and modernise the provincial administration. Young, educated and dynamic princes gradually replaced ineffective provincial governors of the older generation. The new governors, using their royal connections and exploiting the priority given to the rural areas and less developed provinces in the third (1980–85) development plan, expedited the modernisation of their *manatiq* (provinces or districts). Thus, for instance, Khalid al-Faysal, appointed in the 1970s Governor of Asir, began to improve the situation in the backward and neglected Southern Region. No less impressive were the achievements of Prince Muqrin b. Abd al-Aziz, an ex-air force major, appointed (in 1980) as Governor of the Shammar (Ha'il) province (the Shammar tribes were considered Abdallah's matrilineal constituency, whereas Muqrin was probably Prince Sultan's protégé). Besides infrastructure and other development projects which he brought to the region, Muqrin took advantage of the generous subsidies to agriculture and the fossil water reservoirs in the region and brought prosperity to the population (of Muhammad al-Fahd and Al-Hasa, see below).

Obviously the ability to overcome the red tape of the bureaucracy and access to the King, the senior princes and ministers were essential to the success of the new *umara*; yet dedication to modernisation, efficiency and special relations between the rulers and the ruled, unlike in the case of the modern bureaucrats, were important as well.

The previously neglected, mainly nomadic Northern, the largely agricultural Southern, and the Shi'ite-dominated Eastern Provinces, were granted substantial budgets in the third development plan, and are undergoing accelerated development. In recent years their *umara* of all ranks were given additional responsibilities and authority and they were put in charge of the coordination of all projects initiated by the different ministries in their governorates. King Fahd believes, it seems, that this would not only compensate the loyal rural population for past neglect and curb migration to the big towns but that the modernised patriarchal provincial government may also counteract separatist tendencies and offset the influence of his conservative rivals, led by Abdallah, and of the new elites, who dominate the central government.[23]

NOTES

1. Of which 13,000 were enrolled in American universities. See above Table 3.3, p. 53.

2. Tables 3.1–3.5, pp. 51–5 above. Also *Al-Watan al-Arabi*, 28 March

1980; *The Middle East and North Africa 1980/1* (Europa Publication, London 1980), p. 661.

3. M. Al Saud, 'Permanence and Change' (Claremont Graduate School, 1982), p. 115; also O.Y. Al-Rawaf, 'The Concept of the Five Crises' (Duke University, 1981), pp. 364, 366–7, 370–1.

4. J. Kraft, 'Letter from Saudi Arabia', *The New Yorker* (4 July 1983), p. 50.

5. M. Collins, 'Riyadh', *The Washington Quarterly* (1981), p. 207; Gh. Salameh, *Al-Siyassa* (Beirut, 1980), pp. 525, 532.

6. On mutual accusations of corruption by new elites and Sauds: Al Saud, 'Permanence', introduction; Collins, 'Riyadh', p. 202; R. Lacey, *The Kingdom* (London, 1981), p. 491; Al-Rawaf, 'Five Crises', p. 367; T. Sisley, *The Times*, 23 May 1980; Chung In Moon, 'Korean contractors in Saudi Arabia', *The Middle East Journal*, Vol. 40, No. 4 (1986), pp. 626–7. Of regional cleavages about 1980 Ayubi ('Political Economy', pp. 13–14) says: 'Regional differences continue to be significant. The Hijaz-Najd dichotomy is a historical one that is unlikely to disappear overnight, since it still has an impact, especially on important political and military appointments.'

7. *Al-Safir*, 9 January 1980, pp. 9–10.

8. *Al-Watan al-Arabi*, 28 March 1980; *Al-Riyadh* (Saudi Arabia), 10, 13 January 1980; *Al-Siyassa* (Kuwait), 10 January 1980.

9. *Ukaz*, 22 March 1980; *Al-Riyadh*, 10, 13 January 1980; *Newsweek*, 21 January 1980; M.A. Saati, 'The Constitutional Development in Saudi Arabia', unpublished PhD thesis (Claremont Graduate School, 1982), pp. 113–14.

10. *Al-Jazira*, 8 September 1980, 19 March 1982; WP, 22 July 1980: on fermentation over 'constitutional reforms' among Saudi students in America; N.H. Hisham, 'Saudi Arabia and the Role of the Imarates' (Claremont Graduate School, 1982), pp. 301–3; R. Johns, FT, 14 June 1982, supplement.

11. The Kuwaiti Parliament suspended in 1976 was re-established in 1980.

12. Composed of technocrats, bureaucrats, professionals and the middle and upper ranks of the business community. According to Ottaway (WP, 27 November 1984) the number of registered members of the Saudi Chambers of Commerce in 1984 was 100,000.

13. E.B. Gallagher, 'Medical education', *Journal of Asian and African Studies*, Vol. XX, No. 1–2 (1985), p. 12; also H. Lackner, *A House Built on Sand* (London, 1978), p. 72; *The Economist*, 13 February 1982; H. Shaked and T. Yagnes, 'The Saudi Arabian Kingdom', in *Middle East Contemporary Survey*, (New York, 1978), pp. 566–7; A.H. Alyami, 'The Impact of Modernization' (Claremont Graduate School, 1977), pp. 165–6. See Chapter 3 above, pp. 45–6, 47–8, 49–50.

14. O.Y. Al-Rawaf, 'The Concept of Five Crises' (Duke University, 1981), pp. 279–81.

15. M.A.T. Al Saud, 'Permanence and Change' (Claremont Graduate School, 1982), p. 173.

16. A special, even higher, pay scale existed for ministers and those holding equivalent ranks.

17. See above pp. 44–5, 47–8, 125–6. The above salary scale is misleading. Nearly all the middle and upper-rung technocrats earn substantially more from business enterprises, which they or their families own, and from commissions and kickbacks related to their position and connections in the administration especially when connected to development or defence projects. For instance the interests of Hisham Nazir, Minister of Planning (now Petroleum) and of his family were represented by his brother: Moon, 'Korean contractors', p. 624, also pp. 625–7. On kickbacks, ibid., pp. 620–1.

18. Considered *ahl al-hal wa'l-'aqd*, the *umara*'s leadership occasionally participate in the consultations of the royal Consultative Council. On *'umda* see above Chapter 6, pp. 160–1, note 4.

19. Said, 'Saudi Arabia', p. 103; Field, FT, 10 September 1982; Al Saud 'Permanence' p. 114; F. Al-Nassar, 'Saudi Arabian Educational Mission' (University of Oklahoma, 1982), p. 60; T.A.T. Al-Hamad, 'Political Order in Changing Societies, Saudi Arabia' (University of Southern California, 1985), pp. 240–2. On revived influence of traditional rural elites: Chung In Moon, 'Korean contractors', *The Middle East Journal*, Vol. 40, No. 4 (1986), p. 628; Kraft, 'Letter', p. 51. On present standard of living of Bedouin: Craig's confidential report.

20. A royal decree issued by King Abd al-Aziz in 1952 grants every subject the right of access to his ruler, whether a tribal shaykh, a governor or the monarch himself, to present petitions or complaints or pleas for help: Al-Rawaf, 'Five Crises', p. 363; also ibid., p. 361. Al Saud ('Permanence', pp. 135, 155) claims that the stipends paid by Ibn Saud to the royal family were meant to help them exercise their role in grass-root politics. On King Fahd's *majalis*: Al Saud, 'Permanence', p. 137; Field, 'The balancing act . . .', FT, 12 August 1982, supplement; FT, 'Saudi Arabia . . .', 23 May 1984; Niblock 'Social Structure and the Development of the Saudi Arabian Political System', in *State, Society and Economy in Saudi Arabia* (London, 1982), pp. 82, 89; T.R. McHale, 'The Saudi Arabian Political System', *Virteljahresberichte* No. 89 (September 1982), p. 204, 'A prospect of Saudi Arabia', *International Affairs* (1981), p. 639. On King Khalid's *majlis*: R. Lacey, *The Kingdom* (London, 1981), pp. 510–20; H. Lackner, *A House Built on Sand* (London, 1978), p. 174. See also above, Chapter 1, note 13, p. 15.

21. On the attitude of the population to the bureaucracy see: A.D. Al-Mizjaji, 'The Public Attitudes Towards the Bureaucracy in Saudi Arabia', unpublished PhD thesis (The Florida State University, 1982), pp. V, 73–80; A.A. Al-Hegelan, 'Innovation in the Saudi Arabian Bureaucracy: A Survey Analysis of Senior Bureaucrats', unpublished PhD thesis (The Florida State University, 1984); also Said, 'Saudi Arabia', pp. 153, 165–6; Al Saud, 'Permanence', p. 138; D. Holden and R. Johns, *House of Saud* (London, 1982), pp. 460–1; Field, FT, 10 September 1982; Lacey, *The Kingdom*, p. 94.

22. R. Kavoussi and A.R. Sheikholeslami, 'Political Economy of Saudi Arabia' (University of Washington, 1983), pp. 32–5, 54–5; Lackner, *House*, p. 211; Halliday (*Arabia*, p. 69), another writer with a radical bias, explains the failure of the 1969 *coups* by the special relationship existing between the masses and the Saud *hukuma*. Also E.B. Gallagher, 'Medical

education in Saudi Arabia', Journal of Asian and African Studies, Vol. XX, No. 1–2 (1985), p. 11.

23. The new governors of the sparsely populated Bedouin northern border provinces were Prince Abdallah's allies: G.S. Samore, 'Royal Family Politics in Saudi Arabia' (Harvard University, 1984), p. 462. One of the above was Prince Abd al-Majid, until 1985 Governor of Tabuk and thereafter Governor of Al-Madina. On power of traditional elites' sponsors in provinces, especially Asir and Al-Hasa: Moon, 'Korean contractors', p. 628.

8

The Reign of King Fahd (1982–   ): Economic Crisis and Opposition

SUCCESSION, POWER STRUGGLE AND OIL CRISIS

King Khalid died in June 1982 and Fahd was declared King. Abdallah became Crown Prince and first Deputy Prime Minister, and Sultan second in line of succession and second Deputy Prime Minister. Although the prearranged succession went through smoothly, the struggle for power within the royal family soon re-emerged. Abdallah refused to surrender the command of the National Guard 'as Fahd has done [with respect to the Ministry of the Interior] when he became crown prince', thus violating the understanding that the Crown Prince and Deputy Prime Minister should not hold a cabinet portfolio. On his part, Abdallah strongly resented the fact that unlike Fahd, who ruled the kingdom in Khalid's name, he was given a title without real authority. Indeed, it was widely believed that the Sudayris were planning to get rid of him and appoint Sultan as Fahd's successor. Abdallah, moreover, opposed Fahd's inter-Arab and pro-American policy which found expression in his Eight Point Programme for the settlement of the Arab-Israeli conflict (August 1981) and cooperation with the USA during and after the Israeli invasion of Lebanon (1982/83). He disagreed as well with the kingdom's involvement with the GCC and Iraq, and advocated a more balanced policy with regard to Iran and in world politics in general.[1] Known for his integrity, the Crown Prince was critical of the moral corruption and extravagance in the royal family and the administration and was opposed to Saudi Arabia's (and OPEC's) high level of oil production and inflated budgets.

Most conservatives, including many princes, urban *a'yan* and tribal *umara*, supported Abdallah. Ironically, the group of western-educated, third generation princes led by Saud al-Faysal, seemed more openly to side with the anti-Sudayri camp this time, at least in matters relating to foreign affairs and oil policy. It was believed that they, as the majority of the intelligentsia, would have also preferred that the kingdom follow a more neutralist line in world and inter-Arab affairs. They were also displeased with the excesses and extravagence of members of the royal house, led by the 'Fahd clan', in a period of rising economic and social difficulties.[2] As their peers in the older generation of the royal family they were apprehensive of the Sudayris' power and their intentions regarding the succession to the throne in the future, but unlike them they believed that the time had come for the younger generation of the family to take over.

OPEC's substantial price hikes in 1980 caused demand for its oil and its price to decline in the coming years. This was due to the introduction of conservation measures and alternative sources of energy by the industrial countries and rising production of non-OPEC oil. In order to maintain OPEC's shaky unity and its leadership within it, Saudi Arabia gradually became the organisation's 'swing producer' (reducing production as demand for oil declined on the understanding that it would increase it when demand would rise). To the disgust of the majority of the middle class and the royal family, Saudi production thus fell from about 10 million barrels a day in 1981 to about 2 million by September 1985. Hence, the kingdom's revenue from oil, its main source of income, rapidly declined from 1982 onwards (see Table 8.1), due to the fall in production as well as decreasing oil prices. The intense power struggle in the royal family since 1982/83 was thus accompanied by growing criticism of Fahd's 'catastrophic' oil policy which was responsible for the kingdom's economic crisis on the one hand, and his 'inept' foreign policy on the other (America's diminishing credibility and increasingly pro-Israeli policy, declining Saudi role and prestige in the Arab world, and victorious Iran's inimical attitude to the Saudi kingdom).

The Saudi government's budget was largely dependent on its oil revenue because the regime was unable, and unwilling, due to religious and political factors to tax the population. Although Riyadh continued to draw upon its enormous financial reserves (estimated in 1981/82 at over 150 billion dollars), it was obliged, nevertheless, progressively to reduce its annual budget by 1986 to just over one half of its size in 1982/83 (see Table 8.2). Subsequently the kingdom's economic activity, largely dependent on government spending, totally stagnated.

179

Table 8.1: Saudi Arabia's oil revenues, 1981–1987

Year	Billion $
1981	109
1982	70
1983	37
1984	35
1985	22
1986	16–18 (est.)
1987	17.4 (est.)

Source: FT, 22 July 1985, p. 2, 21 April 1986, supplement, 30 April 1986, 2 January 1987; Knauerhase, 'Future', p. 75; IHT, 3 June 1986, 3–4 January 1987; NYT, 8 February 1987.

Table 8.2: Saudi Arabia's budgets, 1981/82–1986/87

Year	Billion $
1981/82	82.7
1982/83	91
1983/84	75
1984/85	75
1985/86	56.3
1986	45 (est.)
1987	45.3 (est.)

Source: Business America, 13 July 1981; Field, FT, 22 April 1985, supplement; Reuter from Riyadh, 5 January 1987.

The private sector, therefore, faced increasing hardships as business contracted and thousands of companies, some among the largest in the kingdom, faced cash-flow difficulties, and even went bankrupt. As their income declined the Saudi population naturally reduced its spending and *per capita* consumption of imported and locally produced goods. This did not affect only importers but also the domestic industry of which Saudi Arabia was so proud. The petrochemical and other oil- and non-oil related industries in which the Saudi government through Saudi Basic Industries Corporation (SABIC) and Petromin invested tens of billions of dollars, also proved far less profitable than expected. Although largely joint ventures with international concerns it is meeting with marketing and other difficulties. Thus, its contribution to the diversification of the kingdom's sources of revenue is still small compared to the enormous investment in it.[3]

For a country of about 8 million people of whom only about 5 million are citizens, the Saudi budget in 1986, in the vicinity of about 45 billion dollars, was still excessive. Yet for political reasons the Sudayris were unwilling to reduce significantly the enormous budgets of the Ministries of Defence and the Interior or halt the development of the poorer Northern and Southern regions and the problematic Eastern Province, neglected until 1980. Nor were they willing to make serious cuts in the enormous subsidies and extensive welfare services which the population enjoyed. Indeed, when the government attempted to reduce the unrealistic subsidies for agriculture and petrol, the move caused such an outcry, both among the 'poor' and the rich, that the regime quickly shelved its plans.[4] That nearly one million foreign workers and experts, including tens of thousands of westerners, left Saudi Arabia between 1982 and 1987 may have pleased the ulama and the nationalists, but it further aggravated the country's economic stagnation. Economic activity further declined — tens of thousands of villas and numerous office buildings in the kingdom's main towns stand empty; rents which provided many Saudis with a handsome income were halved, and in some cases reduced to about a third of their 1982 level.[5]

What at first was believed to be a temporary crisis developed into a prolonged economic recession. Paradoxically, while Saudi Arabia still employed nearly 2½ million foreigners, the phenomenon of unemployment among Saudi citizens re-emerged, due to a rejection of manual work and lack of skills. School-leavers met with increasing difficulties in finding employment, while salaries themselves were substantially reduced.[6] The vocational school system, however, which other than in the Eastern Province had failed to attract students, benefited from the new situation because of the country's continued need for technicians and mechanics. Yet most of the 'lower class' students, who enrolled in, and graduated from, vocational institutions, rather than replacing foreign mechanics and technicians became workshop and garage-owners, exploiting the generous government grants and hiring foreign foremen and workers.[7]

University graduates, who were previously snapped up by the civil service or the private sector, met with increasing difficulties in finding employment, particularly those with humanities and social sciences degrees, despite existing and new Saudi-isation laws. In the early 1980s most graduates of the domestic universities still insisted on employment in the metropolitan towns, although they had to settle for progressively less important positions. By the mid-1980s such graduates were considered lucky to get an appointment in the rural areas, which previously had been socially unacceptable. A higher percentage of students (although still less than a third) turned, therefore, to the more demanding and less prestigious (in Saudi Arabia) engineering and science faculties, the graduates of which could still find attractive employment opportunities. But as the recession became more severe in 1986, unemployment among university graduates became a common phenomenon and was openly discussed in the Saudi press. The universities tightened their admission requirements and reduced the students' grants. They also failed many more students in their final exams, allegedly on government instruction, to reduce the pressure on the authorities to provide suitable employment. (Indirectly this may improve the standards of Saudi universities.)[8]

By 1984 the Association of Chambers of Commerce and Industry (see further below), lobbied the King, albeit unsuccessfully, to disregard OPEC, increase the kingdom's oil production and subsequently government spending. They managed, however, to convince the government to promulgate a law which required foreign contractors operating in Saudi Arabia to purchase Saudi supplies, services and products to the value of at least 30 per cent of their contract. Later on the 'offset' requirements were expanded to include the setting-up of joint ventures with Saudi entrepreneurs in the field of high technology. Indeed, the fourth development plan (1985–90), is based on the assumption that the private sector will take over from the government the burden of diversifying the kingdom's economy.[9]

Apprehensive of the future of their country's economy, many Saudi businessmen preferred to invest their wealth (valued at 100 to 200 billion dollars) in the economies of the major western industrial countries. During the second conference of the Association of Chambers of Commerce and Industry in March 1985, King Fahd, hinting at the flight of capital from the kingdom, invited Saudi businessmen to take advantage of the infrastructure provided by their government and the absence of taxation in Saudi Arabia, to invest in their country's economy. The Saudi capitalists, however, accustomed to government support and subsidies, considered the ruler's request as a warning signal and many transferred additional funds to foreign countries.[10]

By the last quarter of 1985 the kingdom's economic situation had rapidly deteriorated and its oil production bottomed out at about 2 million barrels a day. King Fahd now gave in to the pressure of many senior princes, including his brother Sultan, and of the business community, and decided to abandon the kingdom's role as 'swing producer'. He accepted Zaki Yamani's strategy to step up Saudi production substantially and cause the price of oil to decline to under 20 dollars a barrel, and possibly as low as 15 dollars. This, it was hoped, would discipline OPEC members and coerce non-OPEC oil countries into agreeing to limit their production, enabling OPEC (and Saudi Arabia) to regain its 'fair share of the market'. This strategy, unfortunately for the Saudis, led to a total collapse of oil prices during the first half of 1986.

By the first months of 1986 the Saudi oil industry was generating a fraction of the revenue that it had generated a year earlier. The government, still insisting on providing the citizens with all the services and most of the subsidies that they had enjoyed in the past, was drawing upon the country's financial reserves at an unprecedented rate.[11] Unwilling to reveal its predicament to the public, the Saudi regime postponed the publication in March of its annual budget, still hoping for a surrender of the non-OPEC producers and a recovery of oil prices. Even earlier, it became common to all ministries to delay, as long as possible, payment to contractors and suppliers, a policy that enhanced the difficulties of local and foreign companies active in Saudi Arabia and led to many bankruptcies.

Rumours circulated in the kingdom that the government might be forced to cut its expenditures substantially and that salaried employees would have to forgo part of their pay. In a speech to the nation on 10 March King Fahd assured the population that ample funds were available for salaries and for all the planned expenditures of the government and that a new budget would be published within three months.[12] The promised budget, however, was not published until the end of the year, after the kingdom, in desperation, abandoned its 'fair share of the market' strategy, and sacked Yamani, and after OPEC agreed to limit its production and adopt an average price of 18 dollars per barrel.

Even then the kingdom's budget was based on the assumption that a deficit of about 13 billion dollars (probably about $17 billion) would be drawn from reserves. Prince Sultan, speaking for the government, hinted at opposition among the technocrats to the size of the budget which produced the deficit and justified it by the need to maintain the level of services and the standard of living to which the Saudi population was accustomed.[13] Obviously, at a time when the regime's prestige was at a low ebb, it was essential to keep the Saudi masses content to maintain their support for the Sauds.

FAHD'S POLICIES AND INTERNAL CHALLENGES

The consolidation of the Sudayris' hegemony

Aggravated by budgetary cuts the friction between the major two camps in the royal house reached a climax in the first months of 1983. By March it was widely alleged that Crown Prince Abdallah and the National Guard were involved in an abortive military *coup* against King Fahd. Although grossly exaggerated, the polarisation in the ruling class, as portrayed by the foreign media, seemed so acute that Abdallah broke the usual silence of the Sauds about royal family politics and prudently granted an interview to a Kuwaiti newspaper[14] in which he categorically denied the rumoured *coup* and his involvement in any plot against the King. He admitted, nevertheless, that serious differences existed in the royal house regarding the kingdom's internal (modernisation) and external policies (relations with the West, Iran, Arab affairs and oil) and, indirectly, he accused the King of indecisive leadership. This interview was partly an outcome of endeavours by the *ahl al-ḥal wa'l-'aqd* to reunite the ruling class at a time of growing challenges to the regime.

Faced with a financial crisis, subversion by a victorious fundamentalist Iran and rising discontent among the new middle class, the *ahl al-ḥal wa'l-'aqd* accelerated in 1983 and early 1984 their efforts to re-establish the royal family's wavering external consensus (*ijma'*). The outcome was the consolidation of the 'collective leadership' and the influence of the royal Consultative Council on decision-making, although the King retained his veto power. By 1984, the Sudayris no longer seemed to challenge Crown Prince Abdallah's position as heir apparent and commander of the traditional and relatively weak National Guard and agreed to let the latter grow alongside the armed forces. On his part, Abdallah refrained thereafter from publicly challenging King Fahd's policies and appeared to accept the latter's role as active Prime Minister.[15]

A most significant feature of Fadh's policies in the 1980s was the large-scale appointment of young members of the royal family and offspring of other components of the ruling class to important positions in the civil service, the *imarates* (provincial administration) and the armed and security forces. As mentioned above,[16] the recognised branches of Al Saud are estimated to be about 5000. With the Al-Shaykhs, Jiluwis, Thunayans and Al Sudayri, not counting the other components of the ruling class, they probably number

20,000 or more. Thus, candidates for such appointments abounded. In his previously mentioned PhD thesis, Mashaal Abduallah Turki Al Saud suggested (1982) the involvement of the numerous young members of all branches of the royal family in the administration. The latter, he claimed, are eager to assume an active role in the kingdom's government, are ideologically dedicated to the Saudi-Wahhabi character of the kingdom and, unlike the secular, nationalistic middle-class technocrats, have a vested interest in the survival of the regime. In conjunction with the above, he bitterly remarks that 'it is not enough to be so impressed of a PhD-holder who studied in a western university, without taking account of his ideological inclinations.'[17]

Shortly after the reconciliation in the ruling house, Mishari, one of the late King Saud's numerous sons, was appointed Commander of the National Guard in the crucial Eastern Province. This could be interpreted as an attempt by Abdallah to draw Saud's disgruntled sons into his camp. Yet, inasmuch as such a controversial appointment requires the authorisation of the royal *majlis al-shura* and the King, it was probably above all an outcome of efforts to reconcile the different branches of the royal family and to involve the younger princes and the disgruntled third generation Sauds in the kingdom's administration and the provincial government.[18]

When Fahd was Minister of the Interior (1963–75) he gradually began to implant members of the 'Sudayri Seven' clan, their clients and their 'tribal' relatives in the provincial government. Prince Salman (born 1936), probably the most capable and popular of his full brothers, was appointed amir of the key Riyadh province (*imara*) in 1962. The authority of such *umara* was partly to offset the influence enjoyed by Princes Khalid and Abdallah among the rural population. The gradual 'Sudayrisation' of the provincial government was further accelerated when Na'if took over from Crown Prince Fahd in 1975 the Ministry of the Interior, directly responsible for provincial government and governors (*umara al-manatiq*) and for improving relations with the tribal shaykhs (*umara*). In this Fahd was also occasionally assisted by commoner ministers loyal to him who controlled the budgets of the royal ministries allied with Abdallah (the case of Prince Majid who resigned as Minister of Municipal and Rural Affairs in 1979). In 1977 he exploited the reorganisation of the provinces, expanded substantially the Riyadh province governed by his brother Salman, and implanted Sudayri supporters in other provinces as well. Yet as Crown Prince, Fahd was also able to help appoint and advance his kinsmen and allies to key positions in the government and its administration. Thus, by the early 1980s we find Sudayris and their allies as Governors, Deputy Governors and senior administrators, of many of the kingdom's fourteen provinces and by 1985 of the Eastern Region as well.[19]

The same strategy was used by his full brothers Na'if and Sultan with regard to sensitive positions in the security and armed forces. Nearly all of Prince Sultan's sons serve as senior air force officers. Many sons of his Sudayri brothers and their royal and non-royal traditional elite allies (including the descendants of their uncles and many Al-Shaykhs) also hold key positions in the armed forces, the Ministry of Defence and other ministries. Indeed, the recently organised fourth command of the Saudi armed forces, the air defence command, was entrusted to Sultan's son Prince Khalid who was promoted to major-general. Sudayris and their allies hold as well all the important departments of the Ministry of the Interior and command its various security forces, including the feared *Mabahith*.[20]

The strengthening of the provincial government by Fahd, reversing Faysal's policy, eroded somewhat the authority of the central government, controlled by the new elites, was also consistent with the regime's policy of balancing centres of power. Yet the main thrust of this policy was aimed, it seems, at countering the influence of Prince Abdallah and, until 1982, of King Khalid and his brother Muhammad among the tribes and other rural elements. In addition to the *Mujahhidun* Department which paid stipends to the remnants of the Ikhwan, other early followers of Ibn Saud and their offspring, the Ministry of the Interior is also responsible for the provincial governments and their budgets and for coordinating the activities of their *umara*. Especially since 1980 (the third development plan) the ministry has been increasingly involved, together with the provincial governors, in the accelerated development of rural areas and the improvement of the standard of living of their population. The ministry's special security forces recruited their personnel largely from among the rural or ex-tribal population. These forces were rapidly expanded in the 1980s, after the budget for this purpose was sharply increased, and are approaching in manpower the strength of the National Guard. Plans for a 'security training city' were announced by the Ministry of the Interior in July 1981, giving Na'if a role in the defence and security fields equal to Abdallah and Sultan.[21]

Control of the Ministry of Interior thus enabled the Sudayris to consolidate and expand their influence among the rural and the newly urbanised lower middle class. Not surprisingly, with the resources of the Ministry of Defence, not to mention the monarchy, also at their disposal, the Sudayris have lured to their camp in recent years many Bedouin *umara*, regional *a'yan* and their followers, traditionally considered the powerbase of Crown Prince Abdallah.

The Sudayris, it seems, expanded their control to the media as well. Prince Turki ibn Sultan is the Director of the Department of the Press in the Ministry of Information, whose Minister, General Ali al-Sha'ir, is a Sudayri 'retainer'. Many editors of Saudi newspapers are Saudayris. Indeed, Fahd frequently utilises the Saudi television and radio to inform his subjects of their country's progress and problems. He often also visits universities and answers students' queries, and this policy, and what he says, is always prominently reported by the media.[22]

The consolidation of the Sudayris' powerbase at the expense of the Jiluwi-Al Faysal camp despite the seeming 'collective leadership, and the claimed erosion in the King's prestige, were evident in other areas as well. Prince Ahmad (the Deputy Minister of the Interior), and later his nephew Muhammed al-Fahd, took over after 1981 some of the duties of Abd al-Muhsin al-Jiluwi, the reactionary and ineffective Governor of the crucial Eastern Province. Nevertheless, by giving a free hand to the Wahhabi ulama and their Morality Police, Abd al-Muhsin enhanced the tension in the province where Shi'ites possibly constitute as much as half of the population and where many Americans and other Westerners employed by Aramco and the Ministry of Defence live. After an earlier attempt to get rid of Abd al-Muhsin failed, Muhammad al-Fahd and his cousin Fahd al-Salman (Prince Salman's son), officially replaced the governor and his deputy respectively at the beginning of 1985 and brought to an end the government of the Jiluwi 'dynasty' in Al-Sharqiyya. Another son of King Fahd, Saud, was appointed in 1985 deputy head of external intelligence (*Istikhbarat al-'Amma*) to offset the power of Turki al-Faysal, King Faysal's son.[23] Bandar ibn Sultan, the western-educated ex-pilot son of the Minister of Defence, was appointed in 1983 Ambassador to the United States. Thus, King Fahd provided himself with a direct link to Washington, bypassing the Foreign Office, controlled by Saud al-Faysal.[24]

It is evident that the Sudayris enjoy the support of a number of the 'younger' sons of King Abd al-Aziz and other members of the royal family, who themselves, or their offspring, were appointed to different positions in the government and the '*imarates* system' or granted special concession which enriched them. Even more important is the alliance between the 'Fahd clan' and the descendants of some of the King's paternal and maternal uncles and a major part of Al al-Shaykh. Hence, if a new confrontation were to break out in the royal house in regard to the monarch's authority or the problem of succession, the Sudayris could count on substantial support in the ruling class as well.

Yet, on the other hand, there is intensive opposition in the royal house, both among senior and frustrated 'third-generation' princes, to the Sudayris' dynastical tendencies and endeavours to monopolise power. Moreover, as was the case with Faysal between 1958 and 1960, the support for Fahd among the different components of the aristocracy and the middle class (and, it is alleged, even among the Sudayris) is conditioned on his success as a ruler which has been somewhat tarnished as a result of events in the region and the growing economic crisis in Saudi Arabia. In the last four years, due to the decline of oil revenue which in the past fuelled the kingdom's prosperity and contributed to its stability, government budgets have been halved (excluding those of the Ministries of Defence and Interior) and economic activity has stagnated. Saudi Arabia's prestige has also undergone a marked erosion due to its inability to continue subsidising the other Arab and Third World countries and to what seems to be a failure of its American-oriented policy. The proliferation of royal officials in the provincial government and of royal technocrats in the central government also antagonises the middle-class elites with whom they compete.

Tension within the royal family, though still covert, is on the rise, but is tempered by apprehension in the ruling class about the rising dissatisfaction among the middle class and the fear of Iran's power. The economic crisis experienced by the kingdom is partly attributed, as mentioned above, by elements in the aristocracy and the middle class, to Fadh's shortcomings as a ruler, and to the 'failure' of his foreign policy.[25] Similar accusations led to the dethroning of King Saud in 1964, yet Fahd is by far a better statesman and commands a broad support which he has managed to consolidate in recent years.

The regime and national integration

A 1982 doctoral thesis of Abdallah Ali Al-Ibrahim demonstrates how the modernisation of Saudi Arabia until the 1980s favoured the central province (Najd) and the more developed Western Province (Hijaz).[26] Development has, however, largely bypassed the desert Bedouin-inhabited Northern Region (Ha'il, Qurayat, Tabuk and Al-Jawf provinces), the agricultural Southern Region (Najran, Asir and Jizan provinces) and, to a lesser extent, the Eastern Province. The northern and the southern provinces still had in the early 1980s 'a high rate of illiteracy, inadequate access to social services and physical infrastructure'. Subsequently their population migrated to the more developed Western and Central Regions, where attractive employment opportunities and government services abounded. Minimal development and a very high rate of migration were particularly noticeable in relation to the densely populated Southern Region (over 25 per cent of the total Saudi population).[27] An offshoot of Yemen, it supplied cheap labour to Saudi rural and urban areas. In the sparsely populated north, the settlement of Bedouin nomads gathered momentum with the drilling of water wells by the Tapline contractors in 1949–50 and has been accelerated with government help since the late 1960s. Yet, in both regions jealousy of the prosperity of Najd and Hijaz caused frustration and alienation. In Asir, for instance, support grew for Nasserism in the 1960s and for radical nationalism and separatist tendencies in the 1970s and 1980s.[28]

The appointment of young, dynamic governors such as Khalid al-Faysal (Asir), Muqrin bin Abd al-Aziz (Ha'il) and Fahd bin Khalid al-Sudayri (who replaced his father, the 'Sudayri Seven' maternal uncle, as Governor of Najran), coincided with the third five-year development plan (1980–85) which gave the highest priority to the development of the peripheral rural areas. The generous development allocations and subsidies for agriculture completely changed the above regions by the mid-1980s and halted migration from them. Schools, clinics, hospitals, roads and airfields were constructed, running water, electricity and telephones were introduced, land was redistributed, and the standard of living of the population was noticeably improved. Attempting to promote national integration and win the favour of the rural population, King Fahd insisted that despite the drastic cuts in the government's budget in the mid-1980s, development allocations for the Northern, Southern and Eastern Regions should remain a priority.[29]

Comparatively speaking, the Eastern Province experienced some development in the 1960s and 1970s due to the oil industry and Aramco's operations, yet its Shi'ite population was the most discriminated against in the kingdom. After the 1979–80 riots and the rise of Iranian subversive activities in the Gulf, Prince Ahmad was instructed by Crown Prince Fahd personally to supervise the speeded-up development of the Eastern Province and to improve the treatment and inferior status of its Shi'ite community. Moreover, Fahd and King Khalid (and after 1982 King Fahd) regularly visited Al-Sharqiyya's major towns, meeting with their sectarian leadership and business communities and with the students and faculty of its two universities.

The instability in the kingdom following Fahd's succession and the rise of subversion in the Eastern Province in 1982–83 caused the regime to accelerate its effort to develop the region, improve the standard of living and abolish the inferior status of the Shi'ite community. Following a visit by King Fahd to Al-Sharqiyya in the summer of 1983, it was decided to give priority to developing parts of the Eastern Province with high Shi'ite concentrations, especially the towns of Qatif and Hufuf which did not benefit from the oil boom. Simultaneously, in the face of the intensified activities of leftist supported workers and intellectuals and pro-Iranian Shi'ite organisations, the government accelerated the construction of a National Guard town near Dammam and a 'military town' near Hufuf and reinforced the security forces in the province.[30]

The pace of development activity in the Eastern Province in the years 1980–85 was the most intense in the kingdom, surpassing that of Najd and Hijaz. Airfields, ports, hospitals, schools, roads and other facilities were feverishly constructed all over Al-Sharqiyya. The Jubayl super-modern oil-related industrial centre became operational and was followed by three industrial sites around the town of Dammam.[31]

The appointment of his son and nephew as Governor and Deputy Governor may have been prompted by royal family politics. Yet Fahd probably intended Muhammad, his able (and controversial) son, to accelerate also Al-Hasa's development and reduce sectarian tensions in the province during a difficult period for his regime, when it was vulnerable to the effects of Iran's victories and the economic recession. Prince Muhammad and his deputy introduced a new style in the government's relations with the Shi'ites and endeavoured to convince them that they were now to enjoy full citizen rights. The Governor and his deputy visited members of the community and made Shi'ite leaders welcome in their *majalis*. A special effort was made to win over the Shi'ite new elites and students, who in the past tended to be the most radical.[32]

Prince Muhammad's enlightened policy met with difficulties, however. Predictably, the economic recession gravely affected the Eastern Province. Aramco (and its affiliate companies) the largest single employer in Al-Sharqiyya, was forced to adopt severe austerity measures and substantially reduce its workforce.[33] Moreover, the local Sunni religious establishment exploited the heightened influence of the ulama over the Sauds to incite the Sunni population and administrators against the Shi'ites; the *muttawwa'in* increasingly flexed their muscles when dealing with the Shi'ite community. The attempt by Prince Ahmad, and later his nephew Muhammad, to elevate the Shi'ites to an equal position to that of the Sunnis was totally rejected by the local conservatives. Traditionally strongly anti-Shi'ite, the Wahhabi *'alims'* revulsion for this sect was now rekindled by the Gulf War, Iran's fundamentalist anti-Saudi propaganda and the activities of extremist elements among the Shi'ites. In sermons and lectures in the mosques and public institutions, through publications and even the official media, the local ulama lashed out at the religious habits and beliefs of the Shi'ites, characterising the latter as infidels 'more dangerous than the Zionists and the Communists'.[34] In the mid-1980s, having regained their self-respect and confidence, the Shi'ite leadership and middle class were no longer willing quietly to accept such incitement. Hence, they signed a petition to the King demanding his personal intervention and the punishment of those responsible for the semi-official campaign against them.

The regime and the ulama, 1982–86

It has been pointed out earlier that the events of 1979–80 caused the Saudi rulers to grant the ulama greater latitude in the supervision of the moral-religious conduct of the kingdom's citizens and foreign residents. The ulama's support for the legitimisation of the regime seemed even more important in a period of rising fundamentalism in the Muslim world. Indeed, by the late 1970s Crown Prince Fahd had become convinced of the wisdom of accepting some of the ulama's demands concerning the enforcement of Wahhabi religious practices, as long as the religious establishment did not attempt to interfere with the kingdom's development and conduct of government. In reality, however, the pace of modernisation was slowed down in the early 1980s, and in some areas there was a marked regression from the relative liberalism introduced in the 1970s.[35]

After his succession in June 1982, Fahd, not known for his piety in his younger days, attempted to improve his relations with the ulama. He now met (as did his predecessors) with the religious establishment in a weekly *majlis* and frequently consulted them on various matters. Inasmuch as he encouraged them to 'codify' laws 'in accordance with the needs of modern life' (within the context of the *Shari'a*) he also prudently supported their efforts to protect the kingdom's Wahhabi character and 'Saudi way of life.'[36] This meant, *inter alia*, that the largely uncouth *muttawwa'in* of the Morality Police were permitted to intensify the enforcement of Islamic Wahhabi laws in the kingdom's towns. Even westerners in the Aramco enclaves in Al-Sharqiyya were now exposed to their interference and not immune to *Shari'a* punishment and, as mentioned above, their harassment of the Shi'ites was stepped up. King Fahd's policies also resulted in the expansion of religious studies within the 'secular' education system, stricter separation of sexes in the universities and reduced employment opportunities for women (despite the increase in female school and university graduates and the country's dependency on a huge foreign workforce).[37]

As he advanced in age and gradually assumed the full responsibilities of government, Fahd, it seems, had begun to appreciate the importance to the regime's stability of the conservative orientation of the Saudi populace and its acceptance of the principles of 'Islamic government' propagated by the ulama. Confronted by rising criticism of his regime by the intelligentsia and fundamentalists and increasingly also by the 'lower classes', King Fahd decided to encourage the reorganisation and modernisation of the archaic Directorate for Islamic Propagation in order to improve the 'indoctrination' of the masses. Obviously, the monarch hoped that better trained and educated *muttawwa'in* would also be more palatable to the new elites. His policy resembled, to a degree, that of Faysal who brought the ulama into the fold of the establishment, yet Fahd lacked Faysal's pious reputation and authority and therefore could not force the ulama to accept his wishes.

Fahd's earlier readiness to safeguard the kingdom's 'Wahhabi character' and his declared opposition to 'westernisation' helped win the ulama's cooperation. The Hijazi ulama, exasperated with their dominant narrow-minded Najdi counterparts, and the younger ulama in general, were particularly receptive to Fahd's ideas. Yet even the ultra-conservative Najdi *'alims* were willing, even keen, to modernise the religious propagation apparatus and advance Fahd's indoctrination policy.

At the apex of the religious hierarchy, Shaykh Abd al-Aziz b. Muhammad Al al-Shaykh, the head of the Committees for Encouraging Virtue and Preventing Vice, considered the most reactionary body in the kingdom, was thus co-opted by the King to modernise and upgrade the 'Morality Police'. Returning to the original concept of the *muttawwa'in*, he undertook to train them for Islamic propagation and expand their activities in the different provinces in cooperation with the Ministry of the Interior. Simultaneously, Abd al-Aziz al-Baz, the reactionary President of the Administration of Scientific Study (religious) Legal Opinions, Islamic Propagation and Guidance, also deployed his organisation to help the King's efforts to indoctrinate the rural population.[38]

By the mid-1980s King Fahd not only appeared as the protector of the special character of the 'Saudi-Wahhabi theocracy' but, making up for past reputation, he made an effort to project the image of an ideal Islamic ruler. Indeed, in October 1986 he even officially adopted the title 'servant of the holy places' (*khadim al-haramayn*) instead of 'His Majesty' (yet three months later Dr Abd al-Aziz al-Khowayter, the Minister of Education, a conservative technocrat, replaced Hassan b. Abdallah Al al-Shaykh as Minister of Higher Education); inasmuch as Fahd needed religious legitimacy at a time when his credibility was undermined, the establishment ulama also had a vested interest in the continuity of the stability of his government. This was needed to maintain the kingdom's Wahhabi character and the ulama's position as its guardians in the face of criticism by 'secular' nationalistic new elites and, ironically, also by the militant 'neo-Ikhwan'.[39]

While members of the royal family continued to indulge in excesses, the economic recession was progressively eroding the standard of living of the less affluent Saudis. The newly urbanised masses were particularly affected by the recession and have also become more aware of the extravagances of Saudi princes. The dissatisfaction of members of the rural and urban 'lower classes' is expressed through letters to the editor, often published in the Saudi press. A non-Saudi Muslim scholar, who visited Hijaz during this period, remarked that 'The sermons at Friday prayers in Mecca and Madina are filled with parables of Omar, the second Caliph, who was known for simple living and humility.[40]

RULERS AND OPPOSITION IN THE MID-1980s

The resurgence of militant opposition

The succession of Fahd to the throne, and the struggle for power in the ruling class, signalled a resurgence of the activities of militant fundamentalists and leftist-nationalist circles in the kingdom, but especially in Al-Hasa. To make things worse, Saudi Arabia became the target of subversion and propaganda campaigns initiated by Iran and, to a lesser degree, by Syria, the PDRY (until 1984) and Libya. Radio broadcasts and agents of the above countries agitated against the royal family and the Sudayris in particular, underscoring the reactionary or anti-Islamic character of their regime, their corruption and the squandering by the Sauds of the country's vast oil wealth.[41]

In his press interview in March 1983, when questioned about the imprisonment in previous months of numerous Saudis, Crown Prince Abdallah admitted the fact but claimed they were drug traffickers. Saudi opposition and leftist Arab press on the other hand claimed that students, intellectuals, workers and members of the armed forces in Najran, Hijaz and particularly in the Eastern Province had been incarcerated and accused of participation in an 'abortive *coup*' and that some Saudi students of foreign universities who had returned to their country were also detained. The organisations involved in the 'plots' against the regime, it seems, were largely the Union of Democratic Youth, the Socialist Workers Party, and the Shi'ite-dominated IRO (*Al-Thawra al-Islamiyya*).[42]

By the 1980s, most of the original radical opposition organisations such as that of Nassir Sa'id (who was abducted by the Saudi intelligence services from Beirut in 1980), People's Democratic Party (formerly UPAP), the Free Saudis, and the offshoots of the Arab Nationalists (*Qawmiyyun al-Arab*), were replaced by, or developed into, a number of small, extreme leftist-oriented or Marxist ones. These included the Saudi Communist Party, the Socialist Workers Party of the Arabian Peninsula (related to the Palestinian PFLP), the Union of the Democratic Youth (related to the Palestinian PDFP) and a Syrian-related Ba'thist Party. Each had, it seems, several hundred supporters among students, intellectuals and workers, largely in the Eastern Province but also in Hijaz and Asir (and in the Saudi diaspora whose publications became the main source for information about their existence). The most important, however, judging by its publications and the number of members put in jail, was the Shi'ite-dominated IRO. The latter combines Iranian fundamentalism and radical socialism as its ideology and is probably Iranian supported.[43]

While exerting efforts to develop and improve the standard of living in Asir, the northern border regions and the Eastern Province and striving to mollify and grant equality to the Shi'ite community, the regime intensified its suppression of the militant opposition organisations. This was facilitated by the modernisation of the Saudi security services through closer cooperation with the GCC countries.

As early as 1981 the Saudi government signed an agreement with France for the installation of a central computer with a databank connecting the security services in the capital with terminals in all airports, seaports, and other major towns and the provinces. The project was later entrusted to Americans, who trained 400 Saudis for the National Information Center (*Markaz al-Ma'lumat al-Watani*) of the Ministry of the Interior. With the help of the Center's computers, the Passport Department and the recently introduced identity cards, the ministry is now able to supervise the millions of foreign residents in the kingdom and the Saudi citizens. In addition, the government now requires the *'umda* of each neighbourhood, as it does of the amirs of rural areas, to serve as representatives of the security services, in addition to their normal functions.[44]

Thousands of suspected members and sympathisers of the militant opposition groups, mainly in the Eastern Province, were questioned and hundreds incarcerated between 1982 and 1984. This is evident from a list of several hundred political prisoners from the Eastern Province (but not Hijazis and Asiris), arrested by the authorities between 1982 and 1986 (constantly updated), appearing in pamphlets published by Shi'ite and leftist-oriented Saudi opposition circles in London and New York. These pamphlets distributed in 1986 allege that the number of Saudi political prisoners is about 900.[45]

A new wave of arrests of Saudi and non-Saudi militants residing especially in its Eastern Province and suspected of membership in the IRO and different leftist organisations, began at the end of 1984. Many foreign Arab employees, mainly Palestinians, it is claimed, were deported from the kingdom and replaced by Pakistani and other non-Arabs. Their deportation followed increasing evidence of cooperation between the Marxist factions of the PLO (who broke away from the organisation in the meantime), their Saudi counterparts and Shi'ite fundamentalist organisations in Lebanon and the Gulf. This cooperation led in 1984–85 to hijacking attempts on

Saudi airlines, attacks on Saudi diplomats and embassies abroad, and efforts to smuggle weapons and explosives into Saudi Arabia from neighbouring countries and Lebanon. Among those arrested were, it is alleged, students, intellectuals, members of the armed forces, workers and Aramco employees. The fact that 'Committees for the Defence of Political Prisoners in the Arabian Peninsula', which mushroomed in England, the USA and in some Middle Eastern countries, were supported by the publications of both the Saudi Shi'ite IRO and Arab nationalist-leftist organisations, vindicates the belief of such cooperation in recent years.[46]

The small militant opposition organisations in Saudi Arabia (possibly with the exception of the IRO), focus largely on the Eastern Province. Other than their operations abroad, the main activity of the militant organisations in the kingdom is the distribution of leaflets. Occasionally they also sabotage police and government vehicles, plant bombs and attack the security forces.[47] Their potential danger, nevertheless, is not overlooked by the Saudi authorities. Severe security measures were instituted, therefore, in airports, government and military installations and offices, and even in hotels. Indeed, a special force was established at the end of 1984 to protect such installations, whereas Aramco further strengthened security measures in 1986 protecting the residential enclaves of its American and other western employees.[48]

Despite the above, it is evident that the 'carrot-and-stick' policy of the Saudi regime is proving rather successful. The majority of the Shi'ites are satisfied with the new policy of the regime, although they would like to see further improvement in their status and the job opportunities opened to them. Sympathy for Iran's Islamic revolution among the Shi'ites has declined.[49] The size of the anti-regime organisations operating in the kingdom in the mid-1980s is far smaller than the size of the militant opposition of the 1950s and 1960s. Their operations are inconsequential, and to judge by the tone of the publications of the Committees for the Protection of the Rights of Political Prisoners in the Arabian Peninsula, the authorities were able to arrest most of their activists.

Fear of Tehran's propaganda and its military success, the vulnerability of the Saudi oil industry, and the size of the Shi'ite community in Al-Hasa, were probably responsible for the more liberal policy introduced by the Saudi authorities in the Eastern Province. The success of this new policy, which led to Al-Sharqiyya's rapid development and accelerated the growth of its Shi'ite middle class, will partly depend on the recovery of the oil industry and an improvement in the kingdom's oil revenues.

Middle-class elites in the mid-1980s — from cooperation to confrontation?

Far more serious than the militant opposition is the growing discontent with the regime of the middle-class new elites, whose size and potential power has increased year by year. Their displeasure, especially in the Hijaz, emanates, as was to be expected, partly from the intelligentsia's being excluded from political power, while the ulama were pampered and granted additional authority. Businessmen and entrepreneurs were resentful in the past of the numerous princes who competed with them or often forced themselves upon them as patrons or partners. Yet, as long as the kingdom prospered and everyone got a share of its wealth, they reconciled themselves to the situation. But as recession began to set in, both merchant-entrepreneurs and technocrats became increasingly outraged with the 'corrupt and extravagant Sauds' who were wasting the kingdom's patrimony and increasingly monopolising business opportunities and key positions in the civil service and provincial administration. The Hijazi new elites, moreover, are angered by the obvious preference given by the Sauds to their Najdi counterparts (and to Najdi ulama).

Always the staunchest supporter of modernisation in the inner circle of the ruling class, and sympathising with the middle-class new elites, King Fahd believed that their *de facto* exclusion from any participation in the kingdom's political system was the major source of their frustration. When he had tried to advance their cause in the past, however, he met with strong opposition of the *ahl al-ḥal wa'l-'aqd* and the ulama. The former opposed him because they believed that a change in the kingdom's political system would eventually erode their power, and the latter, because they were convinced that if the new elites were to gain power they would be in the position to accelerate changes in the character of the Wahhabi-Saudi state. Lacking Faysal's power and prestige, Crown Prince Fahd, bound by the golden rule of consultation and consensus, gave in to pressure. He hoped, nevertheless, that in the long run the royal house and the ulama would accept his proposed 'Islamic' national *majlis al-shura* and grant the new elites minimal participation in decision-making. Even when he opted for the ulama's support rather than that of the new elites in 1979–80, Fahd endeavoured to keep the middle class within the regime's powerbase by reiterating his support for elusive National Consultative Assembly.

Fahd was cognisant of the revolution which Saudi society had undergone as a result of the development of a modern educational system. Though far from constituting a cohesive class,[50] the middle-class elites, largely Hijazi and Najdi and to a lesser degree from the Eastern Province, numbered several hundred thousands. Indeed, in addition to bureaucrats (about 200,000) and professionals, the Association of Chambers of Commerce and Industry representing middle and upper-level merchants and entrepreneurs had in 1984 a membership of about 100,000 in 18 branches in the kingdom's main cities.[51]

The growth of the Saudi Association of Chambers of Commerce and Industry is a case in point. The association is a legacy of the pre-Saudi Hijaz. Its nucleus was the Jedda chamber whose members after 1925 served in the new administration and proved most helpful to Ibn Saud and useful to his regent Faysal in dealing with foreign representatives and the kingdom's trade. When Faysal became King in 1964 members of the Hijazi Chamber of Commerce assisted him in developing the economy and modernising the kingdom. The organisation truly blossomed, however, in the 1970s, when it benefited from Saudi Arabia's rapid development and its enormous oil wealth.

The council of the Saudi Association of Chambers of Commerce, representing the upper echelons of businessmen, industrialists and contractors, is located in Riyadh. It **plays an essential role in consolidating middle-class support for the royal family and subsequently is believed to enjoy considerable influence over the regime**. It is the only major organisation in the kingdom to elect its officers (two-thirds of its governing board are elected and a third are appointed by the Minister of Commerce), has its own publications, and is permitted complete freedom within the scope of its interests.[52]

Still opposed to any form of professional organisation, the Saudi government in recent years gave its blessing to professional congresses of university professors, engineers, doctors, pharmacists, chemists and others, whose numbers in the kingdom had grown dramatically over the last fifteen years. In the first congress of engineers, which took place in Jedda, some participants proposed that the congress request government permission to form a professional organisation. Although the proposal was not adopted by the congress, it was another milestone in the process of consolidating the new elites' power in Saudi Arabia.[53]

Even before he was enthroned, Fahd attempted to win the conservatives and the ulama's backing for a watered-down formula that would enable the middle-class elites to participate in decision-making. Using Ibn Saud's tactic of confronting orthodoxy with Koranic precedents (or the lack of them), Fahd instructed Prince Na'if, in charge of the committee for 'political reforms', to extract from the Koran all the verses (about 200) relating to the principle of *shura*. These were to serve as a guideline for the proposed 'Islamic' National Consultative Council. Within a month of coming to power, King Fahd vowed that

> the principles of the basic system of government and the consultative council . . . will, God willing, be in the forefront of the issues of concern to me.. . . This will be accompanied or preceded by moves to bring to completion the necessary measures to put into force the provinces' law.[54]

Obviously Fahd, wishing to consolidate his regime, was keen on winning the support of the middle class. But once again, in the face of the royal family's and the ulama's opposition to a change in the status quo and in view of the stronger role which the royal Consultative Council exercised in decision-making since 1983, the matter was again shelved. Iranian victories over Iraq, the growing unrest in the kingdom, and the deteriorating state of the economy were probably partly responsible for the submission by Prince Na'if of his committee's recommendations in mid-1984. Those included a 'Basic Charter of Government' (Koranic constitution) and the modernisation of the provincial administration. Each province was thus to have a partly elected assembly, some of whose members were to be members of the proposed, largely appointed, National Consultative Assembly.

On 12 September 1984, a tender was issued for the construction of the *majlis al-shura* building. Shortly afterwards, in an interview with the London *Sunday Times*, King Fahd declared that the planned National Consultative Assembly 'whose members will be appointed, will begin to operate in the first months of 1985'. The role of the new 'parliament', Fahd continued, would be to 'express opinion and supervise the execution of government policy' and thus 'ensure the participation of the people in government'.[55] In April 1985 the King again reassured his people that he intended to establish the promised National Consultative Assembly soon, which would be 'composed of members drawn from the proposed partially elected provincial councils'.

Although the King meant well, the delay in the implementation of his promises, it was argued by his supporters, was again largely the result of the strong opposition with which they met in the ranks of the conservative members of the ruling class and the religious establishment.[56] Leading intellectuals, on the other hand, called this explanation a farce, claiming that the rulers could easily overcome the ulama's opposition had they truly wished to do so. Indeed, nothing was said since mid-1985 about the 'Islamic' National Consultative Assembly. Rather, after the militant-nationalistic Kuwaiti Parliament was dissolved in mid-1986, partly under Saudi pressure, the likelihood that the Sauds would voluntarily agree to grant political participation to the middle-class elites further diminished.[57]

The tension between the middle class and the regime and even between the latter and the technocratic upper-crust reached a new climax immediately after Fahd's succession. Not only did the King ignore his promises to grant them political participation while increasingly appointing university-educated princes to high positions, but the economic-financial nexus which held the middle class within the regime's powerbase was also beginning to crumble. As the kingdom's oil revenue plunged from 109 billion dollars in 1981 to about 16 billion in 1986, the Saudi budget was reduced from about 91 billion dollars in 1982/83 to an estimated 45 billion in 1986. The balance was made up from income from other sources and from the kingdom's financial reserves. These, considered by the new elites their national patrimony, particularly in view of the limited success of the costly Saudi industrialisation programme in the 1970s and early 1980s (aimed at diversifying the kingdom's economic base), shrank from over $150 billion in 1982 to about $40 billion at the end of 1986 (liquid assets, not including unredeemable loans to Iraq and Third World countries).[58]

Ironically, while the merchant community and entrepreneurs were displeased with the government for serving as OPEC's 'swing producer' and reducing government spending, the middle-class elites as a whole were critical of the regime's inflated 'political budgeting'. The size of the Saudi budget, many claimed, had no economic justification and was a by-product of the avidity of members of the royal family and the need of the Sauds to 'buy' constituencies (middle-class elites included) and political influence in the Arab countries and the world.

As the kingdom's financial situation deteriorated, leading members of the technocratic upper-crust, largely Hijazis, often disagreed with the royal Consultative Council and the aristocratic cabinet member over policy matters. Some non-royal ministers even dared challenge policy decisions related to finance made by their royal mentors. They, and the middle class as a whole, increasingly resented the excesses of members of the royal family, their 'corruption' and the system of commissions (sponsorship), and coerced partnerships, which enriched the ruling class (and the middle-class elites) but inflated the kingdom's budget and the cost of its development. These excesses continued unabated at the same time that, to the detriment of the population, ministries (excluding Defence and Interior) were instructed to trim their expenditures, salaries were cut and bankruptcies became common.[59] To make things worse, members of the ruling class frequently expressed contempt for the technocrats and claimed that their policy, or inefficiency, were responsible, at least partly, for the difficulties which the kingdom faced.

The dependency of the middle-class elites, the technocratic upper-crust included, on the whims of the Saud rulers, became now even more apparent when cabinet ministers and leading technocrats, previously considered 'the pillars of the government', the majority of whom were Hijazis, resigned, were dismissed and even 'exiled'. In most cases they were replaced by 'loyal' Najdi and other technocrats or by civil servants who were the Sudayris' old retainers.[60]

The first commoner to resign from the government in protest (unheard of in the past) was Abd al-Aziz al-Qurayshi, a member of a prominent Hijazi merchant family and the head of SAMA (holding the rank of cabinet minister). Al-Qurayshi's resignation was caused by his strong objection to the proposed inflated budget for 1983/84, which would further drain the Saudi financial reserves. He was soon followed by Muhammad Abdu Yamani, the Asiri Information Minister, who was dismissed because of the displeasure of the ulama and the Sauds with the way that he handled the domestic media and the coverage of the international press relating to the royal family power struggle. His dismissal was strangely linked to his ignorance of subversive activity in his home province (Asir).[61]

The most significant cabinet change was the dismissal in 1984 of the 'leftist'-oriented Minister of Health (previously of Industry and Electricity), Dr Ghazi al-Gosaybi, universally regarded the leader of the Saudi intelligentsia. Al-Gosaybi, from an Al-Hasa merchant family of Najdi origin which had been instrumental in the province's conquest by Ibn Saud, believed in the ability of the Sauds and the new elites to coexist, yet was critical of the extravagance of the ruling class. He finally clashed with Prince Sultan over his misappropriation (in Gosaybi's opinion) of the enormous defence budget. Always supportive of Fahd's modernisation policy, he also praised him for truly delegating authority to his commoner ministers and his handling of the government, compared to Faysal's era. He naively hoped for the monarch's support in the quarrel with the Defence Minister, which Gosaybi considered a matter of principle. When disappointed, he dared express his feelings in a poem which he managed to publish in a Saudi daily.[62] For this act he was dismissed and practically exiled to Bahrayn when appointed Ambassador to this principality.

The case of Dr Al-Gosaybi notwithstanding, the most publicised dismissal of a senior Saudi technocrat was that of the world-famous Zaki Yamani, the Petroleum Minister, followed by the firing of his Hijazi friend and associate, Abdul Hadi Tahir, the head of Petromin (with the rank of a minister). Yamani's dismissal in October 1986 proved, if proof were needed, of how insecure in their position were the leaders of the technocratic elite and the middle-class elites as a whole, when they incurred the displeasure of the Sauds.

Yamani was hand-picked by King Faysal (in 1962), as were many of the Hijazi commoner technocrats who served in the Saudi cabinets in the last two decades. This in itself did not endear him to the Sudayri ministers and the ulama. Yet his loyalty, expertise and international prestige made him invaluable to Fahd. Despite occasional rumours about his declining popularity in Riyadh since the late 1970s, he persevered in his work. His position was seriously undermined, however, when in 1984, during a period of serious crisis in the oil market, he strongly objected to Prince Sultan's 'oil for Boeings'[63] and similar barter deals. Yamani believed that such transactions, meant to channel commissions to the constituencies of the Defence Minister and to other princes, would jeopardise the kingdom's credibility in the oil market and its financial stability. When in 1986 his strategy for regaining Saudi Arabia's and OPEC's 'fair share of the market', authorised by the royal Consultative Council, proved counter-productive and oil prices declined to as low as 8 dollars a barrel, Yamani was summarily dismissed by his patron Fahd, though the King had supported his plan from its inception.

The Hijazis watched their position slipping away while the power of the new Najdi intelligentsia and royal technocrats grew in the kingdom's economy, bureaucracy, armed services and cultural leadership. This seemed even more threatening because of the continuing pre-eminence of the conservative Najdi ulama (to the detriment of the Hijazi ulama) whose influence, in addition to the traditional political censorship, increasingly stifled intellectual debate in religious and social matters. The Hijazi technocrats, merchants and entrepreneurs viewed Yamani's dismissal as another symptom of the decline of their position and the Najdi-isation of the government and economy, which followed King Faysal's assassination.[64]

The seat of the modern government had been removed from Hijaz to Riyadh during the reign of Saud. It was followed in the 1970s by the migration of the headquarters of most foreign enterprises and several domestic ones from Jedda to Riyadh. The pattern repeated itself with most major banks in the early 1980s. By the mid-1980s, after the Foreign Office moved into its new headquarters in the capital, it was the turn of the foreign embassies, the forerunners of which were established in Jedda in the period preceding the Saudi conquest of the Hijaz, to move to Riyadh.[65] The departure of the last group was received by the sophisticated and traditionally extrovert Hijazis as the supreme insult, particularly because the traditionally introvert and xenophobic Najdis had discouraged westerners until the 1960s even from visiting Riyadh. Some Hijazis bitterly remarked that if possible, the Najdis would have removed the holy towns from the Hijaz to their province as well.

It is unlikely that the Hijazi middle class entertain separatist tendencies (although some tiny groups do), and cut themselves off from the kingdom's oil wealth. Yet constituting the largest element of the new elites, and relatively the most liberal and modernist (compared to their Najdi counterparts), they have become the vanguard of the 'nationalist' middle-class critics of the Sauds' regime (such sentiments also nourish, for some time, on the growing success of the Najdi entrepreneurs and merchants and the total domination of the religious establishment by Najdi ulama). Indeed, as the recession in the kingdom spiralled, the exasperation of the Hijazi-led middle-class elites with 'the traditional royal system of acquiring and distributing wealth', the Sauds' 'feudal system of government', and their handling of the economic crisis, markedly increased. A seasoned journalist[66] visiting Saudi Arabia in 1985, sensing the rising frustration of the intelligentsia with the regime and the power of Najdi conservatism, wrote:

203

A group of university professors in Jeddah watched television in disgust as one of the country's young princes, Abdulaziz, was shown touring Disneyland. 'They're cutting my salary 30 per cent, and I am forced to watch this kid in Disneyland,' one of them said.

The military as a component of the new elites

The modernisation and expansion of the Saudi armed forces[67] since the 1960s made the House of Saud even less dependent on the traditional power brokers. It also reduced, by the 1970s, the importance of the lightly armed, undisciplined and inefficient National Guard, the conservatives' source of power. Younger members of the ruling elites increasingly joined the armed forces, especially the air force, and many were appointed to key positions in the latter.

Despite the enormous investment, which was spent in the 1970s largely on infrastructure for the Saudi armed forces (incidentally enriching many members of the ruling class) and to a lesser degree on the air force, the Saudi military remained weak and inefficient. They were also dependent on a polyglot host of foreign advisers, technicians and mercenaries.

The multi-billion, qualitative and quantitative upgrading of the armed forces planned and executed with American, French and British help, particularly since the mid-1970s,[68] necessitated the recruitment of many thousands of better educated officers, and skilled NCOs, which the oligarchy was incapable of providing. This process was further accelerated in the 1980s as an outcome of Teheran's victories and subversive activities. The chronic shortage of suitable Najdis and related tribesmen to handle the progressively more sophisticated weapons, and apprehensive of turning its armed forces into a 'foreign legion', the regime was forced to enlist educated Hijazis and technically skilled Al-Hasa Sunnis. By setting up extensive security services and appointing many royal officers to key positions, employing numerous foreign advisers and security experts (Americans and Europeans) and foreign mercenaries, the regime hoped to reduce the possibility of a military *coup*.[69] Plans to introduce universal (male) compulsory military service, reiterated by Prince Sultan possibly due to the pressure of the middle class, were repeatedly postponed because the regime prefers to keep the armed forces relatively small, loyal and manageable, through selective recruitment. The army, unlike the trusted National Guard, moreover, is largely kept in military garrisons in the peripheries of the kingdom.

The likelihood of an emergence of 'Young Turks' in the Saudi armed forces seems at present relatively remote, in view of the system of checks and balances instituted by the rulers, the elaborate security services and the substantial benefits enjoyed by officers and ranks.[70] Nevertheless, its many middle-class officers add another dimension to the new elites–ruling-class tension.

As revenue from oil and other sources fall short of the government's expenditures, and the kingdom's financial reserves continue to erode, the exasperation of the middle-class elites with the Sauds continues to rise. The newly cemented alliance of the royal house with the ulama for which the King opted, *inter alia*, to counter the growing power of the middle class, further exacerbates the latter's dissatisfaction, as does the 'Saudi-isation' of the central and provincial government at a time of growing unemployment among the new intelligentsia. In the present circumstances, the *ahl al-ḥal wa'l-'aqd*, apprehensive of the ramifications of change in the kingdom's power structure, are even less likely to voluntarily grant the middle class participation in decision-making which, it fears, could lead to a rapid erosion of the Sauds' hegemony. Yet, their continued exclusion from political participation further antagonises the new elites and militates the younger elements in this powerful and large component of the Saudi society. The ability of the regime to further withstand their growing pressure to share in decision-making will depend largely on what will happen to the oil market in the near future, on the continuous support of the 'lower classes', and on the level of solidarity within the royal family.

NOTES

1. J. Kraft, 'Letter from Saudi Arabia', *The New Yorker*, (July 1983), p. 53; *Al-Tayar* (Iraqi opposition, London), 27 June 1984, p. 1. Fahd's eight-point plan, a departure from the traditionally passive Saudi policy, was abandoned in the face of Syrian opposition. Indeed, despite important steps 'to bring Egypt back to the Arab fold' Riyadh, to this day, refrains from renewing openly its relations with Egypt (unlike Jordan, Oman, Sudan, Morocco and even Iraq), which it badly needs to counterbalance the Iranian threat.

2. R. Johns, FT, 14 June 1982, supplement; WP, 27 March, 31 May 1983; *Al-Tayar*, 27 June 1984; Kraft, 'Letter'; *Al-Hurriyya*, 3 April 1983.

3. On widescale bankruptcies: FT, 21 April 1986, supplement, p. II; IHT, 4 June 1986. On crisis in truck and car assembly industry: *Ma'riv*, 8 March 1987. On SABIC: MEED, Special Report, July 1984, pp. 61, 67; *The Economic Intelligence Unit* (EIU), No. 3 (1986), Country Report — Saudi Arabia, p. 4; R. Knauerhase, 'Saudi Arabia faces the future', *Current History*, February 1986, p. 75. Most of the workforce, other than managerial, of Jubayl and Yanbu is foreign.

4. Ottaway, WP, 27 November 1984; NYT, 28 January 1986; *Al-Shahid* (Teheran), 23 October 1985; WP, 15 February 1987.

5. On foreign workforce leaving Saudi Arabia: WSJ, 8 January 1985; NYT, 28 January 1986. Of 12,500 Americans in 1987 in Al-Sharqiyya, compared to 31,000 in 1982: NYT, 12 February 1987. 'In Riyadh and Jeddah forty per cent of all commercial and residential buildings are empty': IHT, 27–28 April 1985. On same subject: WSJ, 8 January 1985; NYT, 28 January 1986; R. Cower, FT, 21 April 1986, supplement, p. II; *Sunday Times*, 20 July 1986; NYT, 12 February 1987.

6. IHT, 27 November 1985.

7. *Saudi Gazette*, 17 September 1986.

8. *Al-Thawra al-Islamiyya*, August 1986; *Al-Yamama*, 20 June, 4 July, 12 November 1986. According to WP (15 February 1987) the Saudi regime occasionally blocked the universities' efforts to limit enrolment by merit ranking and to cut students' subsidies, because of political considerations. *Al-Thawra al-Islamiyya* (December 1986, quoted by *Haaretz*, 16 December 1986) alleged, however, that the universities, on government orders, rejected thousands of applicants with grades under 85 and failed many of their graduating students.

9. WSJ, 19 July 1985; NYT, 28 January 1986.

10. *Ukaz*, 19 March 1985; *Al-Riyadh*, 26 March 1985. On enormous capital flight: Field, FT, 21 April 1986, supplement, p. I; A. Hottinger, 'Saudi Arabia: entering a new era', *Swiss Review of World Affairs*, Vol. 26, No. 5 (August 1986), p. 24.

11. By August 1986 it was claimed that Saudi financial reserves, once estimated at over $150 billion had declined to about $40 billion (see p. 200 above and note 58 below).

12. *Al-Riyadh*, 11 March 1986.

13. IHT, 7 January 1987, p. 7.

14. *Al-Siyassa*, 22 March 1983. Also on this crisis: *Al-Masa'*, 13 June 1983; Kraft, 'Letter', p. 53.

15. *Al-Sharq al-Awsat*, 22 August 1984; M. Abir, 'Saudi security and military endeavour', *The Jerusalem Quarterly*, No. 33, (1984), pp. 92–3. Of Abdallah negotiating the purchase of airplanes and tanks: *Istratijia* (Beirut), July 1984. On multi-billion National Guard military towns near Riyadh (Khashim al-'Ayn), Taif, Hasa, Dammam and Jedda: EIU, Saudi Arabia, No. 3 (1986), p. 8.

16. See Chapter 1, pp. 9, 13.

17. M.A.T. Al Saud, 'Permanence and Change (Claremont Graduate School, 1982), p. 157.

18. *Al-Siyassa*, 22 March 1983; also *Al-Jarida*, 23 March 1983; WP, 27 March 1983. *Al-Thawra al-Islamiyya*, October 1984, p. 56; FT, 24 April 1984. On alleged army mutiny (?!) in 1982 involving Tabuk's governor Prince

Abd al-Majid: *Merip Reports*, February 1985, quoting a 'Saudi Socialist Labour Party leader'.

19. Al Saud, 'Permanence', p. 127; N.H. Hisham, 'Saudi Arabia and the Role of the Imarates' (Claremont Graduate School, 1982), p. 234; FT, 21 April 1986, supplement, p. VI; *Ukaz*, 29 January 1985; *Al-Jazira*, 5 August 1980 (p. 7), 11, 28 May 1985; *Saudi Gazette*, 1 July, 1 August, 1 October 1986; S.S. Huyette, *Political Adaptation in Saudi Arabia* (Boulder, 1985), p. 82 (note 18); G.S. Samore, 'Royal Family politics in Saudi Arabia' (Harvard University, 1984), pp. 381, 463–4. Nassir bin Khalid al-Sudayri (King Fahd's maternal cousin) is Deputy Governor of the Najran province: *Ukaz*, 29 January 1985. Abd al-Rahman bin Ahmad al-Sudayri is the Governor of Al-Jawf: *Saudi Gazette*, 1 October 1986.

20. The Director of Public Security is General Abdallah b. Abd al-Rahman al-Shaykh: *Saudi Gazette*, 17 July 1986. Deputy Minister of the Interior is Prince Ahmad (Fahd's full brother). General Fahd ibn Abdallah (b. Muhammad Saud al-Kabir, Ibn Saud's paternal uncle) was commander of the air force until September 1985. Princes Fahd ibn Abdallah (b. Abd al-Rahman) and his brother Bandar are Deputy Minister of Civil Aviation (under Sultan) and Assistant Deputy Minister for Provincial Affairs (under Na'if), respectively. On new armed forces' fourth command: EIU, Saudi Arabia, No. 3 (1986), p. 7; also Samore, 'Royal Family', p. 381.

21. On the Ministry of the Interior's 6000-plus strong Special Security Forces and new force to protect crucial economic installations: *Al-Safir*, 9 January 1980, pp. 8–10; Buchan, FT, 5 May 1981, supplement; Lacey, *The Kingdom*, p. 445;' *Al-Yawm* (Saudi Arabia), 21 January 1984; *Al-Thawra al-Islamiyya*, July 1984; also Samore, 'Royal Family', pp. 457–8.

22. *Al-Sharq al-Awsat*, 29 March 1984; *Ukaz*, 4 May 1984; Field, FT, 22 April 1985 (supplement, pp. VI–VII), 15 February 1985; *Al-Jazira*, 2 June 1983, 23 January, 22 February 1985; *Al-Riyadh*, 1 March 1985. Prince Sultan, b. Salman (the first Saudi astronaut) holds a key position in the Ministry of Information.

23. Fahd's eldest son, Faysal, the president of the Youth Welfare Organisation has the rank of cabinet minister.

24. Prince Na'if is in charge of relations with the GCC and its member countries. King Fahd personally directs since 1981 relations with Iraq and Egypt. Saud al-Faysal, the Foreign Minister, and Crown Prince Abdallah, considered 'nationalists' and the proponents of 'normalisation' of relations with Iran, are seemingly in charge of relations with Damascus and Teheran.

25. *Al-Thawra al-Islamiyya*, according to *Haaretz*, 19 February 1987.

26. A.A. Al-Ibrahim, 'Regional and Urban Development in Saudi Arabia', unpublished PhD thesis (University of Colorado at Boulder, 1982).

27. Ibid., pp. 210–11; also pp. 200, 215, 317; I.M. Al-Awaji, 'Bureaucracy and Society in Saudi Arabia' (University of Virginia, 1971), pp. 236, 238. According to *Statistical Year Book* (1980, p. 182), the Northern Province had only 273 hospital beds and Asir 535, out of a total of 10,970 in Saudi Arabia; also Al-Ibrahim, 'Bureaucracy', p. 285; A.M. Al-Selfan, 'The Essence of Tribal Leaders' Participation' (Claremont Graduate School, 1981), p. 128.

28. W. Lancaster, *The Rwala Bedouin Today* (Cambridge, Mass., 1981), p. 18; Al-Ibrahim, 'Urban Development', p. 113; *Merip Reports*,

February 1985.

29. On development: IHT, 12 December 1983, supplement, p. 9; *Al-Jazira*, 22 November 1983, 22 October 1984, 9, 27 January 1985; *Al-Riyadh*, 20 October 1984, 15 November 1984; *Ukaz*, 14 July 1984, 25 January 1985; *Ma'riv* (business section), 5 November 1985; Al-Ibrahim, 'Urban Development', p. 285.

30. MEED, Special Report, July 1984.

31. Ibid., pp. 65–7, 78; MEED, 21 July 1985; *Al-Yawm*, 18 October 1984; *Al-Madina*, 29 December 1984; *Al-Jazira*, 18 November, 3 December 1984, 2 February, 2 March, 22 April, 16 July, 10 October 1985; *Al-Riyadh*, 1 March 1985; *Saudi Gazette*, 23 July 1986.

32. *Ukaz*, 25 March 1984; Field, FT, 21 April 1986, supplement, p. VIII; *Saudi Gazette*, 29 September 1986.

33. R. Cower, FT, 21 April 1986, supplement, p. II; MEED, Special Report, July 1984.

34. *Al-Thawra al-Islamiyya*, April 1985, p. 6.

35. *Sunday Times*, 2 December 1984; J. Miller, IHT, 22 August 1984; Huyette, *Adaptation*, p. 38; Ottaway, WP, 27 November 1984; MEED, Special Report, July 1984, p. 2.

36. *Al-Jazira*, 20 January 1985. King Fahd on his weekly *majalis* with the ulama: *Ukaz*, 4 May 1984; also, Huyette, *Adaptation*, p. 35; IHT, 17 May 1985; *Al-Jazira*, 1 October 1985. On warning to Saudis travelling to the 'corrupt' West: FT, 24 April 1984, supplement, p. XII. On Fahd's international Islamic activities: *Al-Sharq al-Awsat*, 8 June 1983; Ottaway, WP, 27 November 1984.

37. Lacey, *The Kingdom*, p. 178; *Handbook* (1984), pp. 112, 300; Sisley, *The Times*, 23 May 1980; W. Ochsenwald, 'Saudi Arabia and the Islamic revival', *International Journal of Middle East Studies*, Vol. 13 (1981); WP, 20 December 1982, MEED, 1 March 1985; IHT, 16 April 1985, FT, 22 April 1985, p. VI. On rise of *muttawwa'in* activity in Al-Hasa and impact on Gulf states: Field, FT, 21 April 1986, supplement, p. VIII; also, WSJ, 19 July 1985; *The Times*, 15 July 1986, 3 November 1986; FT, 20 May 1986.

38. *Al-Madina*, 29 July 1984, interview with Shaykh Abd al-Aziz Al al-Shaykh; also FT, 21 April 1986, supplement. On reorganisation and training of Morality Police and activity in rural areas of Al-Baz's 'Islamic Propagation' cooperating with Interior Ministry: *Al-Madina*, 30 November 1983; *Ukaz*, 9 February 1984, 8 July 1984, 5 May 1985; *Al-Riyadh*, 17 July 1984, 28 October 1985; *Al-Jazira*, 10 April 1985; Ottaway, WP, 27 November 1984; NYT, 23 May 1985; Field, FT, 21 April 1986, supplement, p. VIII.

39. *Ma'riv*, 29 October 1986; Ottaway, WP, 27 November 1984; FT, 23 May 1984; IHT, 23 November 1983, 6 August 1984; *Handbook* (1984), p. 112; R. Knauerhase, 'Saudi Arabia faces the future', *Current History* (February 1986), p. 78. On curbing of religious extremism: *Ukaz*, 4 May 1984; Field, FT, 21 April 1986, supplement. Fahd and major Islamic foundations: Ottaway, WP, 27 November 1984. On the appointment of Al-Khowayter: *Al-Sharq al-Awsat*, 19 January 1987.

40. IHT, 17 May 1985.

41. WP, 20 December 1982. Interview (1984) with Saudi Socialist Labour Party representative: *Merip Reports*, February 1985. King Fahd

instructed the Interior Ministry to exclude from government contracts and employment people educated in communist countries: *Al-Riyadh*, 29 December 1983.

42. *Al-Siyassa*, 22 March 1983; *Al-Hurriyya*, 3 April 1983; *Al-Nashra* (Syria-left. Athens), 14 November 1983 (quoting *Al-Thaqafa al-Mua'sara*, organ of the Saudi Nationalist Writers Union), 14 July 1986, p. 7; *Daily Telegraph* (London), 25 February 1983, p. 32; Kraft, 'Letter', p. 46; *Al-Masa'*, 23 May 1983; *Economist Foreign Report*, 19 May 1983; *Al-Yasar al-'Arabi* (Leftist. Egypt), March 1984, quoting Saudi leftist periodical *Tariq al-Kadahin*. Also Committee for Defence of Political Prisoners in Saudi Arabia note 45 below. *Sunday Times* (11 January 1984) alleged that the dismissal and arrest of former Information Minister, Muhammad Abdu Yamani, was related to *coup* plots, particularly in his native Najran; also *Ma'riv*, 11 January 1984, quoting *Nidal al-Shabab*, publication of Saudi Union of Democratic Youth. *Al-Thawra al-Islamiyya* excepted, the above are tiny Marxist front groups.

43. *Merip Reports*, February 1985; *Al-Thawra al-Islamiyya*, October 1984, an interview with a leader of the IRO; FBIS, 28 August 1984, Beirut, Voice of Lebanon, 28 August 1984; *Ma'riv*, 29 January 1985: of cooperation between the leftist faction of the PLO and Shi'ite Hizb-Allah elements in smuggling arms into Saudi Arabia. Also *Al-Shahid*, 23 October 1985, interview with IRO representative.

44. *Al-Thawra al-Islamiyya*, July 1985, p. 81; *Al-Yamama*, 2 April 1982, 4, 18 January 1984; FBIS, 10 August 1984, Radio Riyadh, 9 August 1984.

45. Besides names, the pamphlet specified age, occupation, town or villages of origin (in Sharqiyya) and date of arrest and seem authentic. See pamphlets of Committee for Defence of Political Prisoners in Saudi Arabia, London, August–September 1986 and advertisements in *Guardian* (London), 5 August 1986; NYT, 20 August 1986. Also different issues of *Al-Thawra al-Islamiyya*, 1984 to 1986; interviews with leftist and Shi'ite opposition leaders in *Al-Hurriyya*, 2 November 1981, 3 April 1983; *Al-Mawqif al-Arabi*, 22 March 1982; *Al-Shahid*, 23 October 1985, pp. 32–5.

46. *Haaretz*, 7 March 1982; *Al-Nashra*, 7 April 1986, 14 July 1986, 4 August 1986; FBIS, 6 April 1984, Riyadh television, 5 April 1984; FT, 26 July 1984, 25 August 1984; IHT, 26 July 1984, 25–26 August 1984. On widespread arrests and deportations of Palestinian and other foreign employees in Saudi Arabia: FBIS, 2 April 1986, Radio Riyadh, 2 April 1986; *Al-Nashra*, 7 April 1986; *Al-Shahid*, 23 October 1985. Of tension between Sunni nationalist organisations and the IRO: *Al-Thawra al-Islamiyya*, October 1984 (p. 56), March 1985.

47. The Iranian-oriented Shi'ite organisations are more active in Kuwait. Their most publicised operation in Saudi Arabia in recent years was the planting of several bombs in Riyadh on May 15, 1985 for which the 'Islamic Jihad' claimed credit. *Al-Thawra al-Islamiyya*, October 1984, p. 56; *Haaretz*, 19 May 1985; JP, 20 May 1985; IHT, 20 May 1985; FT, 20 May 1985; *October* (Cairo), 3 August 1985. See also pp. 219–20.

48. *Al-Yawm*, 21 January 1984; *Al-Thawra al-Islamiyya*, July 1984, November 1984, p. 4, July 1985; *Al-Dustur*, 30 March 1986; *Saudi Gazette*, 1 August 1986.

49. A. Dawisha, IHT, 25 November 1986; *Merip Reports*, February 1985;

Field, 21 April 1986, supplement, p. VIII.

50. See Chapter 7, pp. 170–1 and note 17, p. 176.

51. Ottaway, WP, 27 November 1984. On the Dammam Chamber of Commerce and its growth: MEED, Special Report, July 1984, p. 67. On Riyadh chamber and royal members: *The Middle East*, February 1987, p. 29.

52. Ottaway, WP, 27 November 1984; *Al-Nashra*, 8 September 1986, pp. 23–4. Pointing out the achievements of the middle class, this leftist publication is calling for the lifting of the restrictions on trade unionism in Saudi Arabia. The second conference of the Association of Chambers of Commerce, opened by King Fahd in 1985, it claims, adopted several decisions relating to the government's economic policy.

53. *Al-Nashra*, 8 September 1986, pp. 23–4; Faheem, 'Higher Education', p. 124.

54. Field, FT, 9 September 1982, p. 12; WP, 20 December 1982.

55. *Sunday Times*, 2 December 1984; FT, 3 January 1985; also MEED, 28 September 1984, p. 32; MEED, Special Report, July 1984, p. 4; Field, FT, 23 May 1984.

56. Field, FT, 22 April 1985, supplement, p. I.; Ottaway, WP, 31 May 1986.

57. FT, 4, 8 July, 18 December 1986; *The Times*, 5, 15 July 1986.

58. On liquid assets, FT, August–September 1986; WP, 15 February 1987. The government reserves are kept by SAMA in addition to assets covering the Saudi riyal and other reserves.

59. Ottaway, WP, 27 November 1984; WSJ, 31 July 1984.

60. Ibrahim al-'Anqari, Ali Sha'ir and Muhammad Ali al-Fayiz: Huyette, *Adaptation*, p. 95; also Samore, 'Royal Family', pp. 270–7, 347–82, 539.

61. *Sunday Times*, 2 December 1984.

62. FT, 25 April 1984; Ottaway, WP, 27 November 1984; Hottinger, 'Saudi Arabia', p. 24.

63. *The Middle East* (September 1984), p. 48; WSJ, 31 July 1984.

64. The Hijazi middle-class elites believe that the Saudi oligarchy which always held them in antipathy, intentionally prefers their counterparts, the offspring of Najdi merchants and civil servants. FT, 25 November 1986; Huyette, *Adaptation*, pp. 95–7, 101. On Najdi-Hijazi social cleavage: M. Field, *The Merchants. Big Business Families of Arabia* (London, 1984), pp. 30, 71–4, 83–4; also Kraft, 'Letter', p. 48; FT, 25 April 1984; WSJ, 31 July 1984; Ottaway, WP, 27 November 1984; Knauerhase, 'Future', p. 78; FBIS, 28 March 1985, Radio Riyadh, 28 March 1985; IHT, 11 November, 17 December 1986; Craig's confidential report.

65. *Saudi Gazette*, 13 July 1986; IHT, 8 May 1985; NYT, 23 May 1985.

66. IHT, 17 May 1985; also WSJ, 19 July 1985.

67. Abir, 'Manpower' (pp. 40–57) and 'Saudi security'.

68. FT, 22 April 1985, supplement, p. VII. Although reduced slightly, Saudi defence allocation comprises of 30 per cent of the kingdom's 1987 budget: *The Middle East*, February 1987, p. 19. The cost of the Tornado airplanes ordered from the UK is about $8 billion, the new submarines tender (which France may win) will cost over $1 billion and the proposed attack and transport helicopters deal with the US is estimated at nearly $800 million.

69. Abir, 'Saudi security', pp. 87–91 and 'Manpower'; Holden and Johns, *House of Saud*, p. 463; Salameh, 'Political power', p. 10; McHale, 'Political system', p. 203. See also note 20 above. The Shiʻites are still excluded from the armed forces. On an alleged abortive air force *coup* at the end of January 1987 involving several princes, including Prince Sultan's son (?!): *Haaretz*, 19 February 1987, quoting *Al-Thawra al-Islamiyya*.

70. T.H.T. Al-Hamad, 'Political Order in Changing Societies' (University of Southern California, 1985), pp. 288–9.

9

Conclusions

Despite the rapid modernisation of Saudi Arabia its rulers managed to avoid the socio-political dislocations that often accompanied development in the Arab-Muslim world and in Third World countries in general. This was to a large extent due to the relative cohesiveness of the wide-based ruling house, the policies of the monarchs and to the inability of the new social forces unleashed by modernisation to mount serious challenges to the Saudi regime. In addition, the modernisation of the kingdom and its government undermined the power of the non-royal traditional elites (tribal *umara* and ulama), and to a lesser degree, that of the royal family's partners, i.e. the Jiluwis, the Thunayans and Al al-Shaykh. Thus today, it is the senior princes of the house of Ibn Saud, Al Abd al-Rahman and the recognised cadet branches of Al Saud, who dominate the kingdom's informal consultative and policy-making organs.

Far from being an absolute monarchy, or a desert democracy, the Saudi regime is an oligarchy, whose cornerstone is the principle of consultation and consensus. Its collective leadership, which became more prominent after Faysal's demise (in 1975) and the 1982/83 royal family crisis, has been strengthened, it seems, by the reported erosion of Fahd's prestige in the wake of the kingdom's economic and political difficulties.

The policies of the Saudi rulers were guided by several 'golden rules' instituted by King Ibn Saud. For instance, whenever possible, the regime endeavoured to 'buy off' the opposition rather than fight it. On the other hand, it crushed with an iron fist the militant opposition which challenged its authority or attempted to overthrow the Sauds' government.

Unlike Iran under the Shah, where only a tiny ruling family and a small, self-indulgent upper middle class monopolised the country's oil wealth, the House of Saud channelled the kingdom's growing oil revenue, however unevenly, to all classes of Saudis. The ensuing modernisation and the rapid urbanisation of the rural population in the 1960s and 1970s helped transform the majority of Saudis into a multi-layered prosperous bourgeoisie, mostly conservative and supportive of the Sauds. Oil wealth also facilitated the process of national integration and gradual emergence of a Saudi identity. Cohesion occurred despite the survival of traditional differences such as those between *ḥadr* and *badu*, Najdi and Hijazi, Sunni and Shi'ite. Indeed, as long as vast oil revenues kept pouring in, such differences seemed relatively unimportant.

Again following the example of Ibn Saud, his successors Faysal, Khalid and Fahd adopted policies aimed at pre-empting the consolidation in the kingdom of alternative power centres. Hence, they strove to incorporate the rapidly expanding middle-class elites into the Saud's powerbase. For its part the middle-class intelligentsia opted on the whole for collaboration with the rulers, gaining in the process prestige, influence and wealth. Yet, despite this collaboration and the greater authority delegated to technocrats since the mid-1970s, the new elites, after about 25 years of faithfully serving the regime, have failed to penetrate the ruling class and are still excluded from policy-making.

The Mecca rebellion in 1979, in which the rebels failed to win even the support of their kinsmen, demonstrated that, in contrast to other Arab and Muslim countries, neo-fundamentalism in Saudi Arabia appeals only to peripheral elements. Most Saudis, especially the conservative rural and newly urbanised population, are quite happy with the apparent synthesis of formal puritanism, modernism and material prosperity, provided by the regime and legitimised by the establishment ulama.

Aware of the deeply-rooted conservative outlook of the masses and apprehensive about the kingdom's uncontrolled development, the rulers have increasingly granted the ulama's demands for stricter observance of Wahhabi doctrine and for the protection of the 'Saudi way of life'. As long as the ulama did not interfere with the kingdom's politics and modernisation programmes, King Khalid and later even King Fahd, preferred to risk the possible alienation of western-educated and other middle-class elites rather than lose ulama support. Indeed, King Fahd now uses the services of the ulama to 'indoctrinate' the masses *inter alia* to uphold the Sauds' regime.

Following the 1979 and 1980 Shi'ite riots in the Eastern

Province, Fahd not only accelerated the development of this region but, ignoring Najdi ulama's objections, initiated a far more tolerant policy towards his Shi'ite subjects. As a result, the majority of the Shi'ite community in Al-Sharqiyya, is far less hostile to the Sauds' regime than in the past. Shi'ites are still discriminated against although they are now benefiting from the kingdom's development and prosperity and their status has been considerably improved.

The replacement of older provincial amirs, since 1980, with younger, modern-educated and capable ones and the proliferation of royal technocrats in the central government, was partly meant to strengthen the Sudayris' position in the royal family and reduce discontent among the younger generation of Sauds. Above all this move was part of the regime's efforts to accelerate the development of the rural areas and improve their standard of living and that of the newly urbanised population. Among other things, it was hoped that this would strengthen the latter's allegiance to the Sauds' traditional ḥukuma at the expense of the middle-class elites who dominate the modern government. The newly cemented alliance between the regime and the ulama was partly meant to serve the same purpose.

The new social forces that emerged with the kingdom's modernisation failed to undermine the bases of the regime. Only a small fraction of the middle class and the oil industry's workforce endorsed radical Arab nationalist and Muslim fundamentalist ideologies. Power and wealth, together with conservative nationalism, served the new elites as a surrogate for the pan-Arab and revolutionary ideologies which they espoused earlier in the 1950s and 1960s. Even the younger Saudi intelligentsia, graduating from local and foreign universities, were keen to join the ranks of their country's bureaucracy or private sector and 'buy their first Porsche' (*Sunday Times*, 2 December 1984).

The limited activity of the small Saudi militant opposition in the 1980s, occasionally evident in Asir and Hijaz, was limited largely to the Eastern Province. There, the Shi'ite 'proletariat', the fundamentalists and elements of the intelligentsia would probably be among the first to join an anti-Saud nationalist uprising if it were to erupt. A Shi'ite uprising in Al-Hasa, however, would probably backfire. The Sunnis would rally in such event behind Al Saud, due to their nearly universal aversion to Shi'ites and their concern lest the Eastern Province's oil revenues, the kingdom's source of prosperity, escape from their hands. The still frustrated elements of the Shi'ite minority continue to represent, nevertheless, a threat, albeit limited, to the regime, underscored by the Iran–Iraq War and

Teheran's subversion in the Gulf.

The rural population in Saudi Arabia, a major source of support for Al Saud (possibly with the exception of the Asiris), has rapidly declined in size in the last two decades but it still comprises of about a third of the population. The newly urbanised masses have also retained, it is believed, their relations with, if not their allegiance to, their traditional socio-political institutions and to the Sauds' *ḥukuma*.

Despite the above foundations of Saudi stability the regime now faces increasing social and economical problems which are a potential source of tensions and instability, as summarised below.

The country's enormous oil reserves and financial resources endowed Saudi Arabia with power and influence in the Arab and Muslim camps and in the international arena out of proportion to its size and level of development. Saudi Arabia demonstrated its solidarity with its Arab and Muslim sister countries by supporting them financially and politically. They in turn helped consolidate the regime's prestige and stability. Yet, as its oil revenues dried up in the 1980s, and correspondingly its grants to Arab and Third World countries, the kingdom's influence in the Arab camp and in the world gradually waned.

Even a drastically reduced budget of about 45 billion dollars seems excessive for a nation of about five million citizens. This is not the case, however, with Saudi Arabia, where the oligarchy has to fund tens of thousands of its members in order to maintain its internal stability and consensus. In order to retain the allegiance of the middle class, the patriarchal regime has, moreover, endeavoured to protect the latter's standard of living through costly subsidies, welfare services and the like.

Saudi Arabia's substantial annual budgetary deficits since 1982 were offset by drawing upon the kingdom's enormous financial reserves. The kingdom's liquid assets, its 'insurance policy', were thus depleted to a level that, unless oil prices soon noticeably recover, they may be totally exhausted within two or three years. Though development programmes, especially related to infrastructure and construction, were slashed, allocations to welfare, subsidies and services have been reduced only marginally until 1986.

Further erosion of its liquid reserves may force Riyadh again to reduce the benefits dispensed to all classes of Saudis. This would not seriously affect the rulers and middle-class elites who accumulated much fat in previous years. As for the less affluent Saudis, the regime will probably exert itself not to cause them unnecessary hardship, although the kingdom's economic difficulties are bound to affect the population unless enormous defence and security budgets (financing the Sudayris' constituencies) and the funding of the royal family are significantly cut.

While members of the royal family continue to indulge in excesses, the escalating economic crisis is beginning adversely to affect the less affluent Saudis who only lately began to benefit more equally from the country's prosperity and services. This problem is exacerbated by the fact that many small businessmen, contractors, taxi and truck owner-drivers, whose enterprises are also encountering growing difficulties, come from among the newly urbanised rural population. The continued support of these groups for the Sauds is conditional, to a large extent, on the regime's ability to shelter them from serious economic hardships. Should the economic crisis persist, and the less affluent components of Saudi society suffer unduly from it, they could suppress their traditional dislike of middle-class elites and join them seriously to threaten the regime's stability. Cognisant of this factor, Saudi rulers exerted themselves, that far, to prevent such a development.

The growth of an unemployed intelligentsia in Saudi Arabia could become a most serious socio-political problem in the near future. As the increase of university graduates coincided with the decline of the Saudi economy in the 1980s, the competition for government positions between graduates of foreign, and of domestic secular and religious universities has become keener. By the mid-1980s, the economic recession peaked and unemployment among school and university graduates grew rapidly, further aggravating the three-sided competition for government appointments.

Allocations to the education system and to universities were reduced in 1985/86 by about one third, compared to previous years. Although the larger part of the saving came from halting spectacular construction, the relevant ministers, it seems, instructed the education authorities and universities in 1986 to reduce their expenditure and simultaneously stiffen admissions and graduation requirements. This was intended also to curb the number of future graduates seeking employment in the administration. From press reports it appears that, indeed, many applicants were rejected by the universities and that numerous students failed the 1986 graduation exams. This situation may reproduce circumstances similar to those of the 1950s and 1960s when the radical opposition won widespread support among the workers and intelligentsia and even the middle-class elites among the workers and intelligentsia and even the middle-class elites led by Hijazis became relatively militant (possibly, *inter alia*, why the Minister of Education Dr Al-Khowayter was appointed also Minister of Higher Education in January 1987). The regime's ability to deal swiftly with this situation will also depend on the renewed growth of its oil income.

The conservative senior princes and the Najdi-led ulama oppose even the seemingly innocuous 'Islamic *majlis al-shura*', proposed by Prince Na'if's committee, lest it become a first step towards a change in the existing Saudi power equation. The conservative ruling class opposition to a 'National Consultative Assembly' was vindicated, it claims, by the example of the dissolution in July 1986 of the militant Kuwaiti parliament. Thus, the likelihood of a voluntary inclusion of the middle-class elites in the Saudi political power system in the near future seems remote.

The gradual 'Najdi-isation' and 'Saudi-isation' of the central and provincial government, and the shift towards greater conservatism by the regime since the late 1970s, are not only causing a narrowing of the regime's powerbase, but could also polarise opposing views and undermine the process of national integration supported by Faysal and Fahd. **Though lacking homogeneity, the growing new elites (commoner officers included) are nevertheless a factor that the Saud rulers cannot afford to ignore, particularly if continued economic recession mobilises the middle class's younger elements, irrespective of region and origin and cultural attitude.**

Many members of the middle-class elites have become disillusioned with King Fahd and his policies and they consider him weak and even incompetent. Prince Sultan's 'corruption' and immense wealth, moreover, have become their favourite target for criticism. The budget of his ministry, about a third of the kingdom's total annual budget (1987), completely out of proportion to the Saudi armed forces' size and power, is largely used to bolster Sultan's powerbase and that of the other Sudayris. Prince Salman, the most able and enlightened among Fahd's full brothers, is nevertheless a Sudayri and part of the system and policy identified with the King. Although more sympathetic to Crown Prince Abdallah's ascetism, and to his inter-Arab and foreign policy, the Hijazi and other elements of the new elites consider him, even more than Sultan and Na'if, to represent traditional, narrow-minded, Najdi conservatism.

Disillusioned with Al Saud, some members of the middle-class

217

elites hope that an alliance with the discontented elements of the third-generation educated princes will lead to political reform. Such an alliance, if at all viable, will resemble, to some extent, the one between the 'Liberal Princes' and the nationalist middle class in the 1950s and early 1960s.

Many younger Sauds, including royal officers and technocrats, increasingly frustrated by the policies of the senior princes, impatiently await their turn to govern the country. Despite the consolidation of the Sudayris' hegemony, it is not inconceivable that continuous economic crisis, or a future clash over succession, may provide them with the opportunity to usurp the hegemony of the family's senior members and attempt to reform the kingdom's political structure.

The above scenarios are unlikely possibilities in the near future. The ruling class is still maintaining its outward unity and consensus and seems to command considerable support among the population. In the expectation of such a challenge and/or the next round of succession the Sudayris, as indicated above, have strongly fortified their position in the government, provincial administration and security and armed forces. It is widely believed that Sultan wishes to replace Abdallah as heir apparent. Even if the anti-western Abdallah were to succeed Fahd, he will have to delegate substantial authority to Sultan, the next in line of succession. It is possible to envisage, however, that in order to please the younger Sauds and the middle-class elites, the liberal, likeable and capable Prince Salman may emerge as a compromise candidate.

Despite the economic recession, Saudi Arabia still has enormous financial and oil reserves and does not owe money to foreign banks or governments. The Saudi regime and many analysts believe that the demand for Middle Eastern oil will grow again, prices will rise and Saudi Arabia's present financial and political problems will disappear by the end of the 1980s. However, no one can predict what course the Iran–Iraq War will take, nor what the impact of its outcome will be on the Middle East and particularly on the societies of the Gulf, Saudi Arabia included. Another important development is the growing interests of the Soviet Union in the area, coupled by its predicted need to increase its oil imports from the Middle East in the late 1990s. Both, it should be stressed, are extraneous factors.

Following the golden rule of winning, whenever possible, the cooperation of every power factor in the society, Fahd attempted to keep alive the powerful middle-class elites' hopes for political participation to prevent a confrontation between them and the regime. However, the rise of Muslim fundamentalism and of Iran's power, the economic crisis in the kingdom and the rivalry in the royal family, are not conducive to maintaining the existing status quo.

Whatever future developments, the Sauds will soon be obliged to reconsider their refusal to grant some sort of political participation to their growing and powerful middle class. Such a reassessment of policy may be forced on the regime, as education and greater mobility will erode historic differences between the new town-dwellers and the ḥadr middle class. The new intelligentsia of rural origin is already gradually merging with middle-class elites. This process is likely to be sustained in the future.

Whilst this book was in production Saudi Arabia succeeded in stabilising OPEC's average oil price at eighteen dollars a barrel and in reconsolidating the organisation's quota system (though cheating still continues). King Fahd's endeavours to re-establish Saudi Arabia's position in the Arab world are partially successful and are finding an expression in the kingdom's renewed role as a mediator between its different camps and in attempts to convene a new summit that would help rehabilitate Arab unity. Finally, apprehension of Teheran's fundamentalist revolutionary rhetoric and continued war against Iraq is also increasingly vindicating the monarch's pro-Western policy, prudently coinciding with a cautious improvement of the kingdom's, and especially its smaller Gulf allies', relations with the Soviet Union.

On the last day of July and the first of August 1987, with more than a million pilgrims conglomerating upon Mecca, Riyadh was sharply reminded of the vulnerability of its oil industry and of Iran's power in the region. Iranian pilgrims had demonstrated in Mecca in the past years, denouncing America and its allies and attempting to influence the huge fathering of Muslims from all over the world. This time, however, with more than 150,000 Iranians present in the Holy Town, the demonstration rapidly turned to violent riots which resulted in the death of 402 people, 275 of whom were Iranian. In the following days, the leaders of the Iranian Islamic republic, participating in huge anti-Saudi demonstrations in Teheran, openly called for the overthrow of the corrupt regime of Al Saud and the 'Islamisation of the oil resources of the Saudi kingdom'. Two powerful explosions, which damaged a major liquification plant north of Ras Tanura (Saudi Arabia's main oil terminal) shortly afterwards, though claimed by Riyadh to be the outcome of an electrical fault, were universally believed to be an act of sabotage by Shi'ite workers of Aramco, members of a clandestine organisation affiliated to the Iranian *Da'wa*. The explosions in the Saudi plant were even compared by the western press to acts of sabotage which occurred earlier in the year in Kuwaiti oil installations and for which Kuwaiti Shi'ites employed in their country's petroleum industry were responsible.

As expected, the above incidents rather consolidated the support of the Saudi Sunni population for their regime, not to mention the solidarity of all the Arab countries (Libya excepted) with Riyadh, enhanced by fear of the rising power of the 'Persian' Shi'ite republic. The blessing given by the Saudi-led GCC earlier in the year to Kuwait's decision to register its tankers in the United States and thus de facto invite America to protect the freedom of navigation in the Gulf, was also further legitimised by the events in Mecca and the Eastern Province.

Moreover, whether a result of sabotage or of an accident, the explosions in the liquification plant near Ras Tanura remained an isolated incident (for the time being) and proved the success of King Fahd's 'carrot and stick' policy in Al-Sharqiyya. Yet, although Riyadh exerted itself to prove the restraint exercised by its security forces during the Mecca rioting and it continues to press Baghdad to refrain from striking at Iran's oil terminals and shipping in the Gulf, the situation in the region, aggravated by the American navy's presence in it, remains tense.

Bibliography

UNPUBLISHED PhD AND MA THESES

Abussuud, A.N., 'Administrative Development in Saudi Arabia: The Process of Differentiation and Specialization', PhD thesis, University of Maryland, 1979.

Al-Awaji, I.M., 'Bureaucracy and Society in Saudi Arabia', PhD thesis, University of Virginia, 1971.

Alghofaily, I.F., 'Saudi Youth Attitude Toward Work and Vocational Education: A Constraint on Economic Development', PhD thesis, The Florida State University, 1980.

Al-Hamad, T.H.T., 'Political Order in Changing Societies, Saudi Arabia: Modernization in a Traditional Context', PhD thesis, University of Southern California, 1985.

Al-Harithi, S.K. Al-Orabi, 'The Mass Media in Saudi Arabia: Present Concept, Functions, Barriers and Selected Strategy For Effective Use in Nation Building and Social Awareness', PhD thesis, Ohio State University, 1983.

Al-Hazzam, F.S., 'The College of Petroleum and Minerals, the Kingdom of Saudi Arabia', PhD thesis, Arizona State University, 1975.

Al-Hegelan, A.A., 'Innovation in the Saudi Arabian Bureaucracy: A Survey Analysis of Senior Bureaucrats', PhD thesis, The Florida State University, 1984.

Al-Ibrahim, A.A. 'Regional and Urban Development in Saudi Arabia', PhD thesis, University of Colorado at Boulder, 1982.

Al-Khudair, I.M., 'Islamic University at Madina, the Kingdom of Saudi Arabia: A History and Evaluation', MA thesis, California State University, 1981.

Al-Mizjaji, A.D., 'The Public Attitudes Towards the Bureaucracy in Saudi Arabia', PhD thesis, The Florida State University, 1982.

Al-Moammar, A.A.F., 'The Manpower Dilemma of Saudi Arabia', PhD thesis, University of California, Irvine, 1983.

Al-Nassar, F.M. 'Saudi Arabian Educational Mission to the US', PhD thesis, University of Oklahoma (Norman), 1982.

Al-Rawaf, O.Y., 'The Concept of the Five Crises in Political Development: Relevance to the Kingdom of Saudi Arabia', PhD thesis, Duke University, 1981.

Al Saud, Mashaal Abdullah Turki, 'Permanence and Change: An Analysis of the Islamic Political Culture of Saudi Arabia With a Special Reference to the Royal Family', PhD thesis, Claremont Graduate School, 1982.

Al-Selfan, A.M., 'The Essence of Tribal Leaders' Participation, Responsibilities, and Decisions in Some Local Government Activities in Saudi Arabia: A Case Study of the Ghamid and Zahran Tribes', PhD thesis, Claremont Graduate School, 1981.

Alyami, A.H., 'The Impact of Modernization on the Stability of the

Saudi Monarchy', PhD thesis, Claremont Graduate School, 1977.

Anderson, G., 'Differential Urban Growth in the Eastern Province of Saudi Arabia', PhD thesis, The Johns Hopkins University, 1984.

Asad, M.T., 'Saudi Arabia: Administrative Aspects of Development', PhD thesis, Claremont Graduate School, 1978.

Assad, M.M.A., 'Saudi Arabia's National Security: A Prospective Derived from Political, Economic and Defence Policies', PhD thesis, Claremont Graduate School, 1981.

Bilmastis, J.S., 'Small States a Major Power: Case Study of Saudi Arabia', PhD thesis, George Washington University, 1980.

Deij, M.M., 'Saudi Arabia's Foreign Policy 1953–1975', PhD thesis, University of Idaho, 1979.

Faheem M.E., 'Higher Education and Nation Building. A Case Study of King Abdul Aziz University', PhD thesis, University of Illinois at Urbana-Champaign, 1982.

Hafiz, F.A., 'Changes in Saudi Foreign Policy Behaviour 1964–75. A Study of the Underlying Factors and Determinates', PhD thesis, University of Nebraska-Lincoln, 1980.

Hisham, N.H., 'Saudi Arabia and the Role of the Imarates in Regional Development', PhD thesis, Claremont Graduate School, 1982.

Jan, N.A., 'Between Islamic and Western Education: A Case Study of Umm Al-Qura University, Makkah, Saudi Arabia', PhD thesis, Michigan State University, 1983.

Kashmeeri, B.O., 'Ibn Saud: The Arabian Nation Builder', PhD thesis, Howard University, 1973.

Kinsawi, M.M., 'Attitude of Students and Fathers Towards Vocational Education in Economic Development in Saudi Arabia', PhD thesis, University of Colorado at Boulder, 1981.

Madani, N.O., 'The Islamic Content of the Foreign Policy of Saudi Arabia. King Faisal's Call for Islamic Solidarity 1965–1975', PhD thesis, The American University, Washington, DC, 1977.

Marks, M.M., 'The American Influence on the Development of the Universities in the Kingdom of Saudi Arabia', PhD thesis, University of Oregon, 1980.

Saati, M.A., 'The Constitutional Development in Saudi Arabia', PhD thesis, Claremont Graduate School, 1982.

Said, A.H., 'Saudi Arabia: The Transition From a Tribal Society to a Nation', PhD thesis, University of Missouri, 1979.

Samore, G.S., 'Royal Family Politics in Saudi Arabia (1953–1982)', PhD thesis, Harvard University, 1984.

Shaker, F.A., 'Modernization of the Developing Nations. The Case of Saudi Arabia', PhD thesis, Purdue University, 1972.

Solaim, S.A., 'Constitutional and Judicial Organization in Saudi Arabia', PhD thesis, Johns Hopkins University, 1970.

Tash, A.T.M., 'A Profile of Professional Journalists working in the Saudi Arabian Daily Press', PhD thesis, Southern Illinois University at Carbondale, 1983.

Zedan, F.M., 'Political Development of the Kingdom of Saudi Arabia 1932–1975', PhD thesis, Claremont Graduate School, 1981.

UNPUBLISHED REFERENCE MATERIAL

Abir, M., 'The Manpower Problem in Saudi Arabian Economic and Security Policy', Colloquium Paper, Woodrow Wilson International Center for Scholars (Washington, DC, April 1983).

Ayubi, N.N.M., 'Vulnerability of the Rich: The Political Economy of Defense and Development in Saudi Arabia and the Gulf', a paper prepared for The Gulf Project, Center for Strategic and International Studies, Georgetown University, Washington, DC (Los Angeles, May 1982).

Cordesman, A.H., 'Saudi Arabia, AWACS and America's Search for Strategic Stability', a working paper, No. 26A (The Wilson Center, Washington DC, 1981).

Kavoussi, R. and Sheikholeslami, A.R., 'Political Economy of Saudi Arabia' (mimeographed, University of Washington, January 1983).

Malone, J.J., 'The Politics of Social Change in the Arabian Peninsula: Observations in Kuwait and Saudi Arabia', a paper published by Near East Center, University of Arizona (Tucson, 4 December 1981).

Schulze, R., 'The Saudi Arabian 'ulama and their Reaction to Muslim Fundamentalism', a paper prepared for a Colloquium on Religious Radicalism and Politics in the Middle East, The Hebrew University (Jerusalem, May 1985).

OFFICIAL DOCUMENTATION

Craig, J. (UK Ambassador to Saudi Arabia until 1984), confidential report No. 5184 to the Secretary of State for Foreign and Commonwealth Affairs: *Glasgow Herald*, 9 October 1986.

Kingdom of Saudi Arabia, Center for Statistical Data and Educational Documentation: *Development of Education in the Ministry of Education During 25 Years 1954–78* (Riyadh, 1978).

Kingdom of Saudi Arabia, Ministry of Finance and National Economy, General Department of Statistics: *Statistical Year Book 1400 A.H.–1980 A.D.* (Jeddah).

Kingdom of Saudi Arabia, Ministry of Finance and National Economy, General Department of Statistics: *The Statistical Indicator* (Jedda, 1981), 6th issue.

Kingdom of Saudi Arabia, Ministry of Information: *Faisal Speaks*.

Kingdom of Saudi Arabia, Ministry of Planning, *Employment by Sector* (Riyadh, 1982).

Kingdom of Saudi Arabia, Ministry of Planning, *Third Development Plan 1400–1405 A.H. — 1980–1985 A.D.*

Kingdom of Saudi Arabia. Saudi Arabia: Education and Human Resources. A booklet prepared for 'Riyadh Yesterday and Today' exhibition, London 29 July–8 August 1986.

Kingdom of Saudi Arabia, Saudi Arabian Monetary Agency, Research and Statistics Department: *Annual Report 1401 (1981)* (Riyadh, 1981. Will be called: SAMA Report 1981).

PUBLISHED REFERENCE MATERIAL

Books

Abir, M., 'Modern Education and the Evolution of Saudi Arabia', in E. Ingram (ed.), *National and International Politics in the Middle East*, (London, 1986).
────── *Oil Power and Politics: Conflict in Arabia, the Persian Gulf and the Red Sea* (London, 1974).

Abu Dhurr (pseud.), *Thawra fi riḥab Makka* (Dar Sawt at-Tali'a, Kuwait, 1980).

Al-Farsy, F.A.S., *Saudi Arabia: A Case Study in Development* (London, 1982).

Almana, M., *Arabia Unified. A Portrait of Ibn Saud* (London, 1982).

Aramco Yearbook (Netherlands, 1960).

Arnold, J., *Golden Swords and Pots and Pans* (New York, 1963).

Assah, A., *Miracle of the Desert Kingdom* (London, 1969).

Blandford, L., *Oil Sheikhs* (London, 1976).

Bligh, A., *From Prince to King. Royal Succession in the House of Saud in the Twentieth Century* (New York, 1984.

Buchan, J., 'Secular and Religious Opposition in Saudi Arabia' in T. Niblock (ed.), *State, Society and Economy in Saudi Arabia* (London, 1982).

Cheney, M., *Big Oil Man From Arabia* (New York, 1958).

Cole, D.P., *Nomads of the Nomads. The Al Murrah Bedouins of the Empty Quarter* (Chicago, 1975).

Daghir, A., *Mudhakkirati'ala Hamish al-qaḍiyya al-'Arabiyya* (Cairo, 1959).

De Gaury, G., *Faisal King of Saudi Arabia* (New York, 1966).

Entiles, J.P., 'Oil Wealth and the Prospects for Democratization in the Arabian Peninsula: The Case of Saudi Arabia', in N.A. Sherbiny and M.A. Tessur (eds), *Arab Oil: Impact on the Arab Countries and Global Implications* (New York, 1976).

Field, M., *The Merchants. The Big Business Families of Arabia* (London, 1984).

Habib, J.S., *Ibn Sa'ud's Warriors of Islam* (Leiden, 1978).

Halliday, F., *Arabia Without Sultans* (Manchester, 1974).

Ḥamzah, F., *Al Bilad al-'Arabiyah al-Sa'udiyya* (Mecca, 1937).

Holden, D. and Johns, R., *The House of Saud* (London, 1982).

Huyette, S.S., *Political Adaptation in Sa'udi Arabia* (Boulder, 1985).

Ibrahim, S.E., *The New Arab Social Order. A Study of the Social Impact of Oil Wealth* (Boulder, 1982).

Islami, A.R.S. and Kavoussi, R.M., *The Political Economy of Saudi Arabia* (Seattle, 1984).

Katakura, M., *Bedouin Village, A Study of a Saudi Arabian People in Transition* (University of Tokyo Press, 1977).

Keegan, J., *World Armies* (New York, 1979).
────── *World Armies* (New York, 1983).

Khalidi, W. and Ibish, Y., *Arab Political Documents* (Beirut, 1964).

Lacey, R., *The Kingdom* (London, 1981).

Lackner, H., *A House Built on Sand* (London, 1978).

Lancaster, W., *The Rwala Bedouin Today* (Cambridge, Mass., 1981).

Layish, A., 'Ulama and Politics in Saudi Arabia', in M. Heper and R. Israeli (eds), *Islam and Politics in the Modern Middle East* (New York, 1984).

Lipsky, G.A., *Saudi Arabia: Its People, Its Society, Its Culture* (New Haven, 1959).

Long, D.E., *The United States and Saudi Arabia: Ambivalent Allies* (Boulder, 1985).

Middle East Record, Volume 2: 1961 (Tel-Aviv University, Israel).

Mosely, L., *Power Play. The Tumultuous World of Middle East Oil 1890–1973* (Birkenhead, 1973).

Moss Helms, C., *The Cohesion of Saudi Arabia* (London, 1981).

Niblock, T., 'Social Structure and the Development of the Saudi Arabian Political System', in T. Niblock (ed.), *State, Society and Economy in Saudi Arabia* (London, 1982).

Nyrop, R.F. (ed.), *Area Handbook Series: Saudi Arabia A Country Study* (Washington, DC, 1982) (Washington, DC, 1984).

Philby, H. St. John, *Sa'udi Arabia* (Beirut, 1968).

Qaḍaya Sa'udiyya (Jabhat al-Taḥrir al-Watani fi'l-'Sa'udiyya' — National Liberation Front in 'Saudi Arabia', n.d., n.p. (probably 1982)).

Rentz, G., 'The Saudi Monarchy', in W.A. Beling (ed.), *King Faisal and the Modernisation of Saudi Arabia* (London, 1980).

Rugh, W.A., *Riyadh, History and Guide* (1969).

––––––– 'Saudi Mass Media and Society in the Faisal Era', in W.A. Beling (ed.), *King Faisal and the Modernisation of Saudi Arabia* (London, 1980).

Safran, N., *Saudi Arabia: The Ceaseless Quest for Security* (Cambridge, Mass., 1985).

Salameh, Gh., *Al-Siyassa al-Kharijiyya al-Sa'udiyya mundhu 1945* (Beirut, 1980).

Sanger, R.H., *The Arabian Peninsula* (New York, 1970).

Shaked, H. and Yagnes, T., 'The Saudi Arabian Kingdom', in C. Legum (ed.), *Middle East Contemporary Survey*, Vol. 1 (New York, 1978).

Shamekh, A.A., *Spatial Patterns of Bedouin Settlement in Al-Qasim Region Saudi Arabia* (Louisville, 1975).

Shaw, J. and Long, D.E., *The Washington Papers: Saudi Arabian Modernization: The Impact of Change on Stability*, No. 89 (1982).

Sheean, V., *Faisal — The King and His Kingdom* (Tavistock, 1975).

The Middle East and North Africa 1980/1 (Europa Publication, London 1980).

Tibawi, A.L., *Islamic Education. Its Traditions and Modernization into the Arab National Systems* (London, 1972).

Van Der Meulen, D., *The Wells of Ibn Sa'ud* (London, 1957).

Wahba, H., *Arabian Days* (London, 1964).

Wenner, M., 'Saudi Arabia: Survival of Traditional Elites', in F. Tachau (ed.), *Political Elites and Political Development in the Middle East* (New York, 1975).

Articles

Abir, M., 'Modernisation, reaction and Muhammad Ali's "empire"', *Middle Eastern Studies*, Vol. 13, No. 3 (October 1977).

―――― 'Saudi security and military endeavour', *The Jerusalem Quarterly*, No. 33 (Fall 1984).

―――― 'The consolidation of the ruling class and the new elites in Saudi Arabia', *Middle Eastern Studies*, Vol. 23, No. 2 (April 1987).

Al-Rikabi, 'Abd al-Amir, 'Al-dawla wa'l da'wa fi'l-'Arabiyya al-Sa'udiyya al-iftiraq shart al-tahaquq', *Qadaya 'Arabiyya* (June 1980).

Assaf, G., 'A constitution for Saudi Arabia', *Plus* (Paris, 1985), No. 1.

Bligh, A., 'The Saudi religious elite (ulama) as participant in the political system of the kingdom', *International Journal of Middle East Studies*, Vol. 17, No. 1 (February 1985).

Braibanti, R. and Al-Farsy, F.A.S., 'Saudi Arabia: A development perspective', *The Journal of South Asian and Middle Eastern Studies*, No. 1 (Fall 1977).

Collins, M., 'Riyadh: The Saud balance', *The Washington Quarterly* (Winter 1981).

Dawisha, A., 'Internal values and external threats', *Orbis* (Spring 1979).

―――― 'Saudi Arabia's search for security', *Adelphi Papers*, No. 158 (Winter 1979–80).

Duguid, S., 'A bibliographical approach to the study of social change in the Middle East: Abdullah Tariki as a new man', *International Journal of Middle East Studies*, Vol. I, No. 3 (1970).

Field, M., 'Society: The royal family and the military in Saudi Arabia', *Vierteljahresberichte*, No. 89 (September 1982).

―――― 'Why the Saudi royal family is more stable than the Shah', *Euromoney* (October 1981).

Gallagher, E.B., 'Medical education in Saudi Arabia: A sociological perspective on modernization and language', *Journal of Asian and African Studies*, Vol. XX, No. 1–2 (1985).

Goldberg, J., 'Abd al-Aziz ibn Saud and the Wahhabi doctrine: Thoughts about a paradox' (in Hebrew), *Hamizrah Hakhadash*, Vol. 30 (1981).

Halliday, F., 'The shifting sands beneath the House of Saud', *The Progressive* (March 1980).

Harrington, C.W., 'The Saudi Arabian Council of Ministers', *The Middle East Journal*, Vol. 12, No. 1 (1958).

Hottinger, A., 'Saudi Arabia: Entering a new era', *Swiss Review of World Affairs*, Vol. 26, No. 5 (August 1986).

Kechichian, J.A., 'The role of the ulama in the politics of an Islamic state: The case of Saudi Arabia', *International Journal of Middle East Studies*, Vol. 12, No. 1 (February 1986).

Knauerhase, R., 'Saudi Arabia faces the future', *Current History* (February 1986).

Kraft, J., 'Letter from Saudi Arabia', *The New Yorker*, 4 July 1983.

Lancaster, W.O., 'The Bedouin and "progress"', *Middle East International* (January 1978).

Lateef, A., 'King Faisal: From obscurity to international status', *Pakistan Horizon*, Vol. 28, No. 4 (1975).

Long, D.E., 'Inside the royal family', *The Wilson Quarterly* (Winter 1979).

Maridi, N., 'State systems and revolutionary challenge: Nasser, Khomeini, and the Middle East', *International Journal of Middle East Studies*, Vol. 17, No. 4 (November 1985).

McHale, T.R., 'A prospect of Saudi Arabia', *International Affairs* (Autumn 1981).

—— 'The Saudi Arabian political system — its origin, evolution and current status', *Vierteljahresberichte*, No. 89 (September 1982).

Mejcher, H., 'Saudi Arabia's "vital link to the West": Some political, strategic and tribal aspects of the Transarabian Pipeline (TAP) in the stage of planning 1942–1950', *Middle Eastern Studies*, Vol. 18, No. 4 (October 1982).

Moon, Chung In, 'Korean contractors in Saudi Arabia: Their rise and fall', *The Middle East Journal*, Vol. 40, No. 4 (Autumn 1986).

Nevo, J., 'The Saudi royal family: The third generation', *The Jerusalem Quarterly*, No. 31 (Spring 1984).

Ochsenwald, W., 'Saudi Arabia and the Islamic revival', *International Journal of Middle East Studies*, Vol. 13 (1981).

Rajab, 'Amr al-Faruq Sayyid, 'Nizam al-ta'lim wa-mutatalibat al-'umalah fi'l-mamlaka al-'Arabiyya al-Sa'udiyya', *Dirasat al-Khalij wa'l-Jazira al-'Arabiyya* (January 1983).

Rugh, W., 'Emergence of a new middle class in Saudi Arabia', *The Middle East Journal* (Winter 1973).

Salameh Gh., 'Saudi Arabia: development and dependence', *The Jerusalem Quarterly*, No. 20 (Summer 1981).

—— 'Political power and the Saudi state', *Merip Reports*, No. 91 (October 1980).

Sams, T.A., 'Education and training in Saudi Arabia', *Business America* (13 July 1981).

Solaim S.A., 'Saudi Arabia's judicial system', *The Middle East Journal* Vol. 25, No. 3 (Summer 1971).

Journals and periodicals

Adelphi Papers

Al-Tali'a or *Sawt al-Tali'a* (Voice of the Vanguard) (Baghdad–California)

Al-Thawra al-Islamiyya (London)

Business America

Current History

Dirasat al-Khalij wa'l-Jazirah al-'Arabiyya

Economist Foreign Report

Euromoney

Hamizrah Hakhadash (Israel)

International Affairs

International Journal of Middle East Studies (IJMES)

Istratejia (Beirut)

Journal of Asian and African Studies

Merip Reports

Middle Eastern Studies (MES)
Middle East International
Mideast Business Exchange
Orbis
Pakistan Horizon
Plus (Paris)
Swiss Review of World Affairs
The Economist Intelligence Unit (EIU)
The Jerusalem Quarterly
The Journal of South Asian and Middle Eastern Studies
The Middle East (London)
The Middle East Journal (MEJ)
The Progressive
The Washington Quarterly
The Wilson Quarterly
Vierteljahresberichte (Forschungsinstitut der Friedrich-Ebert-Stiftung, Bonn)
World Press Review

Newspapers and weeklies

Afrique Action (Tunis)
Akhbar al-Usbu' (weekly, Amman)
Akhbar al-Yawm (Egypt)
Akhir Sa'h (Egypt)
Al-Ahram (Egypt)
Al-Ahrar (FLP, Lebanon)
Al-Akhbar (Lebanon)
Al-Anwar (Beirut)
Al-Bilad (Saudi Arabia)
Al-Da'wa (Riyadh)
Al-Dustur (weekly, London)
Al-Gumhuriyya (Egypt)
Al-Hadaf (PFLP, Beirut)
Al Haqa'iq (Egypt)
Al-Hawadith (Beirut)
Al-Hayat (Beirut)
Al-Hurriyya (PFLP, weekly, Beirut)
Al-Jarida (Beirut)
Al-Jazira (Saudi Arabia)
Al-Jihad (Jordan)
Al-Khalij al-Arabi (Saudi Arabia)
Al-Madina (Saudi Arabia)
Al-Manar (Jordan)
Financial Times (London)
Guardian (London)
Haharetz (Israel)
International Herald Tribune

Ittihad (UAE)
Jerusalem Post (Israel)
Kul Shay' (Beirut)
Le Monde
Ma'riv (Israel)
Mideast Mirror (Beirut)
Newsweek
New York Times
October (Cairo)
Saudi Gazette (Saudi Arabia)
Sunday Times (London)
The Economist (weekly, London)
The Listener
The New Yorker
The Times (London)
Time (magazine)
Ukaz (Saudi Arabia)
Umm al-Qura (Saudi Arabia)
Wall Street Journal
Washington Post
8 Days (weekly, London)

Index

Aba'l-Khayl, Muhammad 121,
128, 133n44, 137, 167
Abd al-Aziz b. Abd al-Rahman
Al Saud; *see* Ibn Saud
Abd al-Rahman b. Faysal b.
Turki b. Abdallah Al Saud 4,
12–14n4, 18n33
Abdallah ibn Abd al-Aziz 14n3,
97, 119, 128, 135, 138–9,
141–3, 146, 159, 162n19,
174, 177n23, 178, 184–7,
194, 206n15, 207n24, 217–18
abortive *coups* — 1969; *see*
coup(s)
Administration of Scientific
Study, (religious) Legal
Opinions, Islamic Propagation
and Guidance 15n15, 16n19,
19, 23, 32n10, 95, 149, 193
ahl al-ḥal wal-'aqd 9–11,
13–14, 16n18, 17n24, 20,
22, 64, 68, 93, 124, 129,
167, 169, 176, 184, 197, 205
Ahmad ibn Abd al-Aziz 106n76,
135, 149, 156–7, 187,
190–1, 207n20
air force (Royal Saudi)
commoner officers,
opposition and attempted
coups 77, 91, 114–17,
131n21 and n26, 144,
219–20
development and upgrading
15n11, 77, 111, 113, 120,
204
Hijazis in 116, 131n26,
132n36, 144
royal officers 120, 174, 186,
204, 207
see also Dhahran (air base)
Al al-Shaykh 4–5, 7–10, 13–14
(also n2), 16n20, 17n24,
27–8, 31n9, 90–1, 95, 185,
186, 188, 212
officials and officers 9,

16n20, 27–8, 37, 90–1,
105n70, 186, 193, 207n20
see also ruling class, ulama
Al-Fahd; *see* Sudayri Seven
Al Faysal; *see* Saud al-Faysal
Al-Hasa (Al-Ahsa); *see* Eastern
Province
Al-Majlis al-A'la li'l-Qada; *see*
The Higher Council of Qadis
Al Saud; *see* royal family
(house)
Al-Sharqiyya; *see* Eastern
Province
Al-Shaykh, Abd al-Aziz ibn
Muhammad ibn Ibrahim 193,
208n38
Al-Shaykh, Hassan bin Abdallah
37, 90–1, 193
Al-Shaykh, Muhammad ibn
Ibrahim 8, 20, 35–7, 41, 125
Al-Shaykhs; *see* Al al-Shaykh
Arab National Liberation Front
(ANLF) 76, 92, 96
Arab Nationalists (*Qawmiyyun
al-Arab*) 28
Palestinians and others 75,
101n35, 110–11, 114,
119, 130n10
Saudi 76–7, 87, 96, 110,
114, 119, 154, 194
see also opposition
organizations (secondary)
Aramco 26, 69–76, 78–80,
83–4, 87, 90, 101n13,
104n51, 110–11, 113–14,
120, 126, 131n15, 144, 153,
155, 164n45, 187, 190–2,
196
and education 35, 40, 43, 47,
65, 92, 98, 123, 153
Aramco (oil) towns 71, 73,
80, 153, 155
Shi'ites 50, 71–2, 74, 87,
100, 101n14, 115, 118,
152–4, 157, 159